AF605827

CANNIBALIZING QUEER

CANNIBALIZING QUEER

Brazilian Cinema from 1970 to 2015

João Nemi Neto

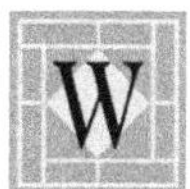

Wayne State University Press
Detroit

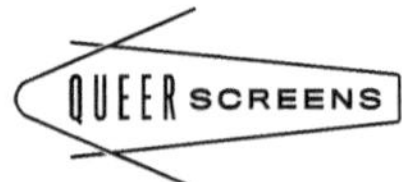

ISBN 978-0-8143-4610-5 (paperback)
ISBN 978-0-8143-4609-9 (hardback)
ISBN 978-0-8143-4611-2 (ebook)

Library of Congress Control Number: 2021943071

Wayne State University Press rests on Waawiyaataanong, also referred to as Detroit, the ancestral and contemporary homeland of the Three Fires Confederacy. These sovereign lands were granted by the Ojibwe, Odawa, Potawatomi, and Wyandot Nations, in 1807, through the Treaty of Detroit. Wayne State University Press affirms Indigenous sovereignty and honors all tribes with a connection to Detroit. With our Native neighbors, the press works to advance educational equity and promote a better future for the earth and all people.

Wayne State University Press
Leonard N. Simons Building
4809 Woodward Avenue
Detroit, Michigan 48201-1309

Visit us online at wsupress.wayne.edu.

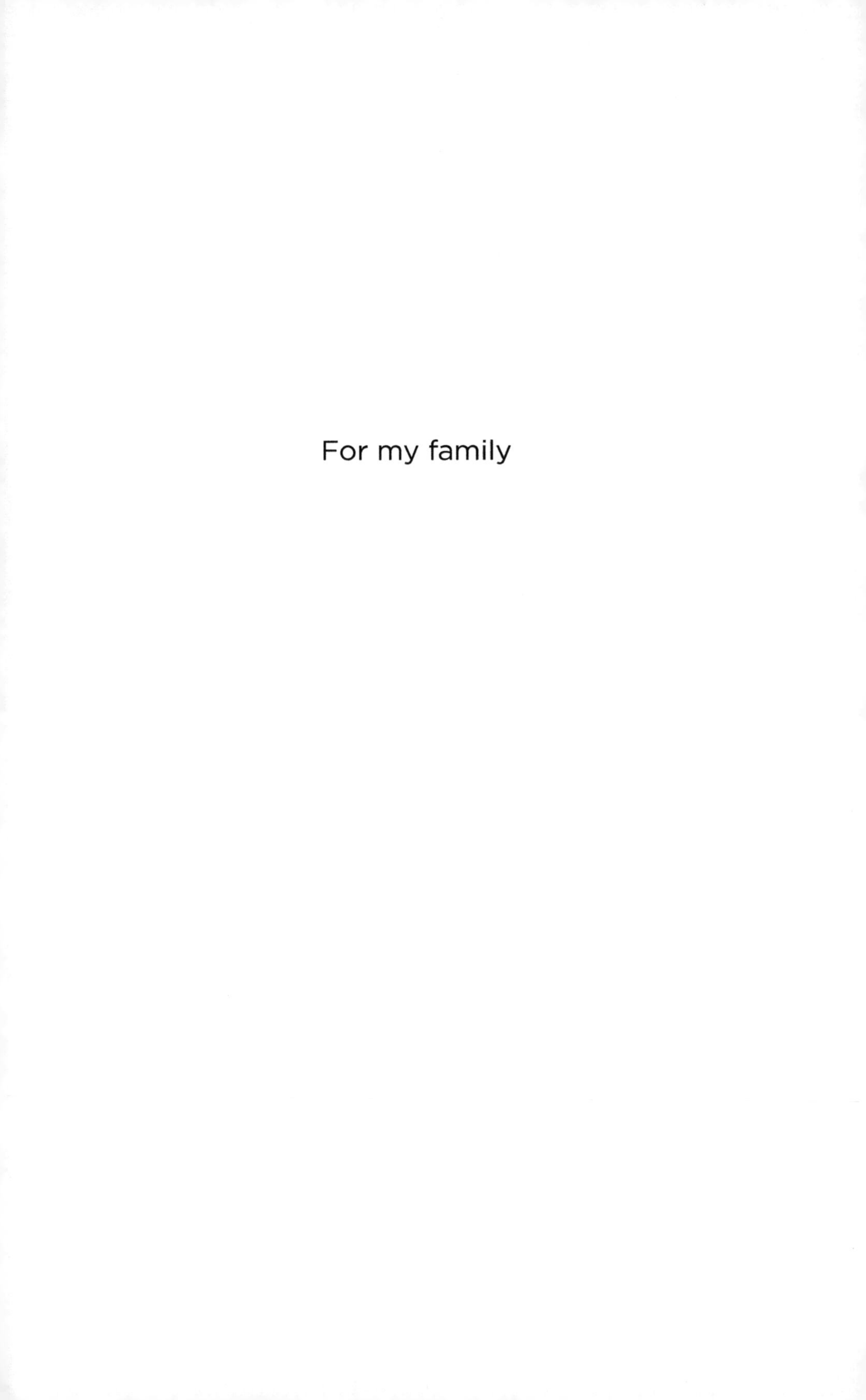

For my family

CONTENTS

ACKNOWLEDGMENTS

First, a special thanks to Ben De Witte, my best reader. He was the first person ever to read this book and the finest "ears" one could have. His dedicated and caring gaze definitely helped me with my writing. This project wouldn't have happened without his encouragement and enthusiasm.

My thanks go also to Paul Julian Smith, my adviser at the Graduate Center of the City University of New York, who guided me through my years at the program and paved the way for this book. I am fortunate to have had the chance to cross paths with him and learn from him. Thanks as well to Professors Magdalena Perkowska and José Del Valle, readers of this project. Their invaluable comments have helped me not only with this project but also with my career. Also, Professors Lídia Santos and Oscar Montero who contributed to the project in its first stages.

Special thanks to David Gerstner, the editor of this book series, who believed in my project since its inception. His support, attentive reading, and long conversations helped me immensely.

Thanks also to the editorial team at Wayne State University Press: Marie Sweetman for her immeasurable help with the editing process from the first stages; Kristin Harpster and Emily Nowak for all the editorial help; Jude Grant for the attentive revisions, comments, and questions; and Carrie Downes Teefey for the cover design.

I would like to thank the LAILAC Department at the Graduate Center and LAIC at Columbia University for their support during the research for this book. Also, the generous support of Columbia's ILAS—the Institute of Latin American Studies—allowed me to conduct part of my research in Brazil.

Gracias mil a Jelena Mihailovic for listening and helping me throughout the years.

Thanks to Shirly Bahar who invited me to join the reading group organized by Sarah Schulman. Along with Noa Hazan, Ilker Hepkaner, and Eva Boodman, their contributions were immensely appreciated and helped me understand this project better.

My greatest and most sincere thanks go to João Silvério Trevisan, the quintessential anthropophagic queer portrayed in this book. João opened his archives to me, allowing me to access unedited materials that are seen here for the first time. He also sat with me for a series of conversations talking about his work, his art, and his life. I cannot express in adequate words my gratitude for his generosity and wisdom. This book is an homage to João Silvério Trevisan's oeuvre and life as an activist and champion for equality.

This book is also an attempt to make all the queer—*travestis, sapatonas, trans, não-binários, bichas, e veados*—bodies visible, individuals who have persistently been erased but nonetheless still fight for visibility. I owe you all my existence as a queer person. *Obrigado!*

INTRODUCTION

It is often said that the history of Brazilian modern cinema starts with the movement known as Cinema Novo. This statement implies that there is no modern film culture in Brazil prior to Cinema Novo. Indeed, it is arguably the most discussed and studied movement in Brazilian filmmaking.[1] This is easy to understand: because Cinema Novo produced award-winning movies that gained visibility and respect on international film circuits and in the broad field of cinema studies, some critics have concluded that there is simply no other cinema worth considering in Brazil prior to the 1960s. However, this book proposes a different genealogy to the study of Brazilian cinema: it follows Guiomar Ramos's (2014) contention that Brazilian literary modernism, as it developed in the 1920s and '30s, indelibly marked the history of Brazilian cinema as a modern form of storytelling poised between nationalism and experimentation. More specifically, I argue that it is by relying on the modernist ideas of Antropofagia that Brazilian filmmakers developed a self-consciously experimental and national style in contemporary cinema.

Antropofagia was a seminal Brazilian cultural movement that, through the works of artists such as Oswald de Andrade, Tarsila do Amaral, and Flávio de Carvalho, proposed cultural and metaphorical cannibalism, blending European avant-garde ideas with Brazilian traditions yet aiming to produce something entirely new. While Antropofagia was a short-lived and socially liminal avant-garde movement, its "anthropophagic" intent to metaphorically "devour" foreign influences to produce uniquely Brazilian art forms in different media fundamentally shaped a Brazilian style in cinema.

This book aims to understand and chart the many manners in which Antropofagia, after its founding in 1928 by Andrade and Amaral, became vital for the development of a uniquely and self-consciously "Brazilian" mode of cultural production from the 1960s and onward and has remained at the center of Brazilian filmmaking. More distinctively, as the title of this book suggests, I contend that Antropofagia is an essential term for understanding queer filmmaking in Brazil; I situate and historicize a tradition in Brazilian queer cinema in the aftermath of Antropofagia and of myths surrounding "the birth of modern cinema" and of Cinema Novo.

A peculiarity of this book lies in its revisiting the history of Brazilian cinema through a modernist avant-garde framework that took place roughly thirty years *before* the era usually identified by critics as the start of modern cinema. Some scholars (Parente

2007; Fernão Pessoa Ramos 2008) will be quick to point out that cinema played a minimal part in Brazilian modernism. In fact, the most well-known figures of Brazilian modernism did not produce film. However, this book joins scholarship arguing that the new medium of cinema was an important source of inspiration for artistic production in literary modernism. Moreover, the modernist era *did* produce a handful films, though these did not enjoy much critical reception at the time. A case in point is Mário Peixoto's avant-garde film *Limite* (Boundary, 1931): now considered by most critics the best Brazilian film ever made,[2] Peixoto's film was scarcely seen or discussed at its release—a situation only remedied in the 1960s when a newly restored copy made the film available to a new generation of moviegoers. The case of *Limite* is telling for the delayed acknowledgment of the avant-garde's investment in cinema and for its understudies' influence on 1960s cinema and onward more generally.

I argue that the continuity between the general ideas of Antropofagia and the development of nascent cinematic modernity has shaped present-day Brazilian cinema. Literary modernism's attempt to write and see/gaze (*olhar*) in the manner of cinema is directly related to the development of modern cinema in the 1960s. Iconic directors such as Glauber Rocha, Rogério Sganzerla, and João Silvério Trevisan wrote cinematic manifestos in the style of literary and cultural modernism in order to contextualize their cinema—hence, the reason this book substantially incorporates discussion of Brazilian modernism as an integral part of the history of modern cinema in Brazil. Modernism, born out of a cross-pollination among various forms of expression, cultural discourses (such as Antropofagia), and new media, shaped practices that would bear new and often controversial (e.g., queer) fruit in the future. I argue that Brazilian cinema studies needs to acknowledge the importance of 1930s modernism, and of Antropofagia in particular, to grasp a particular tradition in Brazilian cinema that developed in the 1960s—especially with regard to queer cinema. In short, this study aims to show that avant-garde ideas about Antropofagia persist even today as a significant cultural mode of queer film production.

Approaching Antropofagia: Cannibalism at Home and Abroad

In the 2018 Netflix show *The Chilling Adventures of Sabrina*, Sabrina (Kiernan Shipka), a witch in training, finds out that her coven annually performs a ritual in which one of the witches is offered as a sacrifice to be devoured by all the other members of the group. The tradition, according to the elder witches, goes back to a time of great persecution, and during a period of starvation and distress, one of the witches offered herself as a meal to the others so that they might survive. While a "disgusting tradition" in Sabrina's eyes, she witnesses one of the witches in her coven cutting her own throat and giving herself to the coven to be eaten. The final shot of this scene is a close-up of the High Priest (Richard Coyle), the male leader of the coven, eating a piece of the witch's insides in ecstasy. In another Netflix series from 2017, the Danish drama series *The Rain*, a group of survivors in a postapocalypse world encounter a community of survivalists who perform a monthly ritual in which one of the members is sacrificed for the others to survive. During a dinner of thankfulness and sacred-like prayers, they eat one of the members who gladly gives himself or herself as the ultimate sacrifice for survival of the human race.

These two recent examples suggest that anthropophagy, or cannibalism, as it is more commonly called, has its place in the contemporary cultural imagination. One need not go far back in time to also find proof of fascination with cannibalism in the archives of cinema. Think, for instance, of the Italian "cannibal boom" from the 1970s and '80s, epitomized by Ruggero Deodato's film *Cannibal Holocaust* (1980), or the Hannibal series (both in cinema and television), which sprang forth from Jonathan Demme's 1991 award-winning *The Silence of the Lambs*. To this list we can add less sensationalist movies, such as Frank Marshall's survivors' drama, *Alive* (1993), or Peter Greenaway's arthouse comedy, *The Cook, the Thief, His Wife & Her Lover* (1989). Literature, too, boasts a long tradition, running from Michel de Montaigne to Herman Melville to Tennessee Williams, which brings the cannibal to life for the eye of the Western reader. Contemporary literary examples also retrieve cannibalism in more subtle and metaphorical senses. The Canadian writer Catherine Mavrikakis, for instance, in her novel *Deuils cannibales et mélancoliques* (*A Cannibal and Melancholy Mourning*, 2009), uses cannibalism as a figure for dealing with loss from AIDS or, more particularly, as a figure that expresses the voracious necessity of mourning: "[B]efore our dead we must be ravenous," she declares, insisting that "we must be cannibals and swallow them whole or tear them apart with our voracious teeth" (212).

Cannibalism seems to have been part of human culture since at least Greek and Roman antiquity. Pliny the Elder made mention of tribes that "feed on human bodies" (Braham 2015, 5). In most myths from antiquity, human devouring is exacted as a revenge (a trope that lives on in Greenaway's *The Cook, the Thief, His Wife & Her Lover*), whereas in the Bible it figures as a sign of condemnation. Eating other humans, however, takes on a wholly different meaning in the Western imagination with the "discovery" of the Americas and the appearance of the "Caliban." Since Montaigne and the first accounts of European travelers in the Americas, elaborate descriptions of cannibalism as an Indigenous ritual provoke condemnation, but not without a fascination tinged with hints of fetishism and eroticism. As Marco Alexandre de Oliveira

(2012) notes, the "(re)presentation of cannibalism in the Americas reveals a hidden fantasy, an imagination that is confused with reality" (9).

The idea that cannibalism at heart defines something essential and primeval about the New World has been a recurring feature in reports on Brazilian culture since its formation during colonial times. The infamous accounts by Jean de Léry and Hans Staden repeatedly mention the existence of anthropophagic practices all over Latin America, as Carlos Jáuregui (2008) explains in *Canibalia: Canibalism, calibanismo, antropofagia cultural y consumo en América Latina* (Canibalia: Cannibalism, "calibanism," cultural anthropophagy, and consumerism in Latin America). Like Jáuregui, but more specifically homing in on the context of Brazilian cinema, I posit that these early modern accounts are critical for understanding some of the most vital cultural innovations of twentieth- and twenty-first-century Brazilian cultural production.

It is not a coincidence that Antropofagia has been commonly translated as "cultural cannibalism." The seminal avant-garde movement reappropriates the discourse of cannibalism as a trope in order to develop Brazilian art that is not totally disconnected from the European avant-gardes but at the same time is invested in creating something unique: Antropofagia.

Since part of my argument contends that the development of a queer tradition in Brazilian cinema stems from the ideas behind Antropofagia, it is necessary to also consider the inevitably Anglo-American provenance of the term *queer* referred to in the title of this book. In this study, I aim to bring into interdisciplinary conversation a number of fields. It is based, first of all, in cinema studies, but it also draws on sights from scholarship on Brazilian modernism and queer studies. Such an approach is necessary to reveal the connecting threads among Brazilian modernism of the 1920s, the rise of a modern cinema in the 1960s, and the tradition in queer filmmaking that ensued. This study is particularly invested in arguing for the existence of a queer and anthropophagic mode in cinema. Queer theory, which puts queer lives and bodies at the center of attention, informs the manner in which I analyze the theoretical, political, and aesthetic ideas explored in the films (a selection of narrative fiction, documentary, and a blend of both). The term *queer* takes on a political dimension in this volume because it represents characters that conform neither to the American narrative of "coming out" politics nor to a clearly delineated concept of identity politics such as that which has currently taken hold in the Brazilian context.[3] The works I study do evoke same-sex experiences and affects, but I do not consider them in terms of conventional gay or lesbian identities per se. In the films I analyze, the characters and subjects do not comply with the clearly delineated conventional norms of sexual identity as either gay or straight: the representation is "queer" in that it challenges not only sexual (hetero- and homo)normativity but also social class and racial divisions.

Hence, Antropofagia invokes queer theory as an anti-identitarian critique, as Eve Kosofsky Sedgwick (1993) explains, of sexual and gender identity as an "open mesh of possibilities, gaps, overlaps, dissonances and resonances, lapses and excesses of meaning when the constituent elements of anyone's gender, of anyone's sexuality aren't made (or can't be made) to signify monolithically" (7). Therefore, this volume deals with the dual perspective of queer that marks Brazilian culture and cinema as both a critique of normative identity and a placeholder for the incongruent identity of sexual minorities (those that are socially "abject" and occupy the "space in-between" [Santiago 2001]). Moreover, this perspective allows me to simultaneously locate Brazilian contexts inside and outside the norms of queer theory in order to situate queer practices within Brazilian theory cinematic production theory.

My reading of queer Brazilian cinema suggests that beyond the Anglo-American model of coming out, these films propose other modes of social and aesthetic affirmation: they are queer in their acceptance of silence and even of failure as a productive mode of representation that challenges both homonormativity and heteronormativity. While discomforting, these films' nonresolute, nondefinitive stance on identity is also an act of resistance—a critique of prejudice and hetero- and homonormativity in contemporary Brazil. In effect, what I call "anthropophagic queer cinema" pushes the terms for representation beyond a declaration of identity. It is precisely in this destabilizing anti-identitarian orientation that contemporary queer theory resonates with those 1930s avant-gardist ideas behind Antropofagia. While the term *Antropofagia* is not by any means synonymous with *queer*, I argue throughout this book that both terms—despite the different cultural contexts in which they originated—can be productively thought of together to illuminate the birth and development of an LGBTQAI+ Brazilian cinematic production.

Anthropophagic Queer: Queering Gay in Brazil

Anglo-American theorizing on gender and sexuality raises particular questions for Latin American and Brazilian scholars. For instance, in "Lo queer en América Latina: ¿Lucha identitaria, post-identitaria, asimilacionista o neocolonial?" (Queer in Latin America: Identity, post-identity, assimilationist, or neocolonial struggle?), Norma Mogrovejo (2011) observes that "[Bradley] Epps, quoting Oscar Montero, affirms that if gay circulates in the Hispanic world in such ways that 'the complexities of its imported status are impossible to edit, and some of its celebratory charge is lost in translation,' the 'uses of queer are still circumscribed in the imperial metropolis'" (237).[4]

Although concerned about the potentially neocolonial effects that might accompany an unquestioned adaptation of the term *gay* in Latin America, Mogrovejo appreciates the possibility that *queer* might retain a certain degree of critical openness.

In 2013, Laerte, a transgender cartoonist from Brazil, wrote a review of Sara Salih's book *Judith Butler* in the form of a comic strip. Drawing on her own experience as a transgender person, Laerte observes that the impact of normative gender expression (i.e., adhering to strictly "masculine" or "feminine" behaviors and attitudes) allows contemporary society to impose a limited sense of self-understanding, restricting people to binaries of gender. In addition, and crucially, Laerte's Portuguese-language comic strip introduced key ideas about queer theory that are particularly revealing and representative for how Latin American intellectuals and artists position themselves not only as scholars and writers but also as citizens and national subjects in relationship to international trends in gay and lesbian studies and queer studies. Mogrovejo and Laerte point to a growing and transnational community of scholars and artists who self-consciously respond to the possibilities and challenges posed by the international dissemination of Anglo-American gay, lesbian, transgender, and queer theories. They emphasize the oppressive effects of normative thinking ("heteronormative," "gender binary," and more recently "homonormative") and foreground, in the spirit of Edward Said's (1983) "Traveling Theories"[5] that find new soil in a Brazilian context. In the same manner, this study also follows Mário César Lugarinho, who in his 2010 "Antropofagia crítica: Para uma teoria queer em português" (Critical Antropofagia: For a queer theory in Portuguese), may have been the first critic to relate queerness to Antropofagia. Lugarinho notes, "To immediately translate the term *queer* from the central society to the peripheral society is a betrayal of the anthropophagy that gives us identity" (109).[6] Lugarinho proposes a queer reading of Brazilian cultural texts that attends to local perspectives and practices. Likewise, my theoretical and methodological aim to propose an "anthropophagic" reading of queer and, reversely, a "queer" reading of Antropofagia follows Lugarinho's and Mogrojevo's efforts to make the most of traveling queer theories, without losing sight of the local realities they are purported to analyze.

To theorize a productive overlap between queer and Antropofagia requires that we attend to the rich but complicated semantic possibilities this terminology offers. *Queer* is certainly not the first Anglophone nomenclature of sexual identity that has traveled to Brazil: for the most part, the Brazilian-Portuguese vernacular has readily adopted the word *gay* for a homosexual person (mostly male), while more recently *queer* has entered the realm of academia and political activism. To what extent *queer* parallels *gay* in the Hispanic Latin America context is a concern Brad Epps (2007) addresses in

"Retos y riesgos, pautas y promesas de la teoría queer" (Challenges and dangers: Guidelines and promises of queer theory). Epps argues that traveling terms "enter" a country to create or uncover existent, latent tensions.[7] For instance, while the adoption of the word *gay* in Brazil has now become widely accepted, a pernicious side effect rests in the heightened negative connotations these outside terms bring to local vernacular, such as *sapatão*, *bicha*, and *veado*.[8] The steady increase of Brazilian scholarship on gender and sexuality studies perhaps suggests that the Brazilian reception of the term *queer* is well under way and perhaps has already solidified in institutional discourse. While it remains to be seen how profound the impact of the term will be in the larger cultural arena, I propose film studies as an area where queer theory can do productive work to illuminate local Brazilian realities with traveling theories. In line with the self-consciously "devouring" tenets of Antropofagia, I, too, highlight the critical value of incorporating and ingesting external theories for shedding light on an understudied tradition in filmmaking. This book is conceptualized as an anthropophagic enterprise, a study as much about reception as it is an active processing: it registers and enacts a reception of foreign theories while probing possibilities tailored to local cultural practices.

If the use of *gay* has become a symbol of social status, a hierarchized word that suggests "better" than one who is *bicha* or *veado*,[9] then perhaps *queer* can continue to trouble the internationalized vocabulary of same-sex (and normatively same-gendered) expression.

Paulo Emílio Salles Gomes, one of Brazil's most important cinema scholars, once said that "of the three great film cultures of Latin America [Argentina, Uruguay and Brazil], we are unquestionably the least impressive, and it is worth reflecting on this situation and searching within it for reasons to hope" (Conde and Dennison 2018, 329). This statement, originally formulated in 1957, certainly comes to mind when considering the generally—some exceptions notwithstanding—peripheral status of Brazil in most scholarship on Latin American cinema. More recently, Robert Patrick Newcomb and Richard A. Gordon (2017),[10] in their introduction to *Beyond Tordesillas: New Approaches to Comparative Luso-Hispanic Studies*, keenly observe that "perhaps no two literary and cultural traditions share such a natural affinity through both language and history, and yet so consistently resist comparative study, as do those of the former Spanish and Portuguese colonial empires" (6). Drawing on a wealth of cultural materials and archives (with themes ranging from history to cinema) from both Hispanic and Lusophone Latin American studies, their book is a conscious effort to investigate and "confront the seemingly paradoxical relationship, the interplay of proximity and distance between these fields and their objects of study" (7).

There are, of course, obvious and legitimate reasons that stymie the disciplinary conversation between scholarship on Hispanic and Lusophone America—reasons that could also be seen as a point of proximity. Differing linguistic realities are a given. Brazil is the only Latin American country with Portuguese as its official language; Spanish dominates most of the continent's national identities (even though Dutch, French, creole, Papiamento, and thousands of other native languages are also spoken in the region). Yet it is not sufficient to simply assume this linguistic dominance nor to insist too much on the role that language programs and academic departments outside Latin America play in conferring high visibility to Spanish-language culture. It is also the case that Brazil's cultural market is to a large extent oriented toward its own national audience: many of its films (like its music, television programs and avidly watched telenovelas) do well in the country, with the exception of art house films, which rarely rely on the local market and are instead generally directly targeted for international festivals.

Anthropophagic queer recognizes from the outset that the history of cinema in Brazil does not occur in a vacuum, least of all vis-à-vis the history and recent development of the medium in Latin America. However, it is not the aim of this book to redress these possible lacunae, although I do place my argument in relation to Latin America and to its always intimate ties with Euro-American ideas and discourses. My main aim with this study is to argue for the existence of a particular queer tradition within the history of Brazilian film practices. But of course I hope this book will invite thoughtful conversation across its own discipline, to kindle and ignite questions that carry over into the ever-evolving field of Latin American studies. In that regard, I concur with Vinodh Venkatesh (2016), who in his recent study on queer (*maricón*) Latin American cinema explains that his decision not to discuss Brazilian cinema does not "necessarily [remove] Brazil or its accompanying cultural critique from the equation of Latin Americanness" (13). Similarly, I do not intend to isolate Brazil using the notion of "yes, but no thanks" (62), as Mauricio Tenorio-Trillo (2014) wryly observes in his presentation on "the question of Brazil" (62) in relation to the idea of Latin America. Hopefully, then, the particular history and theoretical framework that this book proposes will enrich other debates in the spirit of Antropofagia: to articulate (and devour!) new perspectives in a dialectical and open-ended fashion.

This book is divided into five chapters. The first chapter explores the central ideas behind 1930s Antropofagia and its understudied investment in cinematic modes of production. As mentioned, I argue that while the modernist period in Brazil is not usually associated with cinema, literary modernism and particularly the avant-garde were crucial to development of a national style in cinema. In this chapter, I also discuss the resonance between queer theory and Antropofagia, and in doing so, I set the stage for what follows, the queerness of Antropofagia as well as the themes and sensibilities that will be important to the films I discuss in the rest of the book.

Chapter 1 provides a theoretical background to serve my examination of the films in the chapters that follow. I aim to demonstrate that the *antropófagos* (anthropophagites) brought to light the Indigenous social practices as an important part of Brazilian culture. However, this attention to the Indigenous body is not without complications or even a certain degree of contempt. The Indigenous body in many ways figures as a transgressive body, one that is socially liminal and, in that sense, abject; it occupies a liminal space in-between that structurally and symbolically corresponds to queerness. A marginal, cultural queerness is thus embedded in the very idea of Antropofagia.

The brief "trailer" that follows chapter 1 presents historical and cultural background, which is necessary for understanding the context in which the films under discussion were made. As such, it serves as an interlude as well as a transition to chapter 2, which discusses João Silvério Trevisan's film, *Orgia ou o homem que deu cria* (Orgy or the man who gave birth, 1970), a remarkable example of the Cinema Marginal genre developed in Brazil at the end of the 1960s. The film, censored for more than a decade, is what I identify as a quintessential example of anthropophagic queer cinema that anticipates future queer filmmaking. To elucidate Trevisan's anthropophagic queer work, I analyze his film in light of the theories on abjection proposed by Julia Kristeva (1982) and Silviano Santiago's (2001) notion of the space in-between, which he discusses in his theoretical framework on Brazilian representations of homosexuality.

Chapter 3 deals with HIV/AIDS representation in Brazilian cinema. Because each film in this chapter derives from a very different tradition in Brazilian cinema, the AIDS epidemic is portrayed in unique ways. *AIDS, furor do sexo* (AIDS, the furor of sex, Fauzi Mansur [as Victor Triunfo], 1985) is a pornographic movie. *Estou com AIDS* (I have AIDS, David Cardoso, 1985) is a mixture of documentary and *pornochanchada*, a classic Brazilian film genre developed in the 1970s. Finally, *Romance* (Romance, Sérgio Bianchi, 1988) represents the kind of socially marginal "auteur" cinema that follows João Silvério Trevisan's model of marginal filmmaking.

In this chapter, I again draw on Kristeva's (1982) theories on abjection to analyze the stigma of shame, panic, revulsion, and contagion attached the figure of the effeminate (queer) man. Kristeva's work on the fear of "being bitten" (38)—a fear that calls to mind the cannibalism trope in unsettling ways—establishes a close metaphorical relation among biting, eating, and death and dovetails particularly fittingly with the stigma of contagion.

In a second trailer, I turn my attention to "effeminophobia" in Brazilian cinema and in scholarly work. This brief section adds to the anthropophagic queer perspective by bringing to light the system of patriarchal oppression at work in the films analyzed thus far.

Effeminacy continues as a topic of concern in chapter 4, which turns to Brazilian documentary production. Brazil's long tradition of documentary filmmaking explores, and sometimes blurs, the distinction between reportage and fiction. Brazil, as Amir Labaki (2003) emphasizes, "already boasts a rigorous tradition of documentary filmmaking, proof of which can be seen in the excursions made into this medium by every great Brazilian filmmaker" (97). This chapter highlights *Dzi Croquettes* (2009), the prize-winning documentary by Raphael Alvarez and Tatiana Issa, which revisits the famed performances of a group of cross-dressing artists in the 1970s. I argue that *Dzi Croquettes*—which even today remains the most awarded documentary made in Brazil—inaugurates a form of queer documentary that makes room for films such as *Divinas divas* (Divine divas, Leandra Leal, 2016), *Bixa travesty* (Tranny queen, Kiko Goifman and Claudia Priscilla, 2018), and *Carta para além dos muros* (Letter for beyond the walls, André Canto, 2019).

The final chapter analyzes two films that put queer bodies at the center of attention in very distinct ways: Karim Aïnouz's *Madame Satã* (Madame Satã, 2002) and Hilton Lacerda's *Tatuagem* (Tattoo, 2013). *Tatuagem* tells the story of a fictional theater group in 1970s Recife, in northeastern Brazil, using a style and formal language that neatly illustrates the anthropophagic queer mode in filmmaking, which I discuss throughout this book. Lacerda's film displaces the traditional discourse of Brazilian cinema in two ways: First, it relocates its central narratives out of Rio de Janeiro and São Paulo to Recife, the center of film production in the twentieth century. Second, it avoids the *pornomiséria*, or "cosmetics of hunger,"[11] discourse usually associated with the northeastern region of the country. *Tatuagem* is part of a new wave of northeastern filmmakers who show different perspectives in terms of gender, race, class, and language.[12] *Madame Satã*, in its turn, presents the life of a historical legend who as a poor, Black, queer man in the 1920s and '30s defied the norms of his time.

While my selection of films is understudied, its raise important issues pertinent to the study of gender and sexuality in Brazil. Moving these films from the margins (from the space in-between where they currently exist) allows me not only to interrogate "queer" and its applications in Brazil but also to question Brazilian tactics and strategies of filmic representation. More broadly, I wish to discuss which queer representations are erased and which ones are acknowledged or gain prominence over others in the complex process of cultural translation, adaptation, and *devouring* that defines the Brazilian understanding of sexual dissidents and minorities.

DEVOURING CINEMA

Queering Antropofagia

According to Vicente de Paula Araújo (1985), a modest golden age of Brazilian early cinema occurred between 1896 and 1912. By 1912, however, American cinema started to dominate the national market. During the first decades of the twentieth century, only a small number of films were produced in Brazil, although there are notable exceptions that merit attention, including Mario Peixoto's avant-garde film *Limite* (Boundary, 1931), which today is considered the most important Brazilian film made, or *São Paulo, a sinfonia da metrópole* (São Paulo, symphony of a metropolis, Adalberto Kemeny and Rudolph Rex Lustig, 1929).[1] Peixoto's film in particular exemplifies the avant-gardist ideas that directly influenced the emergence of a Brazilian style in film-making. Peixoto lived and studied in Europe, and his film appropriated the techniques and sensibilities of the European avant-garde gaze while effectively turning it toward Brazilian narratives and landscapes.

Maite Conde explains that cinema in Brazil was an important cultural reference for the modernist movement in the 1920s. In *Consuming Visions: Cinema Writing and Modernity in Rio de Janeiro* (2011) and *Foundational Films: Early Cinema and Modernity in Brazil* (2018), she presents an in-depth analysis of the movement's fascination and enthusiasm for this then new technological language and art form. Oswald de Andrade (1928a), the creator and developer of the Antropofagia movement, proclaimed in the *Manifesto antropófago* (Anthropophagous manifesto) that American cinema could be a source of inspiration and innovation for Brazilian art. The ideas embraced by Antropofagia would become a persistent trope in Brazilian modern cinema in the 1960s and the decades that followed. For instance, Antônio Castilho de Alcântara Machado's 1926 novel *Pathé-Baby* (the title itself a reference to cinema) is formally conceived as a cinema journal log. The idea for the novel formed after he met Swiss poet Blaise Cendrars during the latter's visit to Brazil in 1928.[2] Oswald de Andrade, aware of cinema's importance to modernity, wrote the preface to Alcântara Machado's book. Even though the modernist era produced no coherent body of film, cinema was a clear reference for their writing.

The often overlooked centrality of cinema to Antropofagia is not without importance for how we might evaluate the movement's recurrent impact throughout the twentieth century until present time. Several authors and scholars have discussed its endurance (e.g., Cândido 1970; Bosi 1994; Campos 1975; Stam 1997; Helena 1983; Nagib 2003; Guiomar Ramos 2008). Antropofagia is not only a literary movement but also a critical aspect of Brazilian culture more generally (Helena 1983). The impact of Antropofagia can be seen in various artistic manifestations in Brazil and throughout Latin America[3] even today.[4] As Hans Ulrich Gumbrecht (2011, 289) explains, the manifesto has created a cult among intellectuals and writers in the past century who have been stimulated by the movement's ideas and language, and I follow a number of researchers who argue that this is also apparent in Brazilian cinema. Randal Johnson and Robert Stam (1995), for instance, point out that 1960s Cinema Novo is marked by a "cannibal-tropicalist" (37) phase. Throughout the 1970s, a series of films dealt with Antropofagia, often by thematizing cannibalistic practices. Two of that era's most famous examples are *Como era gostoso meu francês* (How tasty was my little Frenchman, Nelson Pereira dos Santos, 1971) and *Macunaíma* (Macunaíma, Joaquim Pedro Andrade, 1969). Luís Madureira explains that "while *How Tasty Was My Little Frenchman* ostensibly subscribes to the *antropofagista* recuperation of the anthropophagic act as a strategy of cultural and economic resistance, it ultimately exposes the 'rhetoricity' of this allegorical solution to the dilemma of development" (17)—a critical dimension, I will argue further on, that João Silvério Trevisan also exploits in *Orgia ou o homem que deu cria*.

This "return to Antropofagia" in Cinema Novo is well documented (e.g., Nagib 2003; Stam 1997; Johnson 1984; Guiomar Ramos 2008). However, in this study I propose that each generation returns to Antropofagia in its own way to "cannibalize," as it were, the movement's principal tenets according to the generation's own needs. This was certainly the case with the 1960s return to Antropofagia, which aimed at a collective consciousness, as Joaquim Pedro Andrade explained in a short statement during the release of his first anthropophagic film, *Macunaíma*. During this period, censorship imposed by the repressive military dictatorship (1964–84) forced artists to look for metaphors that could describe their desire for liberty. Within the same statement, Andrade included a short piece titled "Cannibalism and Self-Cannibalism," in which he noted that "the Left, while being devoured by the Right, tries to discipline and purify itself by eating itself" (qtd. in Johnson and Stam 1995, 83). If Oswald de Andrade intended to devour American cinema and its new language(s), forty years later film director Glauber Rocha would turn to Brazilian modernism to tackle contemporary social problems in a manner, as film scholar Ismail Xavier (1993) explains, indebted to the 1920s.

But Antropofagia also resurfaces more recently, inviting us to inquire about contemporary "cannibal" desires. Besides the selected films and documentaries that I will analyze in this book, several examples of contemporary Brazilian cinema (especially with a queer orientation) come to mind. Juliana Rojas and Marcos Dutra's *As boas maneiras* (Good manners, 2017), for instance, deals with literal cannibalization, as proposed by Pierre Fédida (1972) in "Le cannibale mélancolique" (The melancholic cannibal), a psychoanalytic reading of anthropophagic rituals. *Tatuagem* (Tattoo, Hilton Lacerda, 2013) revisits the creative Tropicália movement's appropriation of the carnivalesque approaches of Antropofagia.

I argue in this book that Antropofagia is crucial to the development of a queer style in Brazilian cinema. This is not obvious in and of itself: while widely discussed, Oswald de Andrade's literary manifestos are not generally read in a "queer" light. This book, which proposes a queer reading of Antropofagia to trace the persistence of that movement in Brazilian queer cinema, tries to strike a tenuous balancing act in reconciling the study of a Brazilian cultural movement with the aid of Anglophone queer theory. Guided by this proposition, I thus turn to queer theories of abjection to analyze how a specific tradition in Brazil resonates with the ideas behind Antropofagia. I thus join with a number of scholars who use queer theory as a mode of analysis for Brazilian cinema (see, e.g., Subero 2014; Foster 1999, 2010), but I more emphatically turn to Antropofagia as an enduring cultural matrix that lends itself to queer readings. More specifically, I propose an anthropophagic queer reading in order to understand Brazilian queer cinema and the ways filmic language has dealt with questions of sexual identity and orientation, stigma, HIV/AIDS, and narrative.

Why Is Antropofagia Important to Queer Cinema?

Andrade's manifesto is one of the most original strategies for resisting colonization, and at the same time, it creates forms of critique of the relationship between cultures. Nonetheless, as an underpinning cultural object, it must be read with a double-sided understanding. While the discourse sets out to resists colonization, it is born out of colonial structures of power: the manifesto originated among the white cultural elite from São Paulo who appropriated Indigenous cultures and languages as if Brazil were one *mestiço* nation.

Still, today the principles of Antropofagia offer a model of cultural translation that remains provocative, having lost, I believe, none of its relevance in the discussion of the adaptation of foreign "traveling theories" (Said 1983) in the Brazilian context. If one considers that a literal translation of *queer* into Portuguese is impossible, and that the process of translation would doubtless prove unfruitful, one strategy might be to reinterpret and reelaborate the term, engaging in what Haroldo de Campos calls *transcriação* (transcreation) (see Tapia and Nóbrega 2015). It is also legitimate to question if such words are relevant to Brazilian (or other cultural) practices. The Brazilian cultural discourse on Antropofagia reminds us that there is an intellectual precedent from which to proceed when considering the relevance of the term *queer* in a Brazilian context; there is a critical methodology to incorporate the exogenous, assimilating the external by devouring it, to afterward produce a meaningful *totemized taboo*, to invert Freud's (1918) classic proposition.

This anthropophagic perspective is important not only because it shaped twentieth-century Brazilian culture but also because it informs this book's project of thinking through the challenging tasks of grasping and translating queer theory and bringing queer bodies into a visible space in Brazilian cinema.[5] Moreover, the notion of the abject resonates with the perceived lack of prestige of Portuguese as a peripheral language in relation to a European center, as often expressed by Brazilian writers and critics (e.g., Santiago 2006; Santos 1997; Lugarinho 2002). The Portuguese sociologist Boaventura de Sousa Santos (1997) in *Pela mão de Alice: O social e o politico na pós-modernidade* (Through Alice's hands: The social and the political in postmodernity) aptly summarizes the issue as follows: for centuries, Portuguese culture could see itself as a center because it *had* a periphery represented by its colonies. However, Portugal today is at the periphery because Europe imposes itself as a center. "For a culture that has never been in one space," Santos concludes, "the cultural identifications originated from that point tend to autocannibalize themselves" (135).[6] Interestingly, Santos chooses the notion of cannibalism as a metaphor for the Lusophone world. Geographically speaking, Portugal lies at the periphery of continental Europe, the most western-situated country. In history books, students in Brazil learn from an early age that this peripheral position was one of the advantages that allowed Portugal to be the first and most successful nation in conquering "new" lands in the fifteenth and sixteenth centuries. Once at the center in relation to its colonies, as a European nation-state, Portugal is now at the periphery in relation to other European countries. If one traces a parallel between this peripheral position and queer theory, an analogous relationship between *lusofonia* and queer becomes visible. Not incidentally, then, Lugarinho (2010, 107) contends that to simply translate *queer* into Portuguese is an act of betrayal to the anthropophagic history that has been so important to Brazilian culture.

With that in mind, I use *queer* in this book as a term that disturbs, destabilizes, and questions ideas of centrality and normativity. As Carla Freccero (2011) says in "Queer Times," "*mestizaje, métissage, spectrality*, the trace, and the uncanny all find themselves in certain ways allied with queer as terms that do the work of *différance* in relation to the identitarian inflections they carry" (17). Freccero's choice of terms is particularly useful to this book's project; *mestiçagem*[7] has been a vital part of Brazilian culture and was one of Andrade's main arguments while developing his anthropophagic theory. Michael Warner (1993), too, in *Fear of a Queer Planet*, uses the word *queer* in a manner that goes along with Antropofagia, proposing queerness to interrogate the heteronomativity of class and gender analysis as categories that are always embedded within a history of sexuality.

Following Warner's example, I apply a queer analysis to a range of topics in line with Antropofagia's original interests, such as the notion of emancipation and inclusion of the Indigenous and people of color, but I also broaden the scope of critical analysis to include women's and abject bodies that have been denied visibility. I argue that such a queer reading of Antropofagia recovers the movement's openness for representing different bodies and social modes of organization (e.g., matriarchal society). This way, the active process "queering" may be seen as an act of "swallowing," or *deglutição*,[8] a term that was highly important for the cultural *antropófagos* as an expression for their desire to emancipate the modernist artists (more about that soon).

Reversely, as I argue throughout this book, queer theory, too, may need to be anthropophagized: adapting Anglo-American terminology to a different cultural context continues an anthropophagic movement of *re-deglutição*. Revisiting what was "swallowed" in the past under the aegis of Antropofagia in "queer" terms today gives shape to self-consciously intercultural, dialogic, and specifically Brazilian theory for studying the issues at hand in this book of sexual liberation and queer visibility in Brazilian contemporary cinema. I argue that queer theory needs to be eaten[9] by Brazilian queer bodies and devoured in ways that will fit their queer needs, thus creating an invigoratingly hybrid *mestiço* and queer encounter between and Antropofagia and Anglo-American theory. Ideally, Antropofagia will at once devour queer while simultaneously being queered. As David William Foster proposes in an interview with W. Daniel Holcombe (2012), "As cultural production, a queer reading is a reading that tries to understand in which ways this production is reproduced while questioning social systems" (199).[10]

Queer theory, as the discipline developed in the United States, tries not to conform to the norm and distances itself from the institutionalized gay and lesbian studies. During the past twenty years, since the time when Teresa de Lauretis (1991)[11] used the term *queer*, there has been much discussion about whether or not the institutionalization of queer theory has defanged the critical, deregulatory queerness the term intended to achieve (Halperin 2011). Also, David L. Eng, J. Jack Halberstam, and José Esteban Muñoz (2005), in their respective manner, hold that queer theory has become a discourse of mostly white male homosexuals, which is precisely one of the issues that scholars were trying to redress in the 1990s.

Problems of legitimacy are even thornier in the case of queer theory's arrival in Latin America, where many critics urgently wonder whether the terms of analysis are not inevitably inscribed in a colonial dynamic: queer theory as a discourse through which the educated will enlighten the less educated. However, queer theory, like any other traveling theory that originates in the United States, is already preoccupied with "the other" (that is, non-US subjects). Such preoccupation with the other transforms the theory into the master of several subordinate bodies. Yet many authors in the Lusophone world have taken queer theory as a model for analysis. As Lugarinho (2002) says:

> Anglophone queer theory does offer interpretive tools and useful insights for the analysis of homosexuality in Portuguese-speaking cultures. At the same time, its attempt at overcoming the binary heterosexuality/homosexuality in order to include other registers of sexuality, class, gender, race, nationality, and political ideologies, provides a valuable and more exhaustive framework for the analysis of peripheral societies such as Portugal and Brazil, at the same time as it links these societies to a much larger transnational framework of concerns uniting sexual and gender minorities throughout the world. (286)

Nevertheless, it is important to understand the vicissitudes of traveling theories and ask in which ways they are truly resourceful for Latin American contexts. After all, since its inception, cinema in Brazil is presented as an international novelty. As the well-known turn-of-the-century writer and journalist João do Rio says, "[E]verybody wanted to see the cinematographers" (qtd. in Araújo 1985, 18). More recently, the critic and writer Silviano Santiago (2002) has proposed a culturally sensitive approach for applying international models to the Brazilian context. In "The Wily Homosexual," he holds that Brazil has in fact produced proper models of acceptance of homosexuality that are not dependent on the North American model of "coming out."[12] The simple adoption of the North American model might negatively affect the acceptance of local registers and terminologies, rendering them abject. In his analysis of a nineteenth-century novel, *O cortiço* (*The Slum*, 1890) by Aloísio de Azevedo, Santiago shows that certain models of social tolerance for sexual diversity have existed in Brazil prior to the importation of US models. Santiago comes back to this point in his 1969 novel *Stella Manhattan*, which considers how an effeminate character is unaccepted and consequently rendered invisible both in Brazilian and American societies. The American model of coming out has thus created gaps in visibility for all those bodies that did not conform to the ideal homosexuality that had been developed during the 1960s and '70s. Santiago wonders if the more silenced way in which Brazilians have tended to reveal their homosexuality could not be as fruitful as the more imposing and assertive American coming-out approach. As I discuss further on, just one year after the publication of Santiago's novel, João Silvério Trevisan's film debut, *Orgia ou o homem que deu cria*, proposes a similar position.

Santiago's reflections are important to this book, which turns to Antropofagia as a founding moment for the posterior development of a Brazilian queer cinema. In aligning the Brazilian anthropophagous tradition with a queer method, I aim to create a theoretical liminal space in-between that takes as the start of Brazilian cinema a critical "devouring" of European and American cinema by literary modernism's proponents. But what are the risks of introducing and applying the still largely Anglo-American concept of queer theory to Brazilian queer cinema?

Anticipating this question, Santiago's (2001) influential "Latin American Discourse: The Space In-Between" pleads with urgency for an anthropophagous, almost ritual-like approach to Latin American literary and cultural production. Santiago believes that "somewhere between sacrifice and playfulness, prison and transgression, submission to the code and aggression, obedience and rebellion, assimilation and expression—there, in this apparently empty space, its temple and its clandestinity, is where the anthropophagous ritual of Latin American discourse is constructed" (38). His formulation evokes the anthropophagic queer movement that I proposed earlier: a space in-between that is created between queer as a traveling theory and local practices. In fact, an anthropophagic "swallowing" of queer theory reveals potential critical gains. Consider, for instance, as Butler (1999) shows in *Gender Trouble*, the commonplace of Anglo-American gender theory that Western culture is phallogocentric and the masculine body remains unmarked (13, 17). Antropofagia, on the other hand, proposes a matriarchal society in which the patriarchal views are eliminated in order to create a surrounding space free from all the taboos that had infected modern society. Antropofagia in the 1930s aimed at combining "civilization" with Indigenous roots, thus imagining new possibilities for social organization. To Andrade, civilization makes the population sad. Happiness can be achieved through *antropofagia* or a *caraíba*[13]—a revolution through the return to the mother. As Freud (1918) suggests in *Totem and Taboo*, "[M]aternal transmission probably always preceded and was only later supplanted by the paternal" (4).

In his 1928 *Manifesto antropófago*, Oswald de Andrade attempts to undermine the patriarchal institutions relied on by white European men to colonize Brazil. For Andrade, then, it is necessary to return to our roots and, using anthropophagy as a metaphor, to turn our eyes to a new form of civilization, a matriarchal one—a *matriarcado de Pindorama*, as the author states in the *Manifesto antropófago*: "Joy is the casting out Nines / In Pindorama's matriarchy" (1928a, 7).[14] *Pindorama*, a Tupi word (*pindó-rama* or *pindó-retama*) meaning "land of the palm trees," was the colonial designation for Brazil, the name used before the arrival of the Portuguese settlers. By invoking Pindorama, Andrade is celebrating the country before it was named Brazil. The *matriarcado*, then, was both a source of reflection for Andrade and a prerequisite for achieving an anthropophagic manner of life. The importance of the Mother to achieve a wholly new Brazilian reality is also evident in João Silvério Trevisan's *Orgia ou o homem que deu cria*, which was initially titled "How I killed my father" (more about that in the next chapter).

Antropofagia / The Anthropophagic Movement

During the 1920s and '30s, a number of manifestos[15] were created in Brazil and Hispanic Latin America in order to discuss new perspectives and ideas, several of which are still relevant today. Most vital to the purposes of this book, of course, is Oswald de Andrade's *Manifesto antropófago*. To understand how queer theory has become integrated into academia and social practices in Brazil, it is incumbent to write a historical account of the modernist movement and its conception of Brazil, *brasilidade*, and *brasilianismos*. Also, an anthropophagic reading of queer is helpful for understanding how queer theory can be fruitful for Brazilian queer cinema.

At the beginning of the twentieth century, Brazilian authors, intellectuals, and scholars looked to European currents of thought to create a Brazilian perspective on the recently independent nation.[16] They did so by relying on the idea that it was a properly local and Indigenous practice in Brazil to "devour" and "swallow" foreign influences. From arts to academia, the anthropophagic principle once proposed by Andrade and the other anthropophagites is, as João Cezar de Castro Rocha, David Shepherd, and Tania Shepherd (1999) observe, "central to Brazilian culture and has been present in three fundamental stages of Brazil's intellectual history, namely, in Romanticism, Modernism and Tropicalism" (6). In 1924, Andrade in his *Manifesto da poesia Pau-Brasil* (Brazilwood manifesto) writes: "[O]nly Brazilians from our time. The essential from chemistry, mechanics, economics and ballistics. All digested" (qtd. in Schwartz 2008, 162).[17] The Antropofagia idea of digestion (*digerido*) attempted to incorporate the European *-isms* in a Brazilian fashion, opening up the artistic and social spheres into what was held to be a true Brazilian representation. Andrade's *Manifesto antropófago* further proposed a *deglutição* of the European vanguards, transforming them to meet our local needs.

Antropofagia and the Brazilian modernist movement can trace their origins to a seminal art week, Semana de Arte Moderna, in February 1922 in São Paulo, which was marked by a series of performances at that city's Theatro Municipal. At the time, a group of poets, writers, painters, and artists gathered together in an attempt to revolutionize Brazilian art. In their view, Brazil was still connected to the old paradigms, and a new perspective was vital in order to modernize the aspiring republic. However, cinema was not included among the art forms in need of "restoration." While at this time European surrealists were explicitly invested in cinema, Brazil modernists were considerably less engaged on this front. Conde (2018) explains this marginalization of Brazilian cinema as the result of a divorce between theory and praxis. Nonetheless, the fact that Brazilian modernists did not extensively practice filmmaking does not mean they had no interest in cinema. In fact, they considered cinema to be the modern art par excellence and took it seriously as a source of reference for modernizing other art forms.

Sponsored by the elites who had become wealthy through the São Paulo coffee industry, the Semana de Arte Moderna was an event that put together many upcoming artists from São Paulo and Rio de Janeiro in order to showcase the modern art created in Brazil. São Paulo, the second-largest city in the country at the time, had received more than half of all the European immigrants who came to Brazil and was a thriving metropolis that saw itself as destined to become a center of modernity, industry, and money. The coffee industry sponsors demanded a city that was modern not only in its architecture but also in its arts. Businessman Paulo Prado, whose wealth financed the artistic week, became the main patron of the modernist generation. As Andrade (2000b) observed, Semana de Arte Moderna was born from an exporter capitalist mentality generated by the industrialism in São Paulo.

In this historical moment, the vanguard movements in Latin America self-consciously sought to integrate themselves into the processes of modernization. Gonzalo Aguilar (2005) explains why the elite may have been interested in financing the modernist artists, outlining three tendencies to attempt integration: the first one is related to powers of domination that are articulated in the state and dominant groups; the other two, following Ángel Rama (1998), are *cosmopolita* and *transculturadora*. For Aguilar, those tendencies are powers of opposition and resistance with the former articulated around the urban vanguard and the latter in the conflict between the "culturas letradas," "learned cultures," and the "indigenous" (41).

The Semana de Arte Moderna, unlike the Armory Show in New York, which showcased European artists and their vanguards, presented only Brazilian artists and their interpretations of both the European vanguards and Brazilian art. Even though it received mixed reviews,[18] this event remains one of the most important in twentieth-century Brazilian cultural history. From the buzz surrounding it, a new generation of artists emerged around a set of shared ideological and aesthetical affinities: the Movimento Antropófago was born.

According to a well-known anecdote narrated by Raul Bopp in *Movimentos modernistas no Brasil, 1922–1928* and *Vida e morte da antropofagia* (published in 1966 and 1977, respectively), it was during a fancy dinner party in São Paulo that the ideas of an anthropophagous movement were first developed. Prior to eating a dish of frogs, Oswald de Andrade made a speech describing humankind's evolution and tracing it back to amphibians. After listening to this speech, Tarsila do Amaral remarked, "[E]ntão somos quase antropófagos" (Then we are all anthropophagous). Oswald continued, quoting sixteenth-century German explorer Hans Staden's famous comment: "[L]á vem nossa comida pulando" (There it is, our food jumping). According to Bopp, it was during that same dinner that Andrade uttered, "Tupi or not tupi, that is the question," a line that would become part of the *Manifesto antropófago* and is now practically codified in the Brazilian popular imagination; it is a question that centers on the issue of being (or not being) Brazilian and the idea of accepting our roots or not.

According to Bopp's account, another anecdote from the founding of the movement has its origin in a painting by Tarsila do Amaral, one of the leading figures of the *antropófagos*. The painting, intended for Oswald de Andrade's birthday and discussed by the attendants at the above described dinner, portrays a person with an enormous foot attached to the earth, whose gender or sex is not well defined; it is titled *Abaporu*—Tupi for "the one who eats people." The painting was reprinted in the first publication of the movement in 1928. If we look closely at Tarsila's artwork, we can see that the movement's first moment of queerness starts with the painting itself. Besides depicting a distinct sense of time and space, different and distant from the common experience, the painting shows an ungendered being who eats other people. Tarsila do Amaral describes the painting—the figure sitting on a green plain and the huge foot, the arm resting alongside the knee, and the hand sustaining the tiny head—as a lonely and monstrous picture. Beyond the foot, a cactus explodes in an absurd flower (Marcelo Guimarães da Silva Lima in Schøllhammer 1999, 188). Marcelo Guimarães da Silva Lima (2018) clarifies the contrasting ideas presented in Tarsila do Amaral's painting: "[A] sense of weight stresses the hieratic tranquility and emblematic stability of this dream-like world. Nonetheless, a sense of expansion of forms, slowly growing to occupy their full limits in space, is also present" (95).

Interestingly, Luis Pérez-Oramas (2017), curator at New York's MoMA, calls Tarsila (as the artist is affectionately known in Brazil) a "melancholic cannibal," taking his cue from Pierre Fédida's 1972 "Le cannibale mélancolique," in which he writes that cannibalism is a truly imaginary transgression of a lack (privation, loss, abandonment, separation, etc.). The psychoanalyst suggests that anthropophagy indicates a need to devour something familiar, a primitive unconscious identification that carries the menace of its own rupture (126). Pérez-Oramas (2018), on his account, understands Tarsila's painting as a modern representation of a classic melancholic position "dating back at least to Albrecht Dürer's *Melancholy I* (1514)"; the image, he continues, is "brutal, barren, asexual, naked, solar. . . . [T]he figure sits beside a monumental cactus, potentially with sexual connotations, in the broad light of midday" (84).

One might further think of the painting as representing a melancholic rupture, even as Tarsila's own personal rupture and new trajectory. As Pérez-Oramas (2018) observes, she was not a "sub-Léger" any longer. From that moment, *Abapuru* comes to stand for the Movimento Antropófago's rupture with the past and active search for new paths. However, far from a total rupture, the painting visualizes an impossible, imperfect departure: a melancholic present that is haunted by a never fully digested past.

Tarsila describes the figure as a "cannibal, solitary monstrous figure" (D'Alessandro and Pérez-Oramas 2017, 51). Tarsila do Amaral's connection with the movement will culminate with her work titled *Antropofagia*. As D'Alessandro and Pérez-Oramas explain, "Tarsila's final step on this path seems to have coincided with her preparations for her first solo exhibition in her home country in 1929. There, she would present neither *A Negra* nor *Abaporu*, but a new work entitled *Anthropophagy*. In a literal culmination of her journey, documented in numerous drawings in preparation, Tarsila painted the figures from *A Negra* and *Abaporu* together, physically transformed and united" (51).

A close association between Tarsila do Amaral's *Antropofagia* and popular images of cannibals published in late sixteenth and seventeenth centuries is near at hand. As Persephone Braham (2015) explains, these images "exacerbated the tendency to localize the savagery of cannibalism in the feminine figure" (61), and according to Bernadette Butcher, they depict a number of female figures with sagging breasts, associated in medieval tradition with "maleficent women"—sagging-breasted women who appear "in the context of Tupinambá cannibal rites" (Butcher qtd. in Braham 62).

Andrade's and Tarsila's ideas on modernist Antropofagia were formed prior to the release of the first issue of the *Revista de antropofagia* (Journal of anthropology) in 1928. It is important to now return to the main topic of the book: the formation of a modern cinema in Brazil. For Andrade, cinema was certainly part of the *paideuma* that would form the movement. If Tarsila's images helped forge the movement, cinema and literature's relationship with the new medium also helped forge the sensibilities around Antropofagia.

The lack of cinematic production during Brazilian modernism does not mean per se that the writers and *modernistas* did not consider cinema and film production as part of their modernist project. Literary modernism was aware of the development of new media; the modernist critic A. de Couto Barros (1922), for instance, at the time wrote in *Klaxon* (the period's first literary journal that came out shortly after the Semana de Arte Moderna) that Oswald de Andrade's novel *Os condenados* "inaugurate[d] an unknown cinematographic technique" (13). In addition, Mário de Andrade and Alcântara Machado used cinematic techniques in their literary works, as Maite Conde (2018) discusses. The title of Alcântara Machado's 1926 novel, *Pathé-Baby*, explicitly invokes that name of a camera used at the time to describes its experimentation with narrative technique.

As Conde (2011) explains, Alcântara Machado "considered film to be key in creating a new Brazilian literature" (199). Oswald de Andrade, aware of the importance of Alcântara Machado's innovation, outlines the main ideas for his future manifesto in the preface for *Pathé-Baby*, arguing that Alcântara Machado breaks with a tradition of Brazilian writers who emulate Europeans and in doing so imitate a scared Hans Staden, as if afraid of facing cannibalism (Machado 12). To Andrade, Alcântara Machado's project was a new form of cinematic literature fundamental to modernism. Three years after *Pathé-Baby*, the *Revista de antropofagia* was the main vehicle for spreading modernist ideas. The journal was published in two phases (*dentições*,[19] as they called it) between 1928 and 1929, the first consisting of ten issues and the second of fifteen. A third and final phase was declared by Andrade in "Informe sobre o modernismo" (Report on modernism, 1945).

The *Manifesto antropófago*, according to Augusto de Campos in *Revistas re-vistas*, the most revolutionary magazine of Brazilian modernism, was published in the first issue, in May 1928. For Alfredo Bosi (1994), the manifesto is the "cornerstone of the movement" (284), and as the *antropófagos* themselves said, just like the birth of Christ brought a new era to civilization, the magazine and the manifesto also brought a new era to Brazil. The manifesto is a short text composed of a relatively small number of *aforismos* (aphorisms), and even though the definition of Antropofagia as a movement is not explicitly spelled out, some of its fundamental principles are to be found subtextually within those aphorisms, as Antônio Cândido (1970) describes. Andrade dates the manifesto as the year "374 da deglutição do Bispo Sardinha," in reference to 1556, the year in which the Catholic bishop, Pero Fernandes Sardinha, was devoured by the Caeté Indians. Furthermore, according to the poet, we should also celebrate October 11, as the last day of freedom on the American continent—that is, the last day before the arrival of the European settlers. Silviano Santiago (1989) writes that "Oswald mixes up chronological data, proposing liberating antecedents and castrating origins. Liberation and castration are at the same level" (86)[20]—*liberação* (liberation) being, then, the Indigenous roots and *castração* (castration), the European colonization.

As I mentioned at the start of this chapter, clearly the *Manifesto antropófago* must also be understood at least in part as a decolonization project.[21] Still, one can argue perhaps that European modernism itself gave the impulse to Antropofagia: European artists searched in Africa and South and Central America for images of the primitive and the savage to fuel their own artistic project of modernist rupture. The ideas of anthropophagy were in the air, reverberating particularly with the Latin American vanguards. Gérard de Cortanze (2005) observes that the avant-gardes on both sides of the Atlantic sought "an art for the man in the limits of love and anthropophagy" (136). George Ribemont-Dessaignes, Alfred Jarry (2004), and Francis Picabia (2007) are some of the most well-known European authors who referred to cannibalism in their texts. Ribemont-Dessaignes (1974), for instance, writes that the purest way to show one's love to one's neighbor is by eating them (105).

The French painter Francis Picabia (2007), whose *Dada manifesto cannibale*, was first published in 1920, seems particularly kindred in spirit to Andrade and his work. Picabia would go on to found the avant-garde magazine *Cannibale* and to collaborate with film director René Clair, designing stage sets for his film *Entr'acte* (1924). Picabia's own aesthetic practice and theory of *instantaneísme* (instantaneity) influenced experimental cinema of the 1920s.[22] Besides Picabia, Blaise Cendrars, who wrote the modernist text *Feuilles de route* (Road maps, 1925), based on his visit to Brazil, is noted for adopting the techniques and structure of film in this prose in a manner resonant with Andrade, who probably was familiar with his artistic vision (Conde 2018, 185). Other texts that influenced Andrade were Alfred Jarry's *Ubu roi* (Ubu the king), published in 1896, and his *Anthropophagie* from 1902. Interestingly, the Colombian writer Luis Tejada also published a short *crónica* titled "Antropofagia" in 1924. This rarely studied text shares a lot of similarities with Andrade's project. In it, Tejada (1977) praises the cannibalistic approach of some Indigenous peoples, saying that human meat has "distributed in the necessary proportions, the most adequate substance for man's nourishment" (265).[23] The pretext of this essay is Tejada's ironic treatment of a recent case of cannibalism that was sensationally publicized in the Colombian newspapers. The Colombian journalist wryly notes that unfortunately (*desgraciadamente*), in his day and age, social prejudice has converted an old ritual into a taboo: human flesh is now all too protected under the law. Tejada finishes his *crónica* stating that it will be for humanity's own good when one day anthropophagy is allowed again (267). Both Jarry and Tejada invoke cannibalism to criticize colonization. Both texts are resonant with the Brazilian manifesto in at least two specific moments: first, when Jarry (2004) claims that "this event, in our opinion, manifests one of the noblest tendencies of the human spirit, its propensity to assimilate what it finds good" (345),[24] and second, when Tejada (1977) finishes his text exclaiming, "I trust that, for the good of humanity, the day of the freedom of anthropophagy will come soon! (267)."[25]

Another text that seems relevant to Andrade's ideas on Antropofagia is less obvious: Joachim du Bellay's early modern programmatic text, *La défense et illustration de la langue française* (The defense and illustration of the French language, 1549), proposes the devouring (*devouration* in the French original) of Latin to improve the formation of French as a national language. He herein takes his cue from the ancient Romans, who imitated ancient Greek authors, "transforming themselves into them, devouring them; and, after having well digested them, converting them into blood and nourishment" (Leitch et al., 287). Formally and structurally, Du Balley's text might be considered a mosaic, a *macheterie,* made by pieces of diverse origins (Henri Chamard in Rouanet 2011, 175). The idea behind Du Bellay's linguistic and cultural program to spark the spirit of the French Renaissance is similar to that of Andrade's attempt to feed a Brazilian modernity. Maria Helena Rouanet (2011) argues that both authors found themselves in almost identical situations—namely, as representatives of a self-aware minor culture. Du Bellay, Pascale Casanova (1999) explains, wanted to improve French because it lacked the status and prestige of Latin—hence, "the importance he attached to appropriation," which he explicitly framed using "the metaphor of devouring, comparing this process to what the Romans did" (54). Almost four hundred years later, Brazilian modernists found themselves in a structurally similar position, trying to create a comprehensive *língua brasileira* (Brazilian language) in opposition to the colonial language imposed by Portugal. Different from Du Bellay, however, Andrade and the *modernistas* were thoroughly invested in reimagining popular forms of Portuguese that were suited to express the social and cultural needs of a non-Eurocentric, decolonial order.

Clearly, a wide array of European ideas influenced the modernist movement in Brazil. However, Brazilian authors never simply reproduced European ideas in Brazil. Andrade's manifesto is more than a rereading of Picabia's manifesto, Jarry's 1902 "Antropophagie," Du Bellay, or even Luis Tejada's "Antropofagia." As Augusto de Campos (1975) explains, "[T]here is nothing in the magazine, not one single text that one can read as a platform for a 'cannibal movement'" (11). Benedito Nunes (2004), following Antônio Cândido (1970), argues that Brazilian modernists learned quickly about the vanguard European art, immersed themselves in psychoanalysis, and created a form of expression that was both local and universal; they found the European influence through an immersion in Brazilian details.

What Is Queer about Antropofagia?

If same-sex practices are not explicitly treated by the manifesto, why, then, is Antropofagia so important? It is vital because it constitutes a mode of thinking and a method for understanding Brazilian practices as a whole. The *Manifesto antropófago* is of interest to queer theory because it revolutionizes the way the other is seen, the way the colony saw itself, the way abject bodies saw themselves, and the way local theory could be analyzed. The sense of devouring brings a new perspective into current theory because it allows us to question our own normative practices. Thus, the lack of explicit homoeroticism in the manifesto does not mean that its text is not queer. Moreover, the manifesto stands as a transgressive moment in relation to notions of patriarchy and sexuality. As Sedgwick (1993) writes, "That's one of the things that 'queer' can refer to: the open mesh of possibilities, gaps, overlaps, dissonances and resonances, lapses and excesses of meaning when the constituent elements of anyone's gender, of anyone's sexuality aren't made (or *can't be* made) to signify monolithically" (7).

Andrade (1928a) proposes the permanent transformation of the taboo in totem. While the Western world looks on cannibalism as one of the most unfamiliar, strange, and shocking habits to the civilized Western world, Andrade would find in it the motif for his formulation of *brasilidade*. Almost thirty years on from the launch of the magazine, Andrade returned to the topic: "[T]he metaphysical operation that is connected to the anthropophagic ritual is the transformation of the taboo in totem" (139).[26] Through his reading of Freud's *Totem and Taboo*, Andrade creates an opportunity to revert the negativity of queer into something positive. What had once been forbidden to be uttered now becomes a political tool for activism and theory. While Freud based his formulation of the formation of patriarchal society on the anthropophagous rite of the sons eating their father, Andrade inverts the totem-taboo dichotomy, proposing instead the return to a (preexisting, as Freud suggested) matriarchal society. Andrade chooses one of the most extreme forms of taboo and abjection—anthropophagy—as the totem of his manifesto, and the acts and consequences of abjection become the *força motora* of the movement that shapes the Brazilian cultural perspective in the twentieth century.

The early accounts of cannibalism divided the Indigenous populations into "good" and "bad" Indians: "Columbus's 'naturally Christian' Tainos and the ferocious Caribs who victimize them" (Braham 2015, 58). Andrade's concern was with the "bad" Indians. The "good" ones had already been appropriated by Brazilian Romanticism, but to Andrade the "real savage" was the one that truly represented Brazil, and it was this other that the Movimento Antropófago was invested in understanding. Andrade was not interested in glorifying the *bon sauvage* from the Romantic period; rather, his focus, an apology to the Indigenous ogre, was on the bad savage (*mauvais sauvage*), the anthropophagous, polygamous, communist white killer. Oswald devoured the foreigner theories, the same way his city, São Paulo, devoured immigrants to make Brazilian flesh and blood (Roger Bastide in Retamar 2003, 104).[27]

Persephone Braham (2015) further observes that anthropophagy was early linked to the other and to female sexuality: "[F]rom the moment when cannibalism was first mentioned in connection with the New World, it was construed as a threat to masculine sexuality" (57). And it was Andrade's intention to reestablish Pindorama's matriarch (i.e., a reincarnation of societal practices in which women were at the front). Taken in conjunction, Tarsila's work, Andrade's matriarchy, and the early accounts on anthropophagy that narrate in detail women as devouring beings (hence, "bad" Indians or, as Columbus specified, non-Christians),[28] it is possible to see an antinormative perspective that Antropofagia intends to "rescue" (for a fuller development, see my discussion of Trevisan's *Orgia ou o homem que deu cria* in chapter 2).

The anthropophagic queer can thus be seen as a mode of intervention: "visibilities within forms of social praxis in the Latino American contexts as modes of intervention that allow different publics to participate in the social sphere" (Quiroga 2000, 3). What is central here is the messiness of sex and gender.

In the following chapters, I propose an anthropophagic and queer approach to the history of modern cinema and argue that cinema—a genre that fascinated modernists, even if they did not leave an archive of films—is a compelling medium with which to uncover the avant-garde's discarded topics and bodies. My aim is to revise the mythical origins surrounding the birth of modern cinema from the point of view of a conceptual space in-between, which, I have argued so far, has in its origin in Antropofagia but comes into being retroactively, when thoroughly "queered" in and through queer practices in cinema. Andrade, we saw, believed that modernism would not have been possible without cinema. Geraldo Veloso (1995), in retrospect, argues that without Oswald it would have been impossible to revolutionize Brazilian cinema history. In turn, I now take Andrade's framework to the task of conceptualizing a particular style and affinity in Brazilian queer cinema.

TRAILER 1

The Revitalization of Antropofagia in the 1960s and 1970s

Prior to Oswald de Andrade's death in 1954, he feared he would be soon forgotten. Most of his books were out of print and only occasionally acknowledged by literary scholars. Yet within a decade, Antropofagia had become a central concept in how Brazilian culture sought to understand itself. Already by the 1960s, Antropofagia had become a rhetorical vehicle through which to discuss pressing political issues, notably the legacy of colonialism and the repressive realities of the government dictatorship. Carlos Jáuregui (2008) points to two events that led to a "renewed interest" in anthropophagy: "first, the 1967 premier of Andrade's play *O rei da vela* (The king of candles, 1933) by the group of José Celso Martinez Corrêa, which ridiculed Brazil's underdeveloped industry and criticized the national bourgeoisie's alliance with international capitalism, and second, the success of the musical and cultural movement Tropicália" (27).

In a country under a dictatorial regime, the resurgence of Antropofagia's ideals suited the era's intellectual and artistic needs to, in Joaquim Pedro de Andrade's words, "reexamine the movement of 1922 in terms of the present situation" (qtd. in Madureira 2005, 122). The rhetorical framing of Antropofagia as "devouring" international or external ideas to thereby "create" something new and wholly unique remained central to the arts in all manifestations, including theater and performance, music, architecture, urbanism, and cinema.

Most critics concur on the importance in this period of José Celso's staging of *O rei da vela*, Andrade's iconic 1933 play, which at that time could not be performed because of censorship.[29] Celso's staging marks a turning point in Brazilian theater: the discovery of anthropophagic ideas revolutionized a theater now seeking critical confrontation with the legacy of colonization by incorporating Indigenous anthropophagic rites, Brazilian popular music, candomblé, and samba to subvert Judeo-Christian taboos (Corrêa 2012). When Andrade wrote *O rei da vela*, his aim was to show the contradictions and ambiguities of a country obeying the impulses of modernization while struggling to maintain the national dictum for *ordem e progresso* (order and progress).[30] In the 1960s, little had changed: Brazil's dictatorship was determined to lead the country to industrial modernization despite a crushing national debt. Moreover, because modernization did not afford equal access to the benefits and opportunities of a growing economy, underdevelopment was quickly becoming a hallmark of the country. Celso, seizing on the resonances between Andrade's time and his own contemporary moment, staged the play in the manner of a carnival procession wholly in the spirit of Antropofagia.

Urbanism, landscaping, and architecture, too, were affected by an "anthropophagic turn," as evidenced by artist and designer Hélio Oiticica's *Tropicália*. For Christine Mello (2009, 190), Oiticica's work is the most anthropophagic piece of Brazilian art because it breaks with universalist artistic practices and creates a path for Brazilian artistic thinking.

Other artists followed suit and developed their own understanding of Antropofagia. Lygia Clark created the decade's most recognizably anthropophagic performance when she developed the "happening" *Baba antropofágica* (Anthropophagic slobber). This performance exploited the literality of the anthropophagic principle of swallowing and spitting. During one of her performances, she had one person lie on the floor while a group of people sat around this person and pulled a reel of thread that they had been chewing on from their mouths and placed it little by little over the incumbent's body, thus covering the person with the "new" thread.[31]

The resurgence of Antropofagia is also seen in the rise and development of a Brazilian modern cinema. The era produced a number of iconic film productions, such as Glauber Rocha's *Terra em transe* (Entranced earth, 1967), José Mojica Marin's *Esta noite encarnarei no teu cadáver* (This night I'll possess your corpse, 1967), and finally Ozualdo Candeias's *A margem* (The margin, 1967). Carlos Diegues, one of the founders of Cinema Novo, summarizes the influence of Antropofagia as follows:

> In Brazil the foundations of this new militant culture were laid for the first time by the modernist movement of 1922. From here came Oswald de Andrade, Villa Lobos, Mario de Andrade, Jorge de Lima, etc. . . . It was necessary to make anthropophagy a system, of disorganization a method, of disorder an organization. Like all anthropophagies, ours too has two movements: it destroys what has been devoured and nourishes the devourer. But it was the Cinema Novo in conjunction with the theater and new music, which introduced political sentiment into this concept of national culture. (qtd. in Siega 2014, 159)

In the sense outlined by Diegues, we might even speak of the rise of a Cinema Antropofágico. Randal Johnson and Robert Stam (1995), for instance, argue that the era's new cinema, Cinema Novo, at the time went through a "cannibal-tropicalist" phase (11). Joaquim Pedro Andrade's film *Macunaíma* and Nelson Pereira dos Santos's *Como era gostoso meu francês* both illustrate for Madureira (2005) the "recuperation of the anthropophagic act as a strategy of cultural and economic resistance" (17). This is also the context in which we need to situate an infamous critique by Paulo Emílio Salles Gomes (Conde and Dennison 2018), at the time arguably Brazil's most important film critic, who in his 1960 article titled "A Colonial Situation?" diagnosed cinema in Brazil as mediocre. In 1973, he wrote a follow-up to this piece, in the tellingly titled "Cinema: A Trajectory within Underdevelopment." For Salles Gomes, underdevelopment informs Brazilian cinema's lack of a fully developed and socially committed vision on filmmaking, mired as it is in ambivalence, confusion, and undernourishment: "[C]ultural progress in a context of general underdevelopment makes filmmakers struggle in the face of adversity instead of truly fighting against it" (qtd. in Conde and Dennison 2018, 290).

At the height of the military dictatorship (1964–84), this was no easy feat: state censorship was regularly imposed on works that were deemed too overtly critical. The return to "anthropophagic modernism" always had to remain strategic and tactical. On the release of *Macunaíma*, Joaquim Pedro Andrade wrote a short statement titled "Cannibalism and Self-Cannibalism," in which he observes that "the left, while being devoured by the right, tries to discipline and purify itself by eating itself" (qtd. in Johnson 1982, 157). In other words, critique hardly ever could be overt. Often in an experimental and opaque manner, the tactical recovery of Brazilian avant-garde modes from 1920s served to create a countercultural position in the 1960s and '70s.

This is also the case with Cinema Novo: not unlike Andrade, who in the 1920s intended to "devour" American cinema as a new language for artistic experimentation, four decades later filmmakers found in the modernist tropes and sensibilities of Antropofagia a style that they could reference and experimentally refigure according to the needs of their political and social agendas. In his *Enciclopédia*, Fernão Pessoa Ramos (2014) observes that modernist experiments in Brazilian cinema fully take off thirty years after literary modernism. Brazilian filmmakers in the 1960s began considering the ambition of developing a "modern" cinema only by first revisiting the modernist movement of the 1920s and '30s. In that regard, Rogério Sganzerla (1970), one of the founders of Marginal Cinema, illuminates the 1960s connection with Antropofagia in "A mulher de todos para o seu autor" ("The woman of everyone," according to the author) as follows: the only possibility for an "underdeveloped" cinema from a "terceiro mundo vomitando filmes péssimos e livres" (third world vomiting terrible and free movies) is to "devour" bits and pieces from so-called further-developed cinema, if even by negation and pastiche.

As important as the avant-garde movement Antropofagia is for understanding Brazilian cultural production in the twentieth and twenty-first centuries, it must also be noted that despite Andrade's attempts to rescue Indigenous practices to create a unique Brazilian form of art, Antropofagia was still very much a movement of the São Paulo white elite. The revitalization of Antropofagia by Cinema Novo was a return to a cis-normative model of understanding art. It is only with João Silvério Trevisan's *Orgia ou o homem que deu cria* that cinema will finally depict nonnormative bodies while reappropriating the persistent Antropofagia as a mode of cultural production.

JOÃO SILVÉRIO TREVISAN'S *ORGIA OU O HOMEM QUE DEU CRIA*

2

The Quintessential Anthropophagic Queer

João Silvério Trevisan in the Context of Cinema Marginal

João Silvério Trevisan's only feature film, *Orgia ou o homem que deu cria*, stands out as an iconic event in the history of Brazilian cinema. *Orgia* not only illustrates the pitfalls and paragons of Cinema Novo but also inscribes itself in the short-lived underground style in filmmaking that critics often refer to as Cinema Marginal. This chapter frames the rise of Cinema Marginal in the context of the turbulent period of the 1960s and '70s, when the material and cultural conditions of Brazilian cinematic production changed drastically.

To understand Trevisan's film, it is important to grasp the restrictive political conditions of the times. The end of the 1960s was marked by the military government's implementation of Institutional Act No. 5 (AI-5), which, along with other measures, expanded censorship and severely curtailed civil liberties and freedom. The *anos de chumbo* (lead years), the country's most trying social period, lasted until "the opening," from 1979 to the redemocratization in 1984.

Cinema, as all other art forms, directly suffered from the imposition of AI-5 regulations: the threat of censorship immediately impacted film production. Already in 1969, Glauber Rocha and Carlos Diegues were discussing the "death" of Cinema Novo. Yet at the same time the government created a Brazilian film company, Embrafilme (Empresa Brasileira de Filmes), a state-run company meant to support the production of Brazilian cinema. By controlling filmic production, Embrafilme would offer the population images "forged" by the state machine. Financed by the government and further benefiting from the economic boom known as *milagre econômico brasileiro* (the Brazilian Economic Miracle), cinema viewership doubled in the 1970s and local production share increased from 15 percent to 30 percent in the same decade.[1] However, the government's direct involvement also limited the variety and

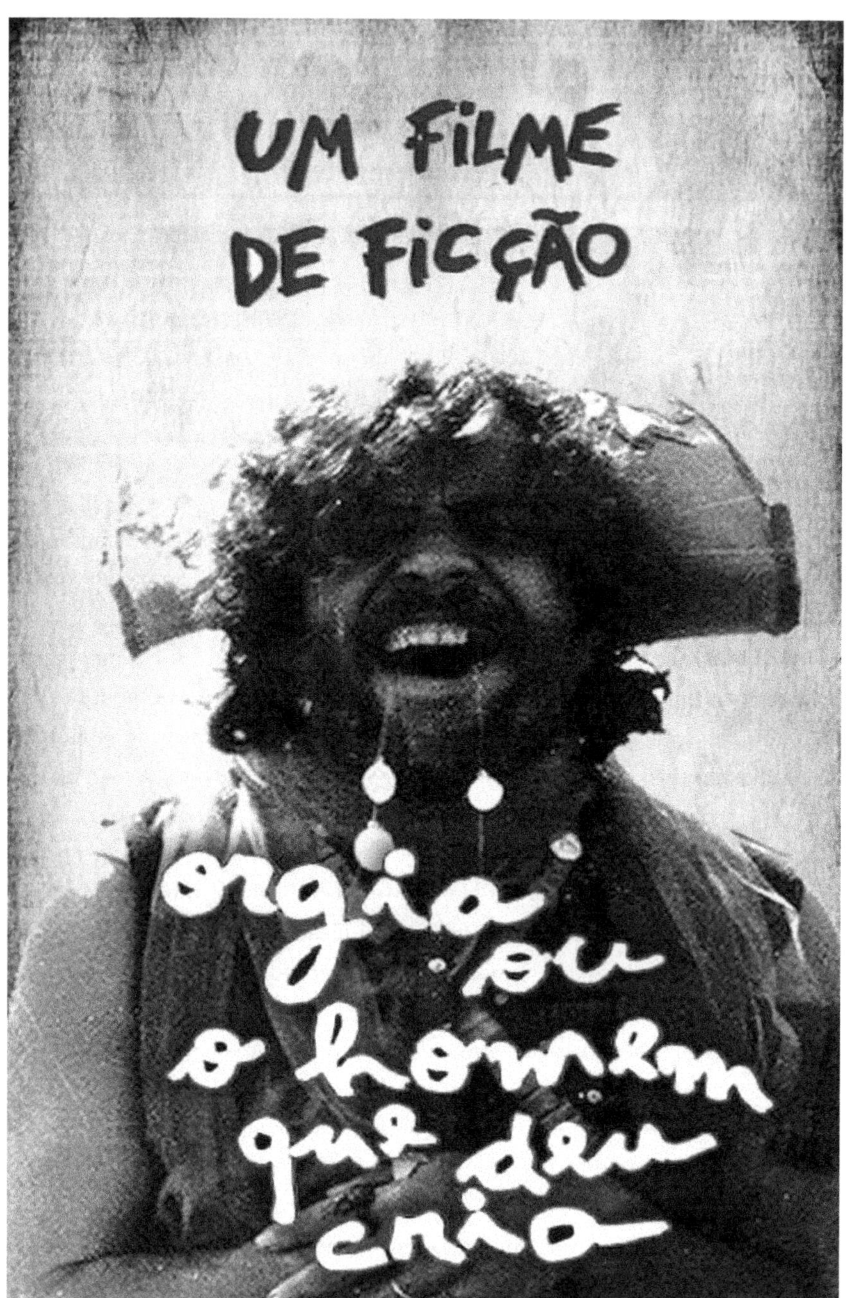

Poster for *Orgia ou o homem que deu cria*

quality of Brazil's national film production (Ferreira 2006), and Cinema Novo was almost completely marginalized in the large offering of state-supported films that were produced from 1969 onward (Johnson and Stam 1995). A great number of erotic comedies—politically inoffensive and culturally conservative—were produced with support of the government, a trend that would culminate in the 1980s, a decade wherein even pornography became a state-sanctioned genre (see chapter 3). Nonetheless, in this context of censorship and anodyne comedies, Antropofagia found its way into cinema as a form for commenting on the historical past of a politically repressive nation.

According to film critic Jairo Ferreira (2006), the first anthropophagic film to see the light was José Mojica Marins's *À meia-noite levarei sua alma* (At midnight I'll take your soul, 1964).[2] At the time, there was little consensus about the appropriate terms for discussing this new direction in author-cinema. Ferreira is one of the first critics to see Marins's film as a take on Antropofagia through the filmmaker's appropriation and resignification of classic horror images into an ugly, crude Brazilian gaze to the body. To the critic, Marins's films mark a still largely unconscious take on the topic, whereas soon thereafter films like Joaquim Pedro Andrade's 1960 *Macunaíma* and Nelson Pereira dos Santos's 1971 *Como era gostoso meu francês* will explicitly invoke Antropofagia as a theme and style. Robert Stam (1997), in this regard, notes that "concurrent with the tropicalist phase of Cinema Novo, there emerged a radically different tendency, variously called 'Udigrudi' (the Brazilian pronunciation of 'Underground'), 'Marginal Cinema,' 'Subterranean Cinema,' and 'Mouth of Garbage Cinema'" (251). As these terms suggest, the countercultural stance of the new trends was clear: "Just when Cinema Novo decided to reach out to the popular audience," Stam observes, "the Underground decided to slap that audience in the face" (251).

Brazil's Cinema Novo has been widely studied and internationally recognized. The filmmakers themselves have theorized about their aims and aesthetics in well-known manifestos and testimonials. In that regard, director Glauber Rocha's 1965 "The Aesthetics of Hunger" (recently published in English as part of a collection of essays in Rocha 2019) is arguably the most important, but other significant statements include Paulo Emílio Salles Gomes's critical essays from the 1960s and 1970s (see Conde and Dennison 2018), Estève Michel's (1972) *Le cinema nôvo brésilien*, Robert Stam's (1997) *Tropical Multiculturalism: A Comparative History of Race in Brazilian Cinema and Culture*, Ismail Xavier's (1997) *Allegories of Underdevelopment: Aesthetics and Politics in Brazilian Cinema*, Darlene J. Sadlier's (2003) *Nelson Pereira dos Santos*, Lisa Shaw and Stephanie Dennison's (2003) *Brazilian National Cinema*, and Lucia Nagib's (2007) *Brazil on Screen: Cinema Novo, New Cinema, Utopia*.

Randal Johnson (n.d.) pegs Cinema Novo as the start of modern cinema in Brazil, and in *Cinema Novo × 5: Masters of Contemporary Brazilian Film* (1984), he details the careers of five filmmakers associated with the movement: Joaquim Pedro Andrade, Carlos Diegues, Ruy Guerra, Glauber Rocha, and Nelson Pereira dos Santos. The movement, according to Glauber Rocha, aimed at raising consciousness among the Brazilian population of their own misery; his tellingly titled "Aesthetics of Hunger" details the rationale behind the movement, declaring the ways in which "[t]he time when Cinema Novo had to explain itself in order to exist has passed" (Rocha 2014, 219). Clearly, like the modernist movement in the 1920s and '30s, Cinema Novo was very invested in defining its position, but as never before in Brazilian cinema, directors now self-consciously took stock of their art and its importance to the cultural field at large. Their manifestos, articles, and ideas were widely diffused on paper and implemented on screen. The directors and creators engaged in debate about their films throughout the decade and afterward. For the first in Brazilian cinematic history, the filmmakers declared, studied, and posited theories about the birth (and ultimately death) of the movement.[3]

Most critics divide Cinema Novo into different phases, starting with the *sertão* (backlands) phase, which produced several landmark films that gained international recognition. It is the final, often-called "anthropophagic" phase, though, that most directly concerns this book. This is the point at which cinema turned to Oswald de Andrade's ideas on Antropofagia as a way to understand Brazil's current political moment. Fernão Pessoa Ramos (1987) observes that by the end of the 1960s, the 1922 sensibility returns, and the "pulso antropofágico" is incorporated in Cinema Novo. This era produced Joaquim Pedro Andrade's iconic film *Macunaíma* (1969), Nelson Pereira dos Santos's internationally known *Como era gostoso meu francês* (1971), and Glauber Rocha's influential *O dragão da maldade contra o santo guerreiro* (*Antonio das Mortes*, 1969). This so-called anthropophagic turn in Brazilian cinema is discussed by Guiomar Ramos (2014), for instance, in her analysis of five anthropophagic films.

Cinema Novo, however important for the development of a national identity in Brazilian Cinema, was also fast lived. As early as 1969, in the wake of the implementation of AI-5 a year earlier, the movement was declared over by Glauber Rocha and Carlos Diegues, and indeed, by 1970 Embrafilme had seized a firm grip on the production and distribution of films. It is against this backdrop that the ideas of Antropofagia a rebirth. Some filmmakers, turning their backs on Cinema Novo, begin reflecting on Brazil's state of "underdevelopment" (in terms that I will later describe as an abject space in-between). Some proponents of Cinema Novo will touch on the state of national and cultural abjection directly in their works. *Macunaíma*, for instance, depicts several forms of abjection—including the cannibalism. The final scene, a Technicolor orgy at a swimming pool, tries to make sense of the new order in the country.

Paulo Emílio Salles Gomes, the era's most important film critic and driving force behind the creation of Cinemateca Brasileira and the academization of film studies at the University of São Paulo, sees a resurgence of anthropophagic themes and concerns at work in the cinema of the time and characterizes Cinema Marginal as a new form of filmmaking that replaces Cinema Novo. Guiomar Ramos (2014) explains that Salles Gomes's criticism rests on reviving Antropofagia's rhetoric of "devouring" national (and mostly mediocre) cinema, such as the 1940s popular comedy, or *chanchada*, or the more recent erotic parodies of this genre, known as the *pornochanchada* (both genres are discussed further in chapter 3). These genres must be "devoured" for new national genres to emerge. Two films from 1968 readily came to mind to illustrate this period of transition: Nelson Pereira dos Santos's *Fome de amor* (Hunger of love) and Rogério Sganzerla's *O bandido da luz vermelha* (The red-light bandit).

If Santos is widely considered as one of the founders of Cinema Novo, he is also the one who closes its curtains: *Fome de amor* initiates the path to Cinema Marginal and "desbunde."[4] The term *desbunde* is of particular importance to this moment of cinema history. Both the noun and the verb (*desbundar*) took on ideological connotations in 1960s and '70s. *Desbunde* was adopted as a term to differentiate those who were involved with the political guerrilla and those who were not, and the verb *desbundar* was used to criticize those who had apparently abandoned left-wing political activism. Péret (2011, 45) observes in her book that the youth of the time were divided into two factions: the politically engaged, on the one hand, and the *desbunde*, on the other, which referred to those not interested in the political fight. Tropicalismo, however, tried to subvert that simple distinction by incorporating both activism and *desbunde* in subtle ways. *Desbunde*, despite its apparent lack of adherence to left-wing activism, was in practice much more critical and political than its critics acknowledged. In fact, in hindsight it is now clear that it *was* a political manifestation that responded to the repudiation of minority positions—referred to at the time as *devenires*, according to Perlongher (1997)—that were often unacknowledged by the traditional left. *Desbunde* opened space for nonnormative manifestations politicizing the body beyond the restrictive views of the left and right. Whereas the politicized youth saw the desbunde generation as a representation of alienation, another faction identified desbunde as a new counterculture proposing a wholly new, anti-aesthetic response to the political and cultural repression in Brazil. At the end of *Fome de amor*, for instance, the protagonist Mariana (Irene Stefânia) says, "I crucified Marxism-Leninism in my head." *Fome de amor* clears the path for dos Santos, who three years later will propose an anthropophagic take on Brazilian culture with his *Como era gostoso meu francês*.

Sganzerla's *O bandido da luz vermelha*, too, initiates a path at the margins of Cinema Novo. His "Cinema de Invenção" (Invention Cinema) as it has been conventionally named, while successful at the movie theaters and international festivals, also registers a break or rupture in tone and style that places his work on the periphery of Cinema Marginal. This also comes to the fore in a double interview with Sganzerla and Helena Ramos in *Pasquim*, a counterculture journal that circulated from 1969 to 1991, in which they call Cinema Novo right-wing conservative, paternalizing and anti-avant-garde (Fernão Pessoa Ramos, 2018a, 178). Glauber Rocha responds in a later interview saying that the bridge of niceties is over. To Rocha (1981, 214), *udigrudi* is a restorative abortion of the decadent formalism.

Often mentioned in the same breath as Cinema Marginal is Cinema da Boca do Lixo (Mouth of Garbage Cinema). Carlos Reichenbach, a filmmaker associated with Cinema Marginal, explains that the two terms reflect two different movements and moments occurring at the same time. Confusion arises because most films associated with Cinema Marginal aesthetics were also produced at the Boca do Lixo, a district of São Paulo at the time mostly connected with the low-end production of *pornochanchadas*. Causing further confusion, some films were able to cross over, gaining popularity and favorable critical appraisal, such as Alfredo Sternheim's *Anjo loiro* (Blond angel, 1973). However, the tone and content of Cinema Marginal can certainly not be reduced to the genre of *pornochanchadas*, nor should its avowed differences from Cinema Novo totally eclipse commonalities with Rocha and the "cinemanovistas." Cinema Margin, for instance, was no less serious in its commitment to exploring social issues such as poverty, bourgeoise morality, and social decadence, and the filmmaking practice "uma câmera na mão e uma ideia na cabeça" (a camera in the hand and an idea in the mind) was present in both genres. Robert Stam (1997) perhaps formulates the clearest distinction between Cinema Novo and the newly emerging Cinema Marginal, observing that "if the early 1960s trope of hunger—as in Rocha's 'aesthetics of hunger'—evokes the desperate will to dignity of the famished subject, token of the self-writ large of the third world nation itself, the trope of garbage is more decentered, post-modern, post-colonial" (20).

Yet at the same time, the persistent association of Cinema Marginal with *pornochanchada* is crucial to this book's understanding of an anthropophagic and queer style of cinema that started to develop the 1970s. To get to the heart of this, a short detour through the golden age of Boca do Lixo cinema is necessary.

Boca do Lixo and Cinema Marginal

Cinema Marginal and *pornochanchada* are two different genres produced at the Boca do Lixo district in São Paulo. Boca do Lixo, literally "Garbage Mouth," refers to prostitution zones. In the 1970s and '80s, the Boca do Lixo district in São Paulo became famous as a center of cinematic production because, according to director Alfredo Sternheim (2005), of the neighborhood's proximity to the old train stations, enabling easy conditions for access and distribution. Most international studios had their offices in this city district since the 1940s, and within the next decades various local production companies made their address in the region as well. For decades, the movie industry shared this part of the city with the prostitutes.[5]

According to Sternheim, it is not possible to talk about Boca do Lixo as a specific genre. In his book *Cinema da Boca*, he uses the term instead to designate several types of films produced in this city district, ranging from the 1960s Cinema Marginal to the 1980s pornographic films, around the time when the flowering production of Boca do Lixo ended. "Cinema da Boca do Lixo" appeared for the first time in print in 1970 in *Jornal do Brasil*. It was claimed not as a movement but rather as a state of mind—a rebellious act against the traditional standards of cinematic production. This lasted until the end of the 1980s, when the financial crisis of that decade, combined with the closing of Embrafilme and the lack of support for national production, made an end to this rich moment in Brazilian film history. Film historians usually identify Agenor Alves's 1987 film, *Eu matei o rei da boca* (I killed the king of Boca), as the last exponent of the Boca vibe.

Crucial to the following study on *Orgia ou o homem que deu cria* is that the rise of Cinema Marginal, and its progeny of a queer and anthropophagic style and sensibility in Brazilian cinema, cannot be separated from the Boca district and its colorful residents. Particularly through its close if often misunderstood and understudied association with *pornochancada* and erotic drama, Cinema Marginal is now viewed as the most radical cinematic experience of the past century in Brazil, which still exerts a direct influence in many productions today. Most of the films analyzed in this book can be inscribed in this tradition. Its name and the origin of its "marginal" status are up for debate. In the past, it was often called Cinema Cafajeste (Scumbag Cinema), although it was later mentioned with Cinema de Invenção (Invention Cinema),[6] before finally being called Cinema Marginal. All these epithets refer to a period between 1967 and 1971 in which the films most clearly associated with the genre were produced. Although there are competing names to address this type of cinema, this book prefers Cinema Marginal not only because it is the most commonly used by scholars and film critics but also, and crucially, because this name nods to the idea of social displacement, which goes to the heart of my understanding of queerness as space in-between in the films I analyze. Certainly, it is also in the margins of social and cultural norms of respectable (middle-class) taste that these films were made and discussed.

In 1968, João Callegaro made an early attempt to identify and situate the movement in its historical moment. At the time of the release of *As libertinas* (The libertines), Callegaro, Carlos Reichenbach, and Antônio Lima, published a short text in the brochure for the film that critics were quick to call a "Manifesto do Cinema Cafajeste" (Scumbag Cinema manifesto). In it, the filmmaker proposes some strategies for a wholly new anti-aesthetic, anti–middle class, and anti-intellectual style of filmmaking. The full manifesto reads as follows:

> Scumbag Cinema is the cinema of direct communication. It is the cinema that takes advantage of the 50 years of exhibition of "bad" American cinema, absorbed by the spectator and not lost in aesthetic research, intellectual thinking, typical of an illiterate middle class.
>
> It is the aesthetic of *Teatro de revista*, barbershop talks, pornographic magazines. It is the language of *Notícias populares*, *Combate democrático*, and "specialized" magazines (Carlos Zéfiro). It is Oswald de Andrade and Líbero Rípoli Filho, it is *Santeiro do Mangue* and *Viúva porém honesta*: masterpieces.
>
> It is typical Brazilian cinema, therefore, it is the *paulista* scumbag Cinema, without *bairrismos*, however with a lucid view of the *paulistana* fauna.
>
> Be aware, frustrated cinephiles, worshipper of *Cahiers* and Godard, for Scumbag Cinema is already a reality. It is the cinema of Rogério Sganzerla, the cinema of Roberto Santos (from *O grande momento* and the genius episode from *As cariocas*), Mojica Marins: it is the real *paulista* cinema.
>
> And its value will be calculated in ciphers, in payment slips, in weeks of exhibition: in audience. And the films will be genius.
>
> São Paulo, 1968.[7]

The manifesto synthesizes many of the points of what Cinema Marginal will attempt to achieve with its marginal aesthetic. With a self-conscious nod to the iconoclasm of Andrade, the manifesto intends to break with the intellectual seriousness of those "worshippers of *Cahiers* and Godard," a reference to the French magazine *Cahiers du cinéma* and its close association with director Jean-Luc Godard. The second paragraph reveals a veneration of popular culture as a source of inspiration for a kind of cinema. The manifesto mentions the *Teatro de revista*, a popular theatrical production of the 1930s and '40s that influenced the commercially successful Brazilian musical comedies of the 1940s and ’50s, a film genre loathed by the cinemanovistas. Cinema Marginal not only sought to revitalize the format of popular comedy but also welcomed pornography as source for innovation, invoking the “specialized” magazines of Carlos Zéfiro, the country’s best-known distributor of pornographic magazines in the 1950s and ’60s. The manifesto’s second paragraph also implicitly references Nelson Rodrigues, at the time Brazil’s most successful playwright, and Líbero Rípolli Filho, a popular theater and cinema director, who brought Rodrigues’s controversial and sexually explicit dramas to the theater. *Viúva, porém honesta* (Widow, however honest) is a Rodrigues play directed by Rípolli, and it is a reminder that many filmmakers associated with Cinema Marginal adapted Rodrigues’s plays and short stories for the screen during the first half of the 1970s. Along these lines, Oswald de Andrade’s posthumously published poem *Santeiro do Mangue*, famous for its “vulgar” language and topic (Mangue, at the time, was Rio de Janeiro’s famous prostitution zone) is mentioned. Callegaro places all these in the context of Boca do Lixo, albeit under the moniker of Scumbag Cinema. Finally, it is also remarkable that Callegaro explicitly identifies Cinema Marginal with the city of São Paulo. Invoking the *paulistas* and *paulistanos* (those who are born in, respectively, the state and the city of São Paulo) as witness to this manifesto, the filmmaker emphasizes the regionalism of the new productions: all is made in São Paulo, by and for *paulistas*.

The manifesto contains all of the characteristics that will become central to Cinema Marginal: sex, eschatology, humor, and debauchery. This group of filmmakers idealizes sexual freedom, as evidenced in Rogério Sganzerla’s *A mulher de todos* (The woman of everyone, 1969), which depicts a woman liberated from the constraining bonds of bourgeois marriage. Cinema Marginal finds in sex a liberating response to the “intellectualism” of the Cinema Novo. More drastically, in Geraldo Veloso’s *Perdidos e malditos* (Lost and damned, 1970), the main character kills his wife searching for a chaotic paradise of total freedom and sexual bliss. In clear resonance with ideas from Antropofagia, the defecating protagonist declares at the end of the film, “O homem é o que ele come” (Man is what he eats). While the manifesto criticizes the worshippers of Godard, inspiration from new trends in European cinema is generally never far away. As Fernão Pessoa Ramos (2018b) explains, “It is the intertextual discovery attracted by the classic varnish that incorporates a nouvelle vague inspiration, from the most precarious Hollywood authorial movie (or scumbag), the Western, the musical, the noir, even the *chanchadas*, now glorified because of its precariousness that once was concerning and the debauchery inherent in them” (183).[8]

According to most critics, Cinema Marginal lasted only three to five years, after which many directors moved on to make *pornochanchadas*. Others, like João Silvério Trevisan and João Callegaro, stopped making films altogether. Government censorship and persecution constrained the creative possibilities of cinematic production, and many artists preferred to abandon the industry. For Sternheim, the end of Cinema Marginal was inaugurated with the prohibition of Trevisan's *Orgia ou o homem que deu cria* and Carlos Alberto Ebert's *República da traição* (Betrayal republic, 1970). Paulo Emílio Salles Gomes finds that "[b]efore fulfilling its suicidal destiny, the Cinema do Lixo movement produced a unique human image in our national cinema. Marginalized to clandestine film showings, this final act of cinematic rebellion is a portrait of a young generation's despair during the last five years" (Conde and Dennison 2018, 308).

The semantic and cultural associations between a "marginal" cinema and a "garbage" cinema are important, as Robert Stam (1998), too, avers: "[G]arbage, like death and excrement, is a great social leveler; the trysting point of the funky and the shi. . . . In social terms, it is a truth-teller" (19). In this regard, we might add that garbage is not unlike excrement, which places it on the same level with the abject in the sense presented in the first chapter: the abject cannot be contained or honored; it challenges mastery and elides all attempts of rational understanding and order. In seeking out the abject as a topic of concern for a countercultural cinema, Cinema Marginal challenges the self-entitled moral seriousness of Cinema Novo. As we will see below, João Silvério Trevisan in *Orgia* relies on both garbage and excrement (portrayed literally in the film and not incidentally censored by the government) to shed light on a hidden, inconvenient "truth" plaguing Brazil's militarily imposed social order.

João Silvério Trevisan and His *Manifesto Entendido*

Prior to my discussion of Trevisan's film, I wish to address the main points of the manifesto the director wrote when *Orgia* was selected for a screening at the Museum of Modern Art in Rio de Janeiro. This unpublished document, part of the author's personal archives, is wholly in the tone and style of the avant-garde tradition but is particularly relevant as founding document of a queer cinema. Trevisan's *Manifesto entendido* delineates some of the criticism toward Cinema Novo and debauchery that he presents in his film.

Manifesto entendido might as well be translated as "Queer Manifesto." *Entendido* is an adjective in Portuguese derived from the verb *entender* (to understand), which before the introduction of the English word *gay* was used by the lesbian and gay communities in Brazil in either masculine (*entendido*) or feminine (*entendida*) form to disclose one's sexual identity. To ask "Você é entendida/o?" ("Do you understand?" or "Are you knowledgeable?") was a way to declare "understanding" as a dissident group.[9] Trevisan self-consciously finishes his manifesto with a provocative question: "By the way, do you understand, too?" The full manifesto:

cinemateca do museu de arte moderna 30.1.71
novos rumos do cinema brasileiro - VI programa 27

1. ...OU MANAUS

Direção, roteiro e montagem de Roberto Kahané e Domingos Demasi + fotografia de Paulo Sérgio Muniz (eastmancolor) + trilha sonora: John Mayal, Villa Lôbos, Ravi Shankar, The Who, Kenneth Gaburo, Chico Hamilton, Akira Miyoshi e Toru Takemitsu + sonografia de Hélio Barrozo + produção de Batoque Cinematographice (Brasil 1970). 10'

+ Um ensaio cromático sôbre a "Cidade-Risonha", onde estão presentes tôdos os elementos que fazem de Manaus uma cidade irreverente, nostálgica e grotescamente bela, do Teatro Amazonas ao radinho de pilha. Um filme talvez incompreensivo, mas apenas para os que habitam o "coração da selva". R.K. e D.D.

2. ORGIA OU O HOMEM QUE DEU CRIA

Direção e roteiro de João Silvério Trevisan + fotografia de Carlos Reichenbach Filho + assistentes de direção: Tânia Goni e Jairo Ferreira + montagem de João Batista de Andrade + sonografia de Jairo Ferreira + intérpretes: Pedro Paulo Rangel (assassino), Fernando Benini (viajante), Oswaldo Candeias (pai), Sérgio Couto (travesti), Marcelino Buru (anjo), José Fernandes (cego), Neusa Mollon (prostituta), Janira Santiago (vedete), Walter Marins (cangaceiro), José Gaspar (rei), Fernando Benini casa (fabricante de bombas), Budes Carvalho (seminarista), Sebastião Milaré e Antonio Vasconcelos (índios), Zenaider Rios, Mário Alves e Eduardo Karan (mendigos) + diretor de produção: Percival Gomes + produção de João Silvério Trevisan/INF-Indústria Nacional de Filmes (Brasil 1970). 90'

+ O cinema só morreu para quem um dia o colocou num pedestal - como eu. Coisas de aprendiz de feiticeiro. O tiro saiu pela culatra e eu acabei fazendo um filme.

+ Meu espetáculo (meu universo ficcional) tá aí prá os entendidos verem. Se alguém quiser saber, eu ainda sou daqueles que fazem cinema prá falar do desespêro que não entendo. Sou ainda mais retrógrado porque falo de um desespêro com causa. Falo como um louco num hospício. Falo, quando ao meu redor a consciência expira orgàsticamente e nossos olhos estão mortos.

+ Acho que um homem tem não apenas o direito mas o dever de pensar.

+ Acho que os modismos não conseguiram me convencer. E aproveito prá acusar minha geração que compra o inconformismo fabricado nas agências de publicidade e vendido nos super-mercados - como se tudo fôsse muito bem.

+ Saúdo a podridão daqueles que estão abrindo mão de tudo, em nome de sua tranquilidade pessoal, num tempo onde a neurose em massa é inevitável.

+ Saúdo os traidores (os da badalação intelectual) que vão prá os festivais jogar cartas na beira da piscina, tomar sauna no Hotel chic e receber aplausos - enquanto vendem o folclore colorido.

+ Saúdo as casas de teatro lotadas aplaudindo o inconformismo de Brecht, que bolou aquêle pensamento edificante pela bôca de Galileu Galilei: "Infeliz o país que tem necessidade de heróis".

+ Os surdos não ouvem mas batem palmas. E os burros só saem do lugar na base da porrada.

+ Amo apaixonadamente meu filme. Não se trata de curtição. Amo simplesmente porque minha consciência tá lá em cada plano, e êle respira o meu tempo. Não obstante, cinema prá mim é um fato acidental e circunstacial.

+ De resto, lamento que só o deserto me ouça. Afinal, eu não venho dizendo nada de novo.

+ Os românticos estão condenados, e a civilização é uma delícia.

+ A propósito, você também é entendido? João Silvério Trevisan

Facsimile of *Manifesto entendido* (João Silvério Trevisan's personal archives)

Cinemateca do museu de arte moderna
30.1.71
Novos rumos do cinema brasileiro—VI
Programa 27

Cinema is only dead for those who put it on a pedestal—like me. Wizard apprentice stuff. The shot backfired and I ended up making a film.

My show (my fictional universe) is here for the *entendidos* to see. If anyone wants to know, I still am one of those who make cinema to talk about the despair I don't understand. I am even more conservative (retrograde) because I talk of a despair with reason. I talk like an insane person in an asylum. I talk while consciousness expires around me and our eyes are dead.

I think that a man has not only the right but the duty to think.

I think that fads couldn't convince me. And I take this opportunity to accuse my generation that buys into the nonconformity fabricated in publicity agencies and sold at the supermarkets—as if everything were fine.

I salute the rottenness of those who are giving everything up for the sake of their personal tranquility at a time where mass neurosis is inevitable.

I salute the traitors (those intellectual dilettantes) who go to festivals, play cards by the pool, have a sauna bath at the fancy hotel, and get applauses—while they sell colorful folklore.

I salute the sold-out theater houses applauding the nonconformity of Brecht, who created that enlightening thought via Galileo Galilei: "Unhappy is the land that is in need of heroes."

The deaf don't hear, but they clap. And the stupid ones will move only when punched.

I love my film dearly. It is not about enjoyment. I love it simply because my consciousness is there in each sequence and it breathes my time. Nonetheless, cinema to me is a circumstantial and accidental fact.

Or else I lament that only the desert is listening to me. After all, I haven't been saying anything new.

The romantic is condemned and civilization is delicious.

By the way, do you understand too? / Are you *entendido* too?

João Silvério Trevisan

Orgia ou o homem que deu cria

João Silvério Trevisan is among a number of filmmakers who turned to Antropofagia to bring visibility to urgent political questions in Brazil. His 1970 *Orgia ou o homem que deu cria* is of particular interest to this book, because it articulates, I argue, a thoroughly anthropophagic and queer view on Brazilian filmmaking, developing as it did in the wake of Cinema Novo. On its release, the film was immediately censured by the Brazilian military government and banned until its first rescreening in 1981. According to the document (see fig. 3), the film was considered almost entirely "inconvenient." The Departamento de Polícia Federal (Federal Police Department), in its official letter sent to the director, states that the film could be released only if some of its most shocking scenes were cut, notably both the delivery and the devouring of the baby, as well as scenes laden with profanities and those depicting characters exhibiting what was considered animalistic behavior. Trevisan instead chose to not make any alterations, keeping the film intact until it could be seen the way he had envisioned.

Apart from being a filmmaker, Trevisan is also an acknowledged scholar, writer, and LGBTQAI+ activist. He wrote *Devassos no paraíso* in 1984 (which was translated into English as *Perverts in Paradise* in 1986), a comprehensive historical perspective on same-sex experience in Brazil. His groundbreaking book (now in its fourth edition) discusses sexual orientation and gender identity from 1500 to 2016 and analyzes the representation of homosexuality throughout Brazil's history. Trevisan is also one of the founding members of Somos, Brazil's first gay organization, established in the 1970s, and a founding editor the county's first homosexual journal, *Lampião da esquina*—all this under the military regime. He has written essays, short stories, plays, screenplays, newspaper articles, and novels. Perhaps because of his prolific career, his sole film feature is regrettably understudied.

I argue that *Orgia ou o homem que deu cria* is a cinematic investigation into the language of literature, film, and Antropofagia. Trevisan's film, described by João Rocha Magalhães Filho (1999) as a *manifesto em celulóide* (manifesto in celluloid) engages a discussion between Cinema Novo and the new Marginal Cinema, on the one hand, and Andrade's seminal text and Tarsila do Amaral's paintings, on the other. The film anticipates a mode of production that I call anthropophagic queer. Antropofagia, clearly represented in Brazil in the 1960s and '70s was seen as one of the main references for filmmakers. As Carlos Diegues, director of *Cinco vezes favela* (Favela five times, 1962), *Ganga Zumba* (Ganga Zumba, 1963), and other films, says, "[I]n relation to Brazilian erudite culture, we find in the most significant

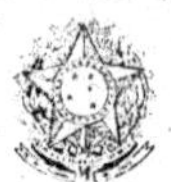

MINISTÉRIO DA JUSTIÇA
DEPARTAMENTO DE POLÍCIA FEDERAL

Brasília, DF.

Em 09 de setembro de 1971

OF. Nº 386/71-SCDP

Do : Chefe do Serviço de Censura de Diversões Públicas

Ao : Sr. Representante da Indústria Nacional de Filmes LTDA.

Assunto : Providência - Solicita

Prezado Senhor:

Com o presente, estamos devolvendo a V. S., o filme intitulado "Orgia ou o Homem Que Deu Cria", dirigido por João Silveira Trevisan, o qual, depois de examinado por êste S.C.D.P.,/ foi considerado inconveniente em quase tôda a sua totalidade.

Esclareço que o assunto poderá ser reexaminado caso V.S. pretenda, desde que devidamente remontado o filme e modificadas as cenas e diálogos considerados atentatórios à moral e aos bons costumes, e como tal, passíveis de corte, a saber: na 1ª parte, sequências nas quais os personagens são focalizados em atitudes animalescas; na 2ª parte, eliminação dos palavrões e corte da tomada que focaliza dois atores limpando as nádegas; na 3ª parte, supressão de pornografias; na 5ª parte, corte das tomadas alusivas ao cangaceiro tendo uma criança e da sequência que mostra os canibais devorando o recém nascido logo após o parto.

Atendidas estas exigências o filme poderá ser reexaminado por êste S.C.D.P..

Atenciosamente,

GEOVÁ LEMOS CAVALCANTE
Chefe do S.C.D.P.

Facsimile of the original censorship letter (João Silvério Trevisan's personal archives) artists after the modernist movement some elements that have served as a base for the Cinema Novo. Very close to the idea of a 'way of saying cinema in Brazil' are Mario and Oswald de Andrade: a new Brazilian language spoken in the corners of streets and countries, so different from that of living rooms and official speeches"[10] (qtd. in Siega 2014, 156).

Guiomar Ramos (2014) argues that *Orgia ou o homem que deu cria* is one of several "anthropophagic films" that combines elements of Cinema Novo and Cinema Marginal, including references to Rogério Sganzerla's *O bandido da luz vermelha* (considered by many critics to be one of the best Brazilian films ever made), which was foundational to Cinema Marginal.[11] Yet, to my understanding, mostly overlooked is Trevisan's pioneering effort in queer filmmaking. In a cultural climate where queer subject matter was often discarded on all sides of the political spectrum, Trevisan's film stands as an attempt to create a culturally liminal but productive—in Santiago's sense—space in-between for queer bodies in Brazilian cinema. *Orgia* offers an anthropophagic queer perspective on the history of Brazilian modern cinema, in particular as a corrective to the conventionally masculinist clichés of the era's cinema. The film's critical intervention is specifically aimed at Cinema Novo's privileging archetypes of Brazilian hypermasculinity, such as the *cangaceiro* (bandit).[12] In an undated PDF document from Trevisan's personal archives, Brazilian historian Durval Muniz de Albuquerque Jr. explains that Cinema Novo had always been a masculine cinema dominated by characters whose virility was articulated through the heroic, courageous, and generally violent manner in which they challenged the world. Trevisan, in response, interrogated hypermasculinity, putting archetypes to work to clear a queer path for visibility.

Trevisan's narrative follows a group of socially marginal individuals who migrate from the rural parts of the country to the city.[13] As Ismail Xavier (1993) has discussed, the idea of migration from the country to the city is a constant presence in Brazilian cinema in the 1960s and '70s, which stems from the high migration movement from the northeastern to the southeastern states during the 1950s and '60s. Space in this film operates as an "in between," as a realm without a recognizable identity; the characters move in transitory, nondescript, and almost empty space, at times reminiscent of the dry areas depicted in dos Santos's film *Vidas secas* (Barren lives, 1963), and then again of lush green landscapes as in Glauber Rocha's *Terra em transe* (1967). Composed as they are of rejects of mainstream Brazilian society, this group of characters form a harsh type of community. *Orgia* is not simply a film with a nonlinear narrative—it is a film that challenges the idea of narrative itself. In a few words, it tells the story of a group of outcasts moving from point A to point B, the latter point being the city. However, they don't make it to the city; they finish their journey instead at a cemetery overlooking the empty city.

Orgia begins and ends as a road movie—a point also made by Ferreira (1986), who describes the film as a story about "antropofagia on the road" (136). Critics often align the road movie with a search for family—a point that is particularly enticing for queer readings. In his comparison of contemporary French and American road movies, Neil Archer (2013) observes that the action in Olivier Ducastel and Jacques Martineau's *Drôle de Félix* (*The Adventures of Félix*, 2000) is structured by intertextual references to *The Wizard of Oz* (Victor Fleming, 1939). To Archer, both films present "the idea of flight and adventure beyond domestic confines, to a place 'over the rainbow,' the accumulation of a surrogate family en route; and finally, the quest for an unseen paternal figure" (81). If at some level this also holds for Trevisan's *Orgia*, the film nonetheless radically breaks with the possibility of finding a father figure: the first scene *kills* the father, precluding such an ending. Nonetheless, the idea of acquiring a surrogate family is also relevant for understanding the queer dimension Trevisan's depiction of an incongruous group of individuals searching for the "city." In fact, Trevisan's group grows in number as they approach the city; family, in Archer's terms, effectively is "accumulated" during the road movie (81). However, unlike in Victor Fleming's classic, the characters remain on the road until the end in Trevisan's black-and-white film.

The Characters

In his 2018 autobiographical novel, *Pai, Pai* (Father, Father), Trevisan opens his story with a line that makes clear how he understands his relationship with his father: "Tudo que meu pai me deu foi um espermetazóide" (Everything my father gave me was a spermatozoid). The sentence sets the tone for the rest of his book, which revisits his life as a teenager in the seminary, where he tries to come to terms with his troubled relationship with his father. Troubled relationships between fathers and son are well represented in the canon of world literature but may also be especially relevant to this book. To Andrade, fatherhood represents cultural decadence; only the ideal of a matriarchy can offer a utopian way out of the problems of Brazilian modernity.

Orgia's main actions are carried out by a nameless protagonist who, after killing his father, leaves his house in search of a new life. Trevisan re-creates Andrade's formulation on parricide while trying to understand the principles of pleasure. The authoritarian father represents Cinema Novo, the figure that immobilized cinema. Carlos Diegues (2014) holds that to most filmmakers Cinema Novo was already dead in

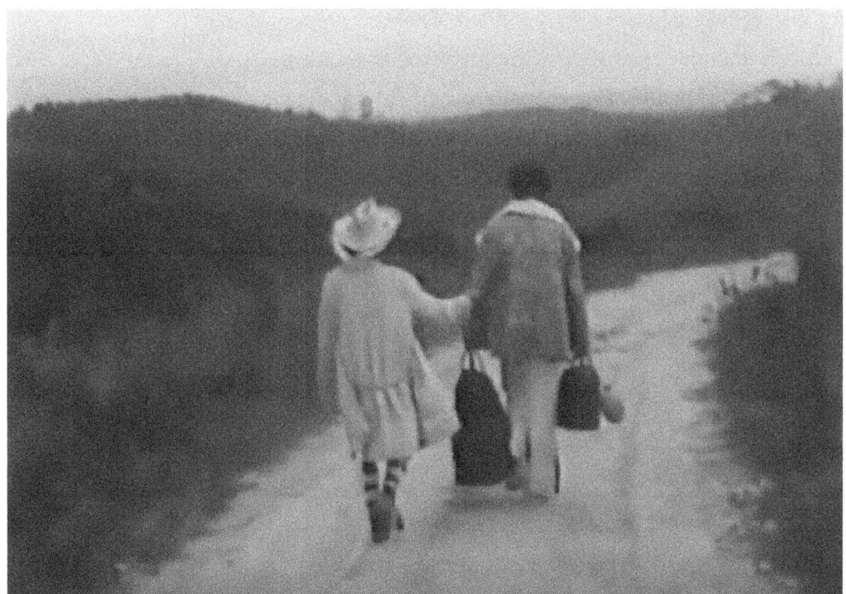

Still from *Orgia*: Accumulation of characters. The first minutes of the film shows two people.

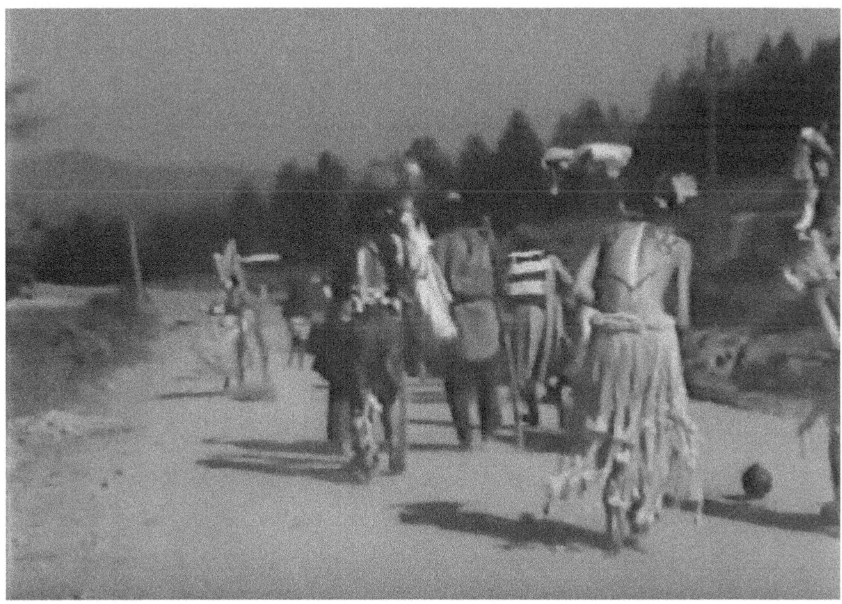

Still from *Orgia*: Accumulation of characters. Throughout the film, different characters join the "troupe."

The first still depicts the beginning of the movie with the two first characters—the parricide and the truck driver. Later, toward the end of the movie, they are joined by "the whole family."

1969: "[S]queezed to the right and left, doubtful of its own validity, shocked by the events it does not control, Cinema Novo begins to decree its own death, perpetrated the death filled by the new generations. I think I was the first one to talk about it in an interview with the *Cahiers du Cinéma* in late 1969" (qtd. in Siega, 158).[14]

By killing the father in *Orgia*, Trevisan delivers the final blow to Cinema Novo. When the director explained in an interview with me for this book (see appendix) that the original title of his film was "Foi assim que matei meu pai" (This is how I killed my father), it reinforced the supposition that the father and Cinema Novo are one and the same, with Glauber Rocha representing heteronormative patriarchy. After all, as noted earlier, Rocha, the most recognized name of Cinema Novo, once compared Cinema Marginal (which he referred to in disdain as "udigrudi") to an abortion of Cinema Novo.

Trevisan in *Orgia* reclaims Andrade's Freudian parricide and initiates his anthropophagic queer journey by killing the authoritarian image of the father. The film's initial scenes, not accidentally, remind the audience of iconic films from the 1960s: a man on his knees in front of a church calls to mind *O pagador de promessas* (The given word, Anselmo Duarte, 1962); a woman cutting manioc, *Deus e o diabo na terra do sol* (*Black God, White Devil*, Glauber Rocha, 1964); and the agricultural scene, *Terra em transe*. The series of sequences with no clear dialogue lead to the death of the father. The beginning of *Orgia* appears to announce a film in the style of Cinema Novo. However, Trevisan parodies this style and content. The nameless father's death at the outset reflects the director's self-conscious distancing from the classic rural images of Cinema Novo. Later, Trevisan's 1996 book, *Seis balas num buraco só: A crise do masculino* (Six bullets in one hole: The crisis of masculinity), revisits patricide, reinforcing the point every cinema creative from Trevisan's generation tried through their filmmaking to kill the father of them all—Glauber Rocha (135). To Trevisan, Rocha's films represent a crisis of masculinity that enacts a logic of homophobia and misogyny. Trevisan, in response, parodies the style and sensibilities of Cinema Novo by referencing Rocha's films. This self-consciously "anthropophagic style" also incorporates what Salles Gomes calls "bad movies"—the classic 1940s *chanchadas*. Trevisan also includes a reference to composer Heitor Villa-Lobos's *Bachianas brasileiras*—just as Rocha does in his movies—but *Orgia* parodies the original when his band of characters come upon a naked woman singing the *Bachianas* in a waterfall.

On his way to the city, *Orgia*'s nameless main character meets an eclectic number of other people, in this order: (1) a truck driver who has just murdered another man, (2) a suicidal intellectual who kills himself, (3) a *travesti* (transvestite)[15] dressed as a Carmen

Miranda *baiana* (Carmen Miranda from Bahia), (4) a fallen angel who falls from a tree, (5) the Black King (a man in a wheelchair carrying the 1970 World Cup trophy), (6) a blind man, (7) a *cangaceiro* (the man who gives birth in the movie), (8) a priest and his choirboy, (9) a nun, (10) two *índios,* (11) three prostitutes, (12) three farmers, and finally, (13) three robbers. Each of these characters seems to belong in the universe of a Cinema Novo film. The truck driver is a reference to Ruy Guerra's *Os fuzis* (The guns, 1964), whereas the *cangaceiro* brings to mind *Deus e o diabo na terra do sol* and *Vidas secas*. These three films, often considered an iconic trilogy of the *sertão,* are pastiched and parodied; or, as I hold, Trevisan's film "devours" and "queers" Cinema Novo in the manner of Sganzerla's "Outlaw Cinema."

Trevisan's characters in *Orgia* form an odd community; they travel together like a moving caravan of archaic and iconic figures who constellate an image repertory of Brazilian history. They form a "queer" community in the sense proposed by Eve Sedgwick (1993): as a group whose common trait is "the open mesh of possibilities, gaps, overlaps, dissonances and resonances, lapses and excesses of meaning when the constituent elements of anyone's gender, of anyone's sexuality aren't made (or *can't be* made) to signify monolithically" (7). This group is displaced, geographically and spiritually: they are on their way, and in flux. On their heels, following but not quite joining, are two Indigenous men. But instead of finding a new life in the city, their journey ends in a cemetery, where the action finds a stultifying conclusion: a baby that the *cangaceiro* had given birth to is devoured by the Indigenous men—a disturbing for its entirely literal tribute to Andrade's cannibalistic vision.

Trevisan's depiction of the *cangaceiro* is important to his critique of Brazilian cinema and the representation / appropriation of popular culture. Jean-Claude Bernardet (2007) argues that *cangaceiros* are crucial to a type of cinema that intends to represent marginality without its social implications (60). This is pleasing to the Brazilian middle-class taste in the 1960s during the rise of Cinema Novo.

The archetypal *cangaceiro* arose in Brazil in early twentieth century, when groups of bandits, such as the one led by Virgulino Ferreira da Silva, better known as Lampião, terrorized the northeast region of the country. In 1938, Lampião's group was finally tracked down and killed by police forces, who cut their heads and paraded them around in different cities in the country, exhibiting them to the population. The image of their heads on display quickly became a classic photograph representing this period of Brazilian history and a recognizable trope in the nation's visual archive. The image of the *cangaceiro* was avidly used in popular cultural and in cinema, for instance, in Lima Barreto's *O cangaceiro* (The bandits, 1953). Trevisan in *Orgia* radically queers and devours the hypermasculinity of this archetypical figure by making the *cangaceiro*

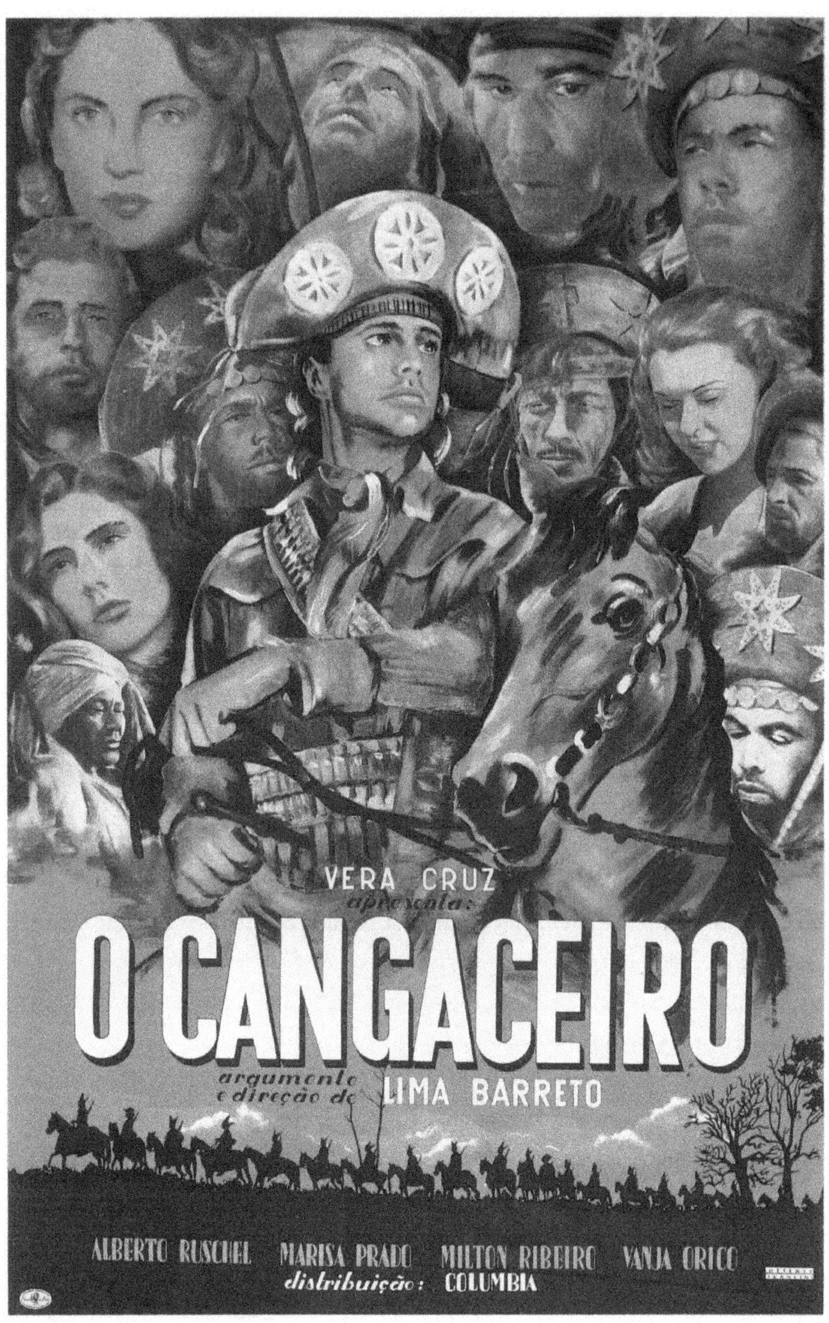

Poster for *O cangaceiro* (Internet Movie Database)

pregnant and giving birth to a baby. Trevisan's radical queering of this iconic image of brutal masculinity is exemplary of his debauchery technique and is also in line with the Cinema Marginal ideal of devouring and revitalizing undervalued, even "bad," genres, such as the classic *chanchadas*.

The plot of *Orgia* is clearly neither realistic nor self-explicatory but instead projects an allegorical dimension. The film presents a fragmented vision on the history of the Brazilian people (or peoples) in a manner resonant with J. Jack Halberstam's (2005) theorizing of queer time and space. The characters travel, stumble, and mumble through the world, often quite literally, reciting poetry by Oswald de Andrade. Not incidentally, then, Melo (n.d.) describes their travel as a kind of "procession," almost in the "epic" Brechtian sense were it not for the complete desultory tone: it is a journey filled with blood, semen, and pain, a journey marked by "abjection." The state of desultoriness and suffering in *Orgia* acquires a religious meaning: its wandering troupe moves as a procession under the *bandeira do divino* (Divino flag). *Divinos* are religious processions and celebrations that date back to the early days of the Portuguese Empire. This kind of procession was introduced by the first settlers and even today are enacted in many parts of the country, usually carrying the same kind of *porta-estandarte* (standard-bearer) with a symbol of the Holy Spirit, such as the one Trevisan uses in *Orgia*. Ironically, the Holy Spirit in Trevisan's *estandarte* is invoked by the Volkswagen symbol—a blasphemous reference to Glauber Rocha's *estandarte* in *Terra in transe*. In two of Rocha's films (the second being *Deus e o biabo na terra do sol*), the *estandarte* accompanies the characters traveling through different landscapes. By carnivalizing it with the German car company symbol, Trevisan's *estandarte* points to how capitalism impoverishes local practices; it is sign of the Holy Spirit in mourning.

If, according to Stam (1997), *Como era gostoso meu francês* is a "didactic lesson in cultural relativism, indirectly posting Montaigne's question, 'Qui sont les vrais barbares?'" (250), Trevisan's film enacts a subversion of this question. The film suggests that it is not important to know who "the real barbarians" are, so in that sense *Orgia* can be read as sign of resignation, almost as a failure of the utopian hopes of Tropicália or Cinema Novo. Trevisan's cinema is not utopian; it is about disappointment, a queer failure. As Trevisan himself commented recently (see appendix), the movie first of all embodied the more anarchistic ideas of the Marginal Cinema, but it was also important for making visible queer bodies who had up till that point been unseen. A case in point is the Travesti Poeta, in Trevisan's words, who, to my understanding, embodies an "abject" position that is both queer and anthropophagic in Oswald de Andrade's sense.

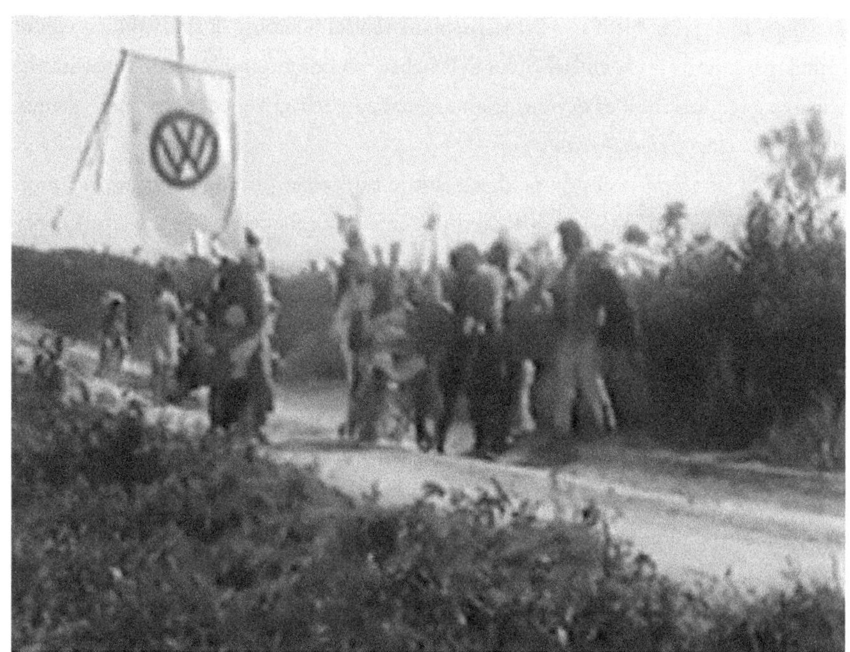

Still from *Orgia ou o homem que deu cria*

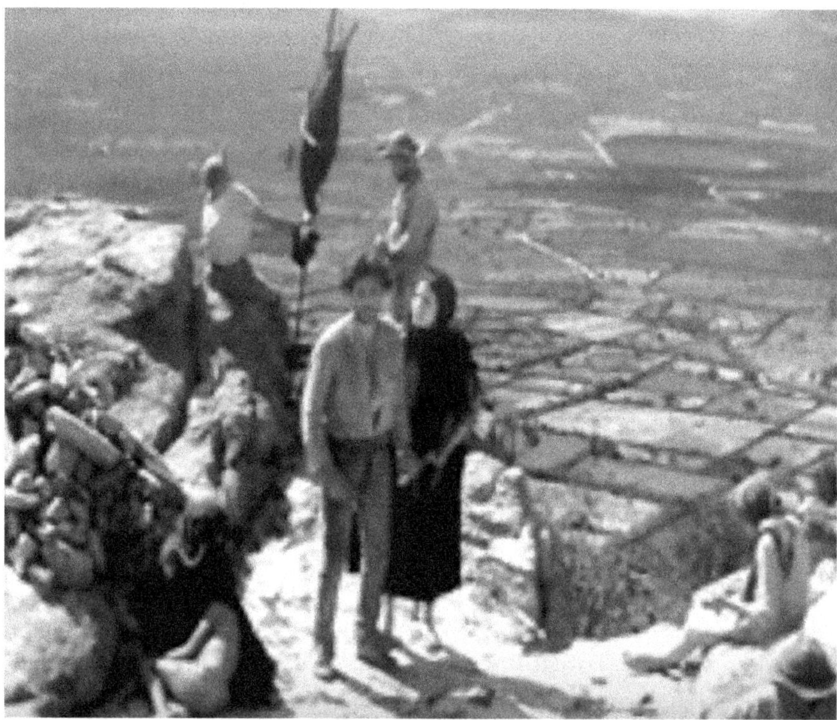

Still from *Deus e o diabo na terra do sol*

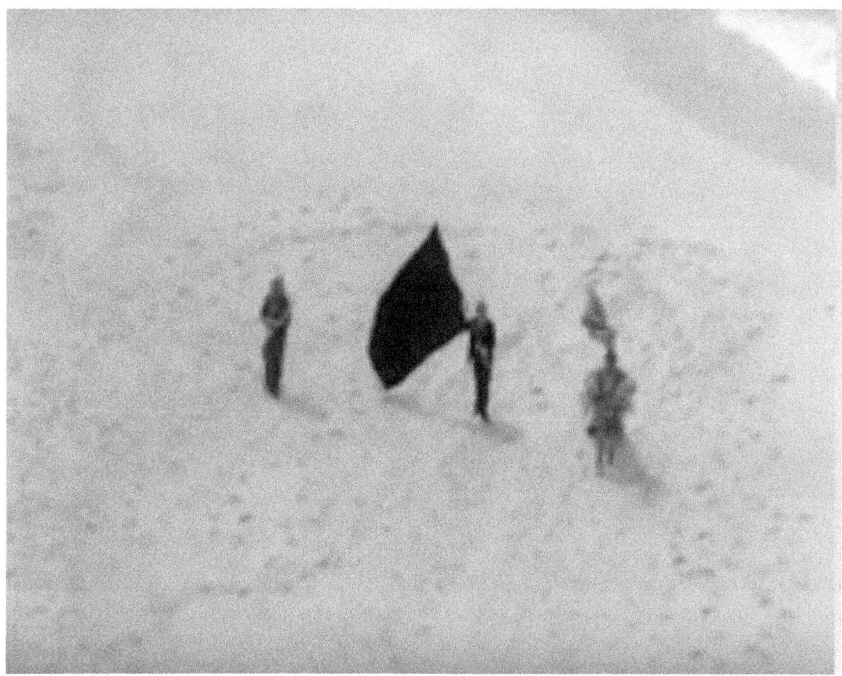

Still from *Terra em transe*

These figures show different depictions of the *estandarte* in the three films.

The Travesti Poeta frequently recites lines from Andrade's poem "Canto do regresso à pátria" (Canto of the return to homeland), part of *Pau-Brasil*, a poetry collection published in 1925, three years before the *Manifesto antropófago*. The poem is a parody of Gonçalves Dias's 1843 poem "Canção do exílio" (The song of exile). In *Orgia*, the Travesti Poeta reads the first three stanzas of the poem, leaving out the last lines that mention São Paulo. The group, the Travesti Poeta, tells us, wants to go to the city, where "there is more life, there are more people." However, it seems unclear at this point in the film whether this is possible. The poem's omitted lines are hopeful yet very melancholy: "Don't let me die God / Before returning to São Paulo / Before seeing Rua 15 / And the progress in São Paulo."[16]

A key moment of the film depicts a religious mass, referencing Humberto Mauro's classic, *O descobrimento do Brasil* (The discovery of Brazil, 1936) and Glauber Rocha's *Terra em transe*. Trevisan shoots the scene in one long, open sequence, placing the priest in the center of the shot and two Indigenous men, who observe his actions, to the left. In doing so, the sequence creates a dialogue with Victor Meirelles's iconic

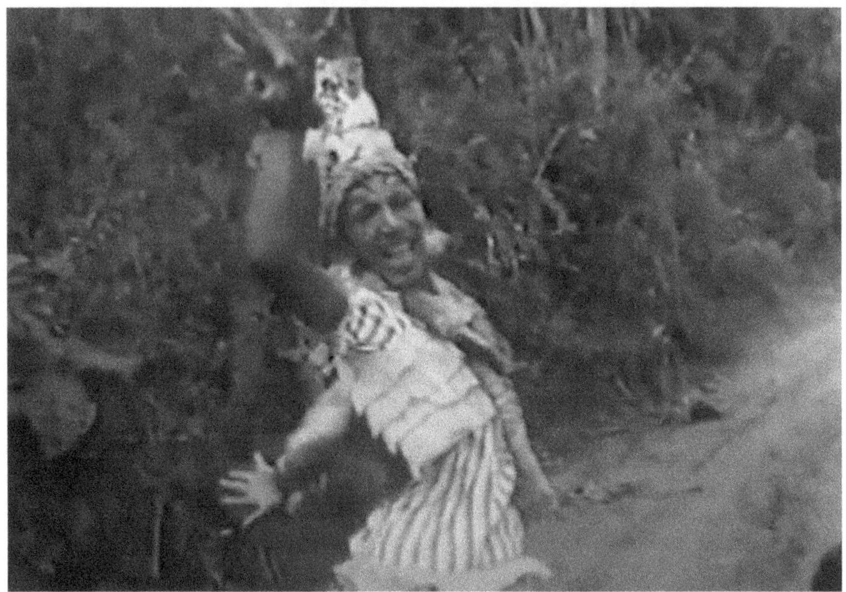

Still from *Orgia e o homem que deu cria*: The Travesti Poeta dancing and singing

painting *A primeira missa no Brasil* (The first mass in Brazil). These images illumine the devouring and carnivalizing of iconic repertoires in a ritual of cultural anthropophagy. Trevisan alters the images, countering their meaning and texture: the mass is set in an extremely dry area, with no proximity to water (unlike in Meirelles's original painting and Rocha's film). The mass takes place in barren conditions, in a nation bereft of humanity and life. Trevisan's chosen landscape, actions, and characters all call to mind a state of national abjection.

I use the term *abjection* in Julia Kristeva's sense. In *Powers of Horror: An Essay on Abjection*, Kristeva (1982) presents an account of abjection as a phenomenon relatable to the topics and personalities of avant-garde artists such as Oswald de Andrade and Trevisan. She argues that "*the writer*, fascinated by the abject, imagines its logic, projects himself into it, interjects it, *and as a consequence perverts language*—style and content" (16, emphasis added). This is resonant with Antropofagia, where movement, so to speak, "perverts" itself to express the abject. To narrate in his film the story of a troupe of characters ostracized by society and family, Trevisan purposefully perverts language: the characters don't speak in a clear manner but instead mumble words, or they scream and talk over one another. Using only one camera to record the film, the camera movement follows the action in a chaotic manner, which Guiomar Ramos (2008), referencing Antonin Artaud's "The Theater and the Plague," has called a "performance of pain" (30).

Trevisan's film is an almost essentially Artaudian piece of theater: "It is like the plague not because it is contagious, but because like the plague, it is the revelation, the bringing forth, the exteriorization of a depth of latent cruelty by means of which all the perverse possibilities of the mind, whether of an individual or a people, are localized" (30).

One of the very rare moments in which the camera remains steady occurs in the film's final minutes: the camera fixes the Indigenous men in the center dancing while a narrator says, "Civilization is delicious. Let syphilis come! We are ready to rot." They are speaking in Tupi. The Indigenous men dance in front of the camera while the main group is in the background. They have never been integrated to the group but "are ready to rot."

Kristeva (1982) explains abjection as the breaching or confusion of the "inside/outside boundary. . . . [T]he threat comes no longer from outside but from within" (114). The taboo act of anthropophagy—where men would eat others as part of a ritual—structurally operates alongside such an inside/outside dichotomy. To the cannibal, the devouring of the body is also an act of cleansing: it will make one stronger or purer. However, cannibalism is also a taboo, other forms of purification—burial, for instance—are developed so that forbidden acts may be avoided. To Kristeva, abjection concerns our intimate beings; it involves what we try to hide or should hide—our sexual practices as much as our excretions. Kristeva's theories invite us to think of the

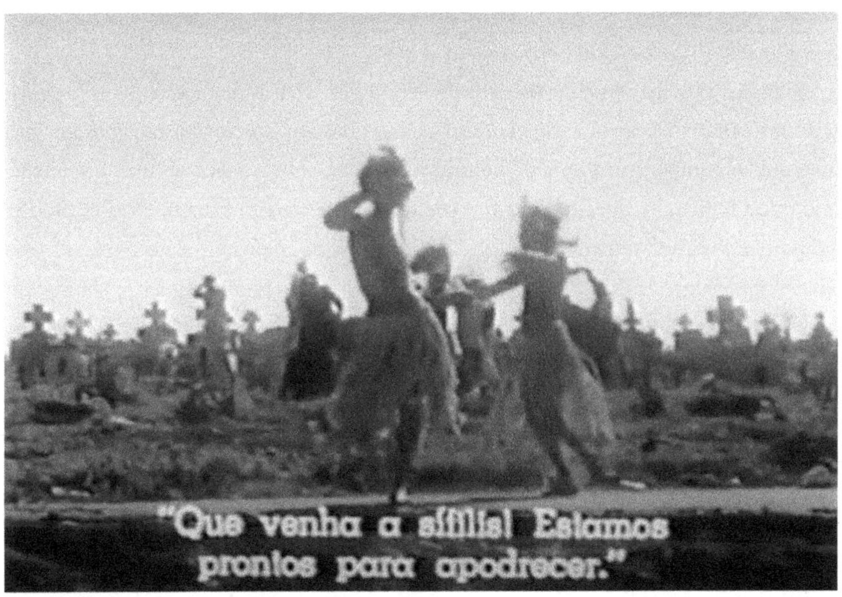

"Let syphilis come! We are ready to rot." Two Indigenous people dance and sing in Tupi, celebrating the ruins of civilization.

abject body in a manner in which sexuality extends beyond sexual practices, identity beyond fixed categories, and shame beyond stigma. As Richard Miskolci (2012) asserts, the abject is something one person is horrified or disgusted by, as if it were polluted or impure. Accordingly, contact with the abject (or with an abject person or feeling) is experienced as contaminating and nauseating (43).

Giving expression to the experience of abjection, observes Miskolci, is fundamental to Trevisan's "queer anthropophagic project; Trevisan's group of misfits live in opposition to a failed patriarchal society in which the feminine is treated as 'the other.' Here too Kristeva's recovery of the 'abject' as a tool for critical analysis resonates with queer antropofagia: 'What we designate as "feminine," far from being a primeval essence, will be seen as an "other" without a name, which subjective experience confronts when it does not stop at the appearance of its identity'" (58). It is this "other" that Trevisan's queer take on Antropofagia attempts to make visible.

It is through the recovery of the feminine that the Antropofagia movement becomes a queer practice. After all, the denial of the feminine is culturally reenacted in prejudice against effeminate men.[17] More generally, the image of a man associating himself with the traits of a woman is reason for distrust, or even disgust—abjection—in the eyes of the traditional male-dominated Brazilian society that Trevisan depicts in *Orgia*. In his film, all the characters, to some extent, represent different versions of this abject state of invisibility and violence. The nameless main character makes this clear in the beginning of the film. Right after meeting the truck driver, he says, "Something is going to end. . . . Yes, I am going to end."

What is it that renders the other abject? Or, rather, what is this abject part of oneself that moves a person against somebody else? The question is as urgent in Trevisan's film as in our contemporary moment. The manner in which *Orgia* enacts an anthropophagic and queer logic puts abject bodies and pleasure at the center of the discussion. Bodies become centers and sources of pleasure, and orgasm can be manipulated, created, and invented through, as Paul Preciado (2011a) explains, "several disciplines of simulation and serial repetition" (29). Preciado, akin to Andrade's fashion, organizes his *Manifesto contrasexual* in terms of a total freedom for the body, unfettered from control by the state. In *The Queer Art of Failure*, J. Jack Halberstam (2011) proposes that "queer studies offer us one method for imagining, not some fantasy of an elsewhere, but existing alternatives to hegemonic systems" (89). When considering that to Heather Love (2007) the homosexual body has historically been associated with "failure, impossibility and loss" (21), then Preciado's (2011a) manifesto indeed imagines (and puts into practice!) alternative modes of living. This alternative world-making is also at work in Trevisan's *Orgia*: the queerness of these loosely assembled bodies is neither silenced nor mourned.

This represents a break with the dominant regime of shame: since its medicalization in the late 1800s, the homosexual body has been marked with shame. Shame, David Halperin (2007) reminds us, is "an effect of the play of the social power" (71). Not surprisingly, LGBTQAI+ individuals in Brazil have historically found it difficult to place themselves between the Right and Left on the political spectrum. The Brazilian gay writer and activist Herbert Daniel, for instance, once reported, "[I]n the 1970s I began to participate politically in the struggle for homosexual rights, because when I fought as a guerrilla I realized that the prejudice of the Left was as strong as that of the Right in relation to homosexuality" (qtd. in Likosky 1992, 300). Trevisan, too, has often expressed similar concerns. *Orgia ou o homem que deu cria* responds to this dichotomy as a film that can't easily be situated on the Left or to the Right. It delineates a transient space in-between as a space of queer visibility—as a space for LGBTQAI+ individuals to come. In his 1982 *Passagem para o sonho*, Daniel argues that up until the 1990s in Brazil the most common way of talking about homosexuality was silence (215). It is precisely this silence Trevisan aims to rupture with his film.

When Andrade formulated Antropofagia, he turned to the abjected Indigenous body as a way to reinvent and realign past traditions with the modernity of his times. In this chapter and throughout this book, I in turn suggest the concept of the anthropophagic queer to attempt to render visible a range of abjected and queer bodies. The idyllic notions that Oswald de Andrade proposed in the 1920s and '30s are not without problems and may no longer be possible. However, the anthropophagic formulations can help us assimilate (or devour) the exogenous in order to reinvent social practices and the filmic experience, as Trevisan proposes. His film, I argue, can help us visualize a precarious but productive space in-between, in the manner of Silviano Santiago (2001): "Since Latin American can no longer close its doors to foreign invasion nor recuperate its condition as a 'paradise' of isolation and innocence, one realizes with cynicism that, without such resignifications, its product would be a mere copy—silence, a copy that is frequently outmoded due to that imperceptible retrocession of time that Claude Levi-Strauss talks about. Its geography must be one of assimilation and aggressiveness, of learning and reaction, of false obedience" (36).

Santiago's discussion of the *entre-lugar* (or "space in-between," as it has been conventionally translated into English)[18] resonates with my understanding of Andrade's metaphorical constructions and placing (or displacing) of abjected bodies and therein reflects the situation of the characters in Trevisan's film: they occupy a space of partial visibility, a space that nevertheless allows limited forms of resistance. Santiago (2013) explains that interest in discussing homosexuality "was not to promulgate a politics of homosexual identity, but rather promote what would later be called queer" (197).[19]

Santiago was well aware of the impossible nature of Andrade's hope for an uncomplicated return to Brazilian ancestral roots. However, like Andrade working against the lasting effects of colonial past, Santiago envisioned a space in-between where Latin American discourse is produced—not to negate external influences or inspiration but to devour and reconnect them with the local and queer practices.

Trevisan's space in-between is neither an abstraction nor a replacement or inversion of positions; the filmmaker aims to question hierarchies, basing himself in a cultural anthropophagy that goes beyond mere representations or mirrors of cultural production. I take my cue here from Denilson Lopes (2014) who sees the space in-between as a strategy of resistance more than an actual (physical) place: "[I]t is from the space in-between that we can include the gay experience in this remodeling of the nation by treating their historical invisibility not only as repression but also as ambiguous resistance" (27).[20] The aim to reclaim abjected bodies[21] that have been denied visibility in the history of the Brazilian public sphere is also pertinent to this book on cinema; in an anthropophagic mode, Trevisan critically incorporates Cinema Novo aesthetics to put on center stage the socially marginal position of abjected bodies in search for a space in-between. In his film, Trevisan appropriates the aesthetics of Cinema Novo (in the use of black-and-white film, long shots, and "a camera in one's hand and an idea in one's mind"), almost as if a foreign aesthetic that is devoured and ingested for queer filmmaking. He revises Antropofagia, a concept widely referenced by Brazilian filmmakers, turning it into an anthropophagic queer mode and paving the way for other queer filmmakers.

Perhaps Trevisan's film, like the characters in it, fails to construct a livable, hospitable queer reality. In this sense, too, *Orgia* projects a bleak and abject universe. The film registers the lack of space in terms of politics for LGBTQAI+ individuals who cannot find a place either on the Right or the Left. But, ultimately, the film perhaps understands failure as quintessential queer—as in recent theorizing on failure as a defiant queer stance (see Halberstam 2011). *Orgia* understands failure as a critical trope. Cultural shock, debauchery, irony, and failure—in a queer sense—were the only possibilities for bodies who were not conventional subjects deemed worthy in the arts. I argue that Brazilian cinema required the anthropophagic descent (*descida antropofágica*, in Andrade's [1928a, 7] terms) and the *tropicalista* revolution to enable a cultural and aesthetic vocabulary to project such bodies into visibility with voice and agency. Hence, along with José Celso's *O rei da vela*, Hélio Oiticica's *Parangolés* and *Tropicália*, Caetano Veloso and Gilberto Gil's Tropicalismo, Lygia Clark's *Baba antropofágica*, and Jairo Ferreira's films and criticism, João Silvério Trevisan is crucial to the anthropophagic queer project that I am proposing in this book and that I will further trace in the following chapters.

3

HIV/AIDS IN 1980S BRAZILIAN CINEMA

Abjection and Shame in Documentary, Fiction, and Pornography

During the 1980s, four Brazilian film genres prevailed at the box office: (1) children's movies, such as those produced by Os Trapalhões and Xuxa;[1] (2) pornographic films, which by 1982 had become a viable commercial genre; (3) "erotic dramas" and "serious" films originating from Cinema Marginal and/or Cinema Novo, which were well received by critics but not always commercially successful; and (4) *pornochanchadas*, which originated in the 1970s and continued to draw large crowds to the movie theaters. In this chapter, I focus on three films produced between 1985 and 1988 that present very different responses to the Brazilian political moment, particularly to the AIDS crisis of the 1980s. These films come from three different traditions mentioned above: the pornographic genre, *pornochanchada*, and Cinema Marginal. None of them were box-office hits, but their depiction of the AIDS epidemic is crucial to our understanding of the articulation of the anthropophagic queer and their experience with abjection.

The 1980s are, of course, an important decade in the history of Brazil: the dictatorship ended in 1984, and in the following year, José Sarney was appointed as the first civil president. In 1989, Fernando Collor de Mello became the country's first democratically elected president. By that time, the country's economic state was quite disastrous, hitting a yearly inflation rate of 5,000 percent by the early 1990s. During Fernando Collor's presidency, Embrafilme closed down, leading to an almost complete halt in cinema production in Brazil in 1992. That year, only three Brazilian films were released, and local production corresponded to 0.05% of the market in the same year (Ortiz and Autran 2018).

In the onslaught of the economic chaos that occurred throughout the 1980s, one cinema genre that survived and even flourished was pornography. Sex was a topic that was easy to sell a wide audience. Between 1985 and 1991, the majority of films in Brazil were pornographic releases. A brief look at the 1988 box-office chart further reveals that some of the most successful movies, with the exception of six children's films, had explicitly sexual titles, and many among them were indeed pornographic—for instance, *Eles comem cu* (They eat/fuck ass, 1988) (Johnson 1993).

It is in this climate of increasing permissiveness of the representation of explicit sex that the three films I have chosen for discussion need to be situated. This chapter's main focus is mapping the response to AIDS in Brazilian cinema, with particular attention paid to *Romance* (Romance, Sérgio Bianchi, 1988), *AIDS, furor do sexo*[2] (AIDS, the furor of sex, Fauzi Mansur [as Victor Triunfo], 1985), and *Estou com AIDS* (I have AIDS, David Cardoso, 1985).[3] Bianchi comes from the Cinema Marginal tradition; Mansur's *AIDS, furor do sexo* is a pornographic movie, and Cardoso's *Estou com AIDS* is a hybrid of *pornochanchada* and documentary. All three directors, working in Brazilian mainstream cinema, captured the early years of AIDS in unconventional and often shocking manners that to this day remain unparalleled in Brazilian cinema.

As in many places throughout the world, the AIDS crisis in Brazil created a sense of moral panic, and accusing fingers quickly pointed to gay men, who at the time had only recently gained more social visibility. As João Silvério Trevisan (2004) observes, homosexuality in Brazil at the time quickly transitioned from being ostracized to being condemned; a poll organized by Brazil's leading newspaper *Folha de São Paulo* in 1988 revealed that 60 percent of the population of São Paulo disapproved of homosexual depictions of affection (449). Cinema responded to this state of affairs in different ways in terms of aesthetic, politics, and morality. Whereas *AIDS, furor do sexo* instills its storytelling with a damning moral sense and guilt, *Romance* connects AIDS with the greater political turmoil of the country in the 1980s. *Estou com AIDS*, finally, presents the "reality" of the disease by intertwining real-life interviews with doctors with fictional characters set against the backdrop of the Boca do Lixo district in São Paulo.

I use the concept of abjection as a premise to explore the association among AIDS, homosexuality, death, and marginality. In Trevisan's (2018) terms, gays during this decade are considered *maldito* (cursed or condemned), and even in cinema, gay sex and characters are represented as abject and marginal to society. However, this marginal position may also be imagined as a creative space of contestation: in the manner of a foucauldian power game, some of the films I analyze in the chapter *allow* the abject to challenge normative morality, shedding light on how power structures are produced and/or challenged. Others, nonetheless, will remain at the margins. The films here, therefore, provide contrasting images of the abject. Yet to make a cinema of abjection is always an ambivalent, uneasy position. All three films analyzed in this chapter wrestle with the shameful "choices" that led infected gay man to such "destiny," and especially flamboyantly gay and effeminate men stand in as damning figures of the contagious HIV-positive body.

Still, following Julia Kristeva (1982), abjection concerns what we try to hide or feel we should hide, and this does not involve only sexual practices or excretion, as one might think.[4] When dealing with abjected bodies in cinema, my concern is thus to think of sexuality beyond sexual practices, identity beyond fixed categories, and shame beyond stigma. As Richard Miskolci (2012), in *Teoria queer*, asserts, "[T]he abject is something one person is horrified or disgusted by as if it were polluted or impure. Furthermore, the contact with such abject is feared as contaminating and nauseating" (43).[5]

The abject becomes the other then. In the films observed here, the abject is the representation of the effeminate man. To me, the idea of the feminine is connected to the effeminate man since prejudice against the effeminate man is intrinsically related to the prejudice against woman and misogyny. Thus, the effeminate man and the view of the gay man as a "lesser" man would respond to these anxieties in relation to male heteronormativity. That is, by accepting a normalized identity, gay men accept the "other" view and a lesser abject position while still remaining an abject body. The rejection of the effeminate man—or "the feminized fag" or "the phallicized dyke," in Butler's words (1993, 96)—becomes a tool for acceptance for those who seek visibility, a practice that sends us back to Freud's *Totem and Taboo*: "[W]e also know that anyone who has violated a taboo by touching something which is taboo becomes taboo himself, and no one may come into contact with him" (46). The response of the AIDS epidemic reinforces the necessary erasure of the abjected effeminate man and in the moral panic of the 1980s transforms the anthropophagic queer into a sick abject.

We can see how distance thus becomes a powerful tool for maintaining one's visibility. This was the case after the initial years of the AIDS epidemic, as the affected bodies began to represent the ultimate abjection, the shame of "choices" that led to such a "destiny." The implicit figurative contagiousness of the effeminate man becomes an explicit fear of real contagions in relation to the HIV-positive body. This idea of the contagious can be associated with Kristeva's (1982) work; she asks if one is "afraid of being bitten" or "afraid of biting" (38). Hence, what is it that a person brings in his or her body that makes him or her render abject the other? What is this abject part of oneself that moves one against another? Leo Bersani (1987) states a troublesome truth: "[O]n the whole, gay men are no less socially ambitious, and, more often than we like to think, no less reactionary and racist than heterosexuals" (205).

Bersani's work is important here because he will locate the abjection within the homosexual body. As Adrianne Davis (2011) says, "Abjection is classically associated with Julia Kristeva's work in psychoanalysis but gained political traction in queer theorist Leo Bersani's call for a subversive sex-based queer identity" (103). Bersani's work complements Kristeva's text since it brings to light the repudiation of some gay-identified sexual practices. Bersani moves the personal and internal tone of Kristeva's text into a political one.

In further discussing abjection, David M. Halperin, on the other hand, attempts to distance the abject from psychoanalysis in order to approach it as a queer concept. Halperin (2007) traces a genealogy of the term from the 1930s in France, observing that for French writer Marcel Jouhandeau "abjection was a social concept rather than a psychological one" (72). However, Halperin seems to focus on the internal aspects of abjection, that is, on its "inside" effects, as Kristeva (1982) mentions, of abjection into a socially abjected body. Halperin's project aligns with Butler (2011) when she writes that "the public assertion of 'queerness' enacts performativity as citationality for the purposes of resignifying the abjection of homosexuality into defiance and legitimacy" (21); or, as Kristeva (1982) puts it, "from its place of banishment, the abject does not cease challenging its master" (2). Also, it is important to note that the goal of normativity is not and has never been the total banishment of the abject since it is very existence of abjection that guarantees the existence of the norm. Abjection is, therefore, the attempted controlling form of the norm, whether it is heteronormative or of any other kind. Abjection is intrinsically related to the idea of projection of "unwanted" fluids. In my view, abjection enters the discussion alongside with shame. By making visible abjected or shamed bodies, we might be giving visibility to queer abjected practices and bodies, as David Cardoso attempts in *Estou com AIDS*.

The three films I discuss in this chapter clearly also struggle with sense of distance and shame, although they do so in their respective manner with different agendas in mind. Whereas Bianchi's *Romance* continues this book's threading of the anthropophagic queer body, *AIDS, furor do sexo* pays lip service to the master narrative of shame. In turn, *Estou com AIDS*, while attempting to give legitimate visibility to abject bodies, ultimately reproduces the shame and stigma it tries to avoid. Because the three films emerge within different genres, it is first important provide some information about the context of their production.

Understanding the Genres: *Chanchadas*, *Pornochanchadas*, and Pornography

One of Cinema Marginal's favorite genres to revisit with new meaning was the then obsolete (and in that sense, too, culturally marginal), *chanchada*, which I argue, was devoured and cannibalized in an anthropophagic fashion to subvert the moviegoer's expectations. The term *chanchada* was coined by Brazilian journalists in the 1930s to describe a type of musical comedy based on Hollywood musicals. With the invention of sound technology in cinema in the 1930s, the insertion of Brazilian music in locally produced films quickly became a successful formula, notably in the *chanchada*. The online *Oxford Dictionary of Film Studies* (Kuhn and Westwell 2012) describes the genre as films that include "carnival celebrations combined with a backstage musical plot featuring the social or career advancement of an underdog character, with an overlay of comic wordplay and parodies of high culture." A good example is *Alô alô, carnaval* (Hello, hello carnival, Adhemar Gonzaga, 1936), featuring Carmen Miranda, who in the next decade will have a successful international career as the highest-paid actor in Hollywood of her time. With its carnivalesque theme, this film exemplifies Lisa Shaw's observation that "the counter-culture of malandragem, a lifestyle of pleasure-seeking, idleness and roguery, and a pole of identity in Brazilian popular culture, is central to the chanchada" (2003, 73). Atlântida Cinematográfica, a film company in Rio de Janeiro, in particular made a large number of commercially successful *chanchadas* between 1941 and 1962, when it ceased production.

Chanchadas enjoyed great popularity until the end of the 1950s, before the rise of Cinema Novo, although Glauber Rocha and other filmmakers considered them "bad cinema." In *Revisão crítica do cinema brasileiro*, Rocha (2003) asserts that the biggest hurdle Cinema Novo had to overcome was the outdated *chanchada* (15). Guilherme Maia and Euro Prédez de Azevedo (2018) enumerate some of the adjectives Rocha used to describe the genre in a variety of texts he wrote: "vulgar," "colonized," "miserable," "immoral," "a cancer conformed with underdevelopment," and "cheap pornography" (108).[6] For Rocha, the *chanchada* had to be extinguished in order for a new cinema to exist.

Yet by the end of the 1960s, Paulo Emílio Salles Gomes (1980) in *Cinema: Trajetória no subdesenvolvimento* has rediscovered the *chanchada*, finding it significant as a unique Brazilian genre—and perhaps not even so bad after all. Under the sway of Tropicalismo and the counterculture, and the revitalization of ideas from Antropofagia, critics and artists revisited the past to understand the present. As Caetano Veloso's song "Tropicália" puts it, "Viva a banda-da-da / Carmen Miranda-da-da-da-da." The comedy and laughter of *chanchada* is placed in a more positive light, informing the moment's critical understanding of the genre's contribution. As Lisa Shaw (2007b) explains, the *chanchadas* often struck a tone of irreverent criticism that playfully ironized the problems of Brazil as a country caught between modernization and underdevelopment. This humoristic, deliberately lighthearted genre was thus also well suited, as Shaw observes, to be revisited and—in an anthropophagic manner—devoured to create something new and that was already perceived by the national audiences as authentically national in essence (69).

In the same spirit of playfulness, the anthropophagic reuse of the *chanchada* in Tropicalismo and Cinema Marginal would also take an overtly erotic turn. Even Cinema Novo was not immune to the genre's love for laughter and sexiness, as comedy and debauchery made its way into *Macunaíma* and the last phase of Cinema Novo, not accidentally known as the anthropophagic phase. The increasingly liberal attitudes concerning sexuality were, of course, more generally a sign of the times: the late 1960s saw a growing openness and interest in sexuality in European and American cinema as well, where it was often underwritten by a revolutionary ideology. Sex and sexuality became a key directors used for unlocking the restraints of the times. Many filmmakers blurred the line between pornography and art productions. One such example is Serbian director Dušan Makavejev's *W.R.: Misterije organizma* (*W.R.: Mysteries of the Organism*, 1971), a film about Wilhelm Reich (W.R.), the revolutionary psychoanalyst who in the 1927 wrote one of the most iconic studies on human sexuality, *The Function of the Orgasm*. Reich's work and ideas became more popular than ever in the 1960s and '70s, in Brazil and elsewhere.[7] Iconic films like Vilgot Sjöman's 1967 *I Am Curious (Yellow)* and Damiano Gerard's 1972 *Deep Throat* challenged pornographic laws and current moral standards with their frank depiction of explicit sexuality. At the time, the nature of pornography in cinematic representation was widely debated. Erik Skoglund, director of the Swedish Institute for Cinema defended Sjöman's film, commenting that while some isolated scenes could be considered pornographic, the director's attention for normal love scenes in the context of an artistic work should never be condemned for being pornographic (cited in Gerace 2015). These films defiantly blurred the lines between pornographic production and mainstream movies. Perhaps the main difference between the "sexualized" films of the 1960s and '70s in Europe and Brazil lies in the understanding of the pleasure principle, as discussed by different philosophers and psychoanalysts. European cinema was trying to understand the visuality of pleasure through the lens of cinema; however, most Brazilian films were interested in the exploitation of sex in order to attract large audiences. (*Dona Flor e seus dois maridos* [*Dona Flor and Her Two Husbands*, Bruno Barreto, 1976]—until 2012 the most watched Brazilian film in history—is one of the few exceptions in Brazilian cinema among all the *pornochanchadas*.)

In this regard, the Brazilian film critic Fernão Pessoa Ramos (2018a) takes the explicit image as a point of departure for delineating the difference between pornography (most *pornochanchadas*) and art (e.g., *Dona Flor e seus dois maridos*): the explicit image imposes a dilatation (*dilatação*) to the fictional plot and mise-en-scène, but when such dilatation becomes the main attraction, it dilutes the narrative structure and abandons the storyline. The pornographic film empties the plot, using the cinematic apparatus as its own masturbatory kindle. For Ramos, the rise of a pornographic wave in Brazilian cinema thus also corresponds to its self-centered collapse and dissolution, against the backdrop economic crisis. Umberto Eco (1989), too, sees the dissolution of a meaningful storyline as a crucial indicator of the difference between pornographic movies and films with explicit sex scenes. In an essay titled "How to Recognize a Porn Movie," the semiotician identifies "pornoflicks" as films whose "true and sole aim is to stimulate the spectator's desire, from beginning to end," and "the rest of the story counts for less than nothing" (222).

In Brazil, Cinema Marginal intentionally and often confrontationally discussed and depicted sexuality in overt terms, directly investigating it as part of the plot or story to be told. Understanding Ramos's and Eco's logic is important for visualizing the distinction between the films observed here. *Romance*, while it utilizes sex to enhance its narrative, is not a pornographic film; *AIDS, furor do sexo* is.

Many critics have associated Cinema Marginal with *pornochanchada* films, which deflated the representation of sex into mere commercial sexiness. Distinguishing one trend from the other is rather complex given the close association between Cinema Marginal and the golden era of Boca Lixo production. Sganzerla, for instance, cites the *chanchadas* as one of his influences while making *O bandido da luz vermelha*, the film manifesto for Cinema Marginal.

The almost self-explanatory term *pornochachada* shows up in critical discourse about sexually explicit cinema around the 1970s. An erotic genre inspired by classic 1940s and '50s *chanchada*, these sexual comedies often became box-office hits. In fact, *pornochanchadas* represented the bulk of Brazil's cinematic production of the 1970s. To many, the genre was the expression of the liberation of the times, constituting a sexual revolution à la mode brésilienne, with oxymoronic like *A viúva virgem* (The virgin widow, Pedro Carlos Rovai, 1972) or suggestive titles like *As cangaceiras eróticas* (The erotic bandits, Roberto Mauro, 1974—a clear reference to Cinema Novo). Under the *pornochanchada* umbrella, we find such diverse genres as detective films, adventure movies, drama, thrillers, and horror movies. The unifying aspect was eroticism and debauchery. Sternheim argues that many producers slid from making acclaimed films to less ambitious, commercially safe *pornochanchadas*. Oswaldo Massaini, for instance, early on in his career, produced Anselmo Duartes's *O pagador de promessas*, winner of the Palme d'Or in Cannes, but ended up producing a large number of *pornochanchadas* during his time at Boca do Lixo. José Mario Ortiz and Arthur Autran (2018) argue that in the early 1970s the first wave of *pornochanchadas* were still naive and respected limitations imposed by censorship on the graphic exposure of nudity. In fact, these early comedies, focusing as they often did on repressed and hidden sexuality and on women's bodies, had a critical edge despite their largely male-oriented and often misogynistic gaze. Later on, this genre of film became less narrative oriented and more sexualized, easing the way for the pornographic industry, which in the 1980s would flourish at the expense artistic cinema.

João Silvério Trevisan also sheds some light on the similarities between the two types of films produced at Boca do Lixo. To the filmmaker, *pornochanchadas* used the same commercial box-office formula. The most important aspect of the film, to Trevisan, was the title. It had to be catchy, and for that, sex was the main aspect of the title (cited in Lamas 2013, 117).

There are two issues I want to point out about *pornochanchadas*. First, although they have an apparent façade of liberation, freedom, and open sexuality, most of these films are, in the end, conservative depictions of heteronormativity, marriage, and female oppression. Women, if liberated, were savages. Homosexuality was portrayed as a joke or punch line and sometimes prompted punishment by heterosexual characters. Trans women and *travestis* were treated with masculine pronouns and depicted as a joke or with disgust. Female bodies were explored through the male gaze (the viewing audience comprised mainly men). Even critical and commercial successes, such as the erotic dramas *A dama do lotação* (Lady on the bus, Neville de Almeida, 1978) and *Dona Flor e seus dois maridos*,[8] insisted on the male gaze.

Second, there existed a complicated relationship between these films and their financing by the government dictatorship, which sought to censor them. As Benjamin Cowan (2016), explains, "The incongruity can be attributed, in part, to bagunça itself, to the several government agencies and individuals whose divergent agendas converged at this site. Censors, bound to stamp out eroticism, were equally or perhaps more bound to support the national film industry. Indeed, the confusion became so apparent that even the government's critics noted the irony of state finance for pornochanchadas" (221).

Nonetheless, as with most cultural products, one cannot categorially say whether *pornochanchada* was good or bad, though in discussions of the time, it was viewed in binary terms as either alienating or revolutionary, *desbunde* or militant, as I have mentioned earlier. It challenged the status quo, reinforced normativity, and, at times, did both. In the end, *pornochanchada* served as anthropophagic turn as proposed by the Tropicalistas. Its means of production allowed for films like *Orgia ou o homem que deu cria* to exist. So, whether good or bad, it is undoubtedly the most successful enterprise in Brazilian cinema and has generated hundreds of films, profits and an avid audience for local production.[9]

In the 1980s, the *pornochanchadas* transitioned into hard-core pornography. Producers had in their hands a long list of successful films that exploited the female body, and anxieties on sexuality with easy stories and repetitive scenarios (e.g., the virgin widow, the unsociable housewife, the cuckold, the secretary/boss, revenge sexuality, etc.). By 1982, the heightening economic crisis and a series of economic shifts, such as the middle-class consumer transitioning shopping habits from the urban center to suburban malls, changed the way film was produced in Brazil.

The political democratic opening in Brazil also allowed films to be produced more freely with the lessening of censorship. In 1981, *In the Realm of the Senses* (Nagisa Oshima, 1976) was finally released, creating a buzz among moviegoers and producers alike. Raffaele Rossi, a famed Boca do Lixo producer and director, saw in the liberation of the Japanese classic an opportunity to bring back popular audiences into the theater by producing the first pornographic movie in Brazil, *Coisas eróticas* (Erotic things, 1981). Filmed in less than three weeks, the movie gathered in Brazil an astounding four hundred thousand viewers and remained in the theaters for six years. It remains until today among the top twenty most viewed films in Brazil. Its release is considered a point of no return for Boca do Lixo and local production. Producers now turned their attention to making pornographic films with no concern for script, acting, or mise-en-scène. Some renowned directors started making films under pseudonyms in order to maintain their alternative productions at the margins. One of the most productive years was 1984: out of 125 films produced, 69 were pornographic. As Johnson (1995) reports, "Between 1981 and 1988 hardcore pornography accounted for an average of almost 68 percent of total production" (363).

Denise Godinho and Hugo Moura in *Coisas eróticas—A história jamais contada da primeira vez do cinema nacional* (Erotic things—The untold history of national cinema's first time, 2012) narrate the story of the production of *Coisas eróticas* and in parallel the story of the pornographic genre in Brazil in the 1980s. In their account, José Mojica Marins and José do Caixão (known internationally as Joe Coffin), creator of the first anthropophagic film still in 1964 and developer of Brazilian horror films, pointed out that *Coisas eróticas* was the beginning of the end. Marins, revolted by the pornographic genre, himself produced two films in the genre. However, his intention was to create disgust in the audience and put an end to the genre. Toward this end, he made an eschatological, anti-sexy film with scenes of zoophilia. His intentions backfired, though: his film, the first one to include sex scenes with animals was a hit and opened the space for the "animal" subgenre at Boca do Lixo. Pornography took Boca do Lixo by storm, leaving other, nonpornographic productions with no distribution. No longer a market for them, "Serious" or "Double Reading Films," as José Mario Ortiz and Arthur Autran (2018, 203) call them, suffer the consequences. In addition, by the end of the 1980s, VHS became the safe solution for the porn industry. The economic crisis, growing violence in the urban centers, and a number of other factors forced the producers to close their doors. It was the end of the pornographic genre along with the end of Boca do Lixo.

It is under this thematic that I turn my attention to three films produced in the 1980s that deal in their own ways with HIV/AIDS representation. First is Bianchi's *Romance*. Bianchi is part of a group of filmmakers who would produce under the Cinema Marginal genre reflecting on Brazil's underdevelopment and social crisis. Mansur's *AIDS, furor do sexo* is part of the pornographic tradition. The film, produced in 1985, is a pornographic detective film that takes advantage of the AIDS crisis to tell a story of guilt, shame, and abjection with explicit sex scenes. Finally, Cardoso's *Estou com AIDS* is an effort to inform the audience about the "dangers" of the new disease. Its director is arguably one of the most prolific from Boca do Lixo and *pornochanchada*, and the film is a mix of documentary and fiction that draws from the *pornochanchada* tradition.

Romance and the Future in the Past

Romance is Sérgio Bianchi's second feature-length film. It was released in 1988 and ended up winning several awards and being released in different countries. A director for more than forty years, Bianchi is, according to João Vieira dos Santos (2003), "one of the very few independent filmmakers in Brazil who have succeeded in producing feature films on a regular basis, despite the political upheavals and economic crisis that have marked the post-dictatorial 1980s" (86).

The original idea for *Romance* is Bianchi and Eduardo Albuquerque's. The final script was written by Fernando Coni Campos, Mario Carneiro, Cristina Santeiro, Claudia Maradei, Suzana Semedo, and Caio Fernando Abreu. It is not a coincidence that Abreu collaborated with Bianchi. In the 1980s, they shared a house in São Paulo and were close friends. Abreu, a prolific writer, was one of the first personalities to publicly talk about his HIV-positive status. In 1994, he published "Carta para além do muro" (Letter for beyond the wall) in the newspaper *O estado de São Paulo* (The state of São Paulo) in which he declares his status by, among other things, quoting other people who had recently died.[10]

Romance tells the story of three people—Maria Regina (Imara Reis), Fernanda (Isa Kopelman), and André (Hugo Della Santa)—whose lives had been affected by Antônio César (Rodrigo Santiago), a leftist intellectual who has died in a car accident. The opening sequence of the film consists of a speech by César in which he talks of political and sexual liberation. This speech is followed by his funeral. The circumstances of his death are suspicious since, according to his own testimony, he had written a book that leveled accusations against politicians, corporations, and multinationals. César is the representation of the charismatic intellectual, and the audience comes to know him through images from home videos and TV interviews, which are interspersed throughout the film, thus reconstructing the past. His death affects the three main characters in different ways. Maria Regina follows César's political path, Fernanda follows his libertarian views, and André is apparently infected by a virus (an allusion to the HIV virus). The film, then, tells of their search for a possible life after Antônio César's death.

Throughout his career, Bianchi has developed a unique style, which can already be identified in his first films. Editing and soundtrack are intrinsically part of the narrative and reinforce his critique of Brazilian contemporary society. In an analysis of *Cronicamente inviável* (*Chronically Unfeasible*, 2000), Bianchi's most acclaimed and commercially successful film, João Vieira dos Santos (2003) uses the metaphor of a knife to explain the director's editing style (88). The transitions between scenes are not smooth, nor are they meant to be; they are cut as if with a knife, switching characters and spaces while still intertwining stories.

Sound, too, is crucial to *Romance*'s experimental aesthetic. With a score that blends synthetized sound effects with dissonant chords and fragments of classical and folkloric music, the musical group Chance contributed to the film's suspenseful and at times alienating and broody atmosphere. Even the sound and rhythm of samba, perhaps the quintessential Brazilian musical tradition, is distorted with dissonant chords that create a sense of estrangement and disorientation. This happens, for instance, when Fernanda prepares her suicide to the tune of the song "Samba do morro." After first recording her voice on tape—"Não muda nada, não muda nada. Vai continuar tudo como está" (Nothing changes, everything will remain the same)—she proceeds to put a speaker on the balcony of her apartment, turns up the volume, and plays both the tape and the samba song. The song's lyrics resonate with the message of her tape: "Morro. Morro cedo. Morro. Morro cedo. Levo embora um segredo" (I die. I die soon. I die. I die soon. I'll take a secret with me).

There is a significant wordplay at work with the song's use of "morro." In Brazil, the word is used to refer to the slums and calls to mind a division between *asfalto* (asphalt) and *morro* (hill) and its concomitant class and racial associations. Those who live in the *morro* (on the "hill" or the "mountain") are from the lower classes. The word *morro* is also the first person of the verb *morrer* (to die). While the song plays, the camera first adopts Fernanda's point of view, looking down from the balcony into the street, where a group of people have gathered. The camera then shows her sitting on the edge of the balcony, preparing to jump, while the roaring crowd downstairs screams, "Pula, pula" (Jump, jump).

During these shots, the double meaning of *morro* (first, as the opposite *asfalto* and, second, as the first-person conjugation of *morrer*) is crudely illustrated. Those gathered on "the asphalt" moments earlier have followed Fernanda home from the street market, begging for food and comforts she cannot provide. Arriving exhausted and exasperated through the gates of her apartment building, Fernanda realizes that she alone cannot redress the social inequalities and problems of her country. Her good intentions notwithstanding, she is the one who has gone up the hill, "subindo o morro," in a twisted allegory of Brazilian social inequality. While she does not belong up there, her life (her devotion to Antônio César's utopias of liberation) does not belong on the asphalt either, and since there is no place for her ideological commitments, she must fall to her death below.

According to Carlos Augusto Calil (cited in Soler 51), in *Romance* Bianchi realized that the main social problem at the time of shooting the film was AIDS. For Bianchi, the epidemic and the silence and marginalization of those affected by it reinforce the destructiveness and corruption of the state. Politics, ecology, and sexuality are thus interwoven into the lives of the main characters. As Amir Labaki explains, "[I]ntertwining the trajectory of four protagonists—Antônio César, dead since the beginning of the movie, and the three others, alive—Bianchi deals with three basic concerns of the moment: moral degeneration, of which political corruption is the most explicit symptom, life quality degeneration (that is, systemic ecological violation), and the real sexual McCarthyism developed with AIDS" (qtd. in Moreno 2002, 153).[11]

Hence, sexuality in the film is also a political act. André, Fernanda, and Antônio César seem to live out a romance in which their pleasure goes beyond sexual identities. Their connectedness is reinforced by the characters sharing the same dialogue at different points in the film.

Antônio César's death marks the end of their relationship. Fernanda and André can no longer remain a couple since they functioned as such only with the intermediation of César. César's death also represents the death of the possibility for liberation, be it sexual or political. For the first time in Brazilian cinema (and one of the few times up to this day), Bianchi portrayed AIDS, capturing a unique moment in the early years of the epidemic. As João Silvério Trevisan (2004) says: "[A]t first, abominated, homosexuality becomes damned" (449).

Maldito (damned) is an important word. The scenes in which André has sex in the bathroom or in the dark alleys highlight that these practices were condemned at the time, and by reproducing them, Bianchi calls attention to the position André occupies in society in order to criticize and combat it. Group sex, gay sex, or any nonnormative practices are thus shown to have been exiled to the dark sides of society.

Antônio César's discourse of liberation has died, and now André is left only with masturbation due to the fear of contamination. He says to Fernanda, "Continuo com tesão, mas não posso mais trepar. Às vezes, me sinto como um assassino das pessoas" (I am still horny, but I cannot fuck. Sometimes I feel like a murderer).

André's words echo Caio Fernando Abreu's assertion that it did not really matter if gay men had the virus or not, since they were all already infected by the fear of contamination (Callegari 2008, 103). This fear, therefore, constitutes the death of liberation and the death of nonnormative practices. As Antônio César affirms in one of the flashbacks, "Há um novo moralismo no ar" (There is a new type of morality in the air). Bianchi finds it more difficult to live as an abject, and death is thus the answer for the characters. As mentioned earlier, AIDS thus reinforces the rise of a stronger sense of heterosexism and normativity. Antônio César's ideas can now find no place of liberation in a society that has embraced a new moralism. As Karl Posso in *Artful Seduction* (2003) says of this time, "[I]n short, the arrival of AIDS and the keen assimilation of medical concepts into religious and moral discourses in Brazil rearticulated national heterosexism into a reinforced and coherent onslaught" (11).

The combination of Bianchi's editing, score, and lighting bring a sense of loss and disorientation to the film. The dissonant chords, the darkness of André's apartment, and the black tarps in Fernanda's apartment (indicating that it is under construction) represent Antônio César's death and the way the surviving characters are dealing with their own imminent deaths.

Of the three films analyzed in this chapter, *Romance*, with its jarring cuts and nonlinear narrative that alternates between past and present, comes closest to the avant-garde technique of João Silvério Trevisan and Cinema Marginal. Bianchi also includes Brechtian-like didactic interludes that explain Brazilian socioeconomic policies. For instance, while Regina takes a taxi from Curitiba to São Paulo, a narrator explains all the levels of misery and poverty that have afflicted the population of the area her car is passing through. Bianchi adds an ironic perspective: while the narrator explores the topic in voiceover in the background, we hear an instrumental version of "Aquarela do Brasil" by Ary Barroso, a classic nationalistic anthem made internationally famous after Walt Disney included the song in his 1942 animated film *Saludos amigos*.

In *Romance*, the editing style is not so obviously marked, cutting at some points in a disorienting style between fiction and documentary scenes. Beyond this formal technique, on an ideological plane, *Romance* shows the impossibility of utopias for queer representation. Queer imaginings, to Bianchi, are all incorporated by the normative regime. Nonetheless, the ideas remain in the air, and Antônio César's videos still represent a queer voice.

AIDS, furor do sexo

Since the first detected cases, HIV and AIDS were associated in the public mind with sexual practices among men. The anxieties that permeated the American imagination in the 1980s were also present in Brazil where terms like *GRID* (gay-related immune deficiency) and *gay cancer*[12] were frequently used by the media. In Brazil, however, AIDS was considered a foreign disease, and the first news articles there talked about a "mysterious disease" among homosexual men in places like New York, Paris, and San Francisco. In November 1984, *Revista veja* published the first statistics about the disease, noting that 70 percent of the infected were homosexuals. Even when statistics later proved that there was not one particular "risk group," the stigma quickly attached to the homosexual body and to the emergent gay identity. For instance, in 1993 the National Research Council in the United States published a study stating that AIDS would have a small impact on the lives of the majority of Americans (Bersani 1996, 21).[13]

There have been several studies about AIDS in Brazil in the past forty years (among others, Galvão 2000; Nunn 2009; Marques 2003; Bastos 1999; Nemi Neto, 2018). What these studies have in common with US studies is a concern with the socially structuring role of shame and stigma to those infected with the disease. To "get AIDS" meant to be revealed as part of a risk group, a pariah community (Sontag 1988, 29). In Brazil, Herbert Daniel, Caio Fernando Abreu, and singer-songwriter Cazuza are among many artists and activists who discussed the stigma associated with the disease. Daniel is perhaps the most important AIDS activist of the 1980s in Brazil. As Trevisan (2004) observes, he was one of the first to become engaged in national campaigns against AIDS (366). As early as 1983, Daniel mentioned the syndrome of prejudice—*síndrome do preconceito* (Guimarães et al. 1988, 5).

Fauzi Mansur's film *AIDS, furor do sexo* uses stigma, shame, prejudice, and guilt to tell a pornographic story in which AIDS is a weapon. Rodrigo Gerace (2015) in his study on explicit sex in mainstream cinema, *Cinema explícito* (2015), observes how the film associates eroticism with paranoia and death (203). The plot is simple: After a transgender woman (Michele) falls sick during a sex party on a millionaire's island, a private detective (Alan Fontaine) from the Departamento de Investigações Especiais AYDS (Special Investigation Department AYDS) is called to the island to solve the mystery. Upon arrival, the detective declares, with no medical evidence, that Ney (Walter Gabarron), the millionaire, is infected: "He has AIDS." Seeking the criminal responsible for spreading the disease, the detective interrogates four women with whom Ney has had sex in the past six months. He determines that the guilty criminal is the butler (Custódio Gomes), a closeted gay man. A plot twist occurs when it is discovered that the butler is also in a relationship with the maid (Samira), a transgender woman. Now there is no doubt in the detective's mind: the maid is "patient zero." Having solved the "crime," the detective departs from the island with the four women, who had not been infected, leaving the diseased men and his staff isolated in their mansion.

The film understands AIDS as a type of fast-spreading zombie virus. In the detective's words: "After the first contact thirty people are infected, the second, three hundred . . ." The detective sees it as his mission to halt the spread of the disease as quickly as possible. As most heroes in cinema, the detective is the guardian of truth; he is the one who is able to ascertain everyone's HIV status based solely on his investigation. The film is not interested in understanding the epidemic and its social connotations; AIDS is not a vehicle for a "whodunnit" crime drama / comedy but rather a weapon of mass destruction used to kill the victims. The objective of the detective is to find the patient zero, the criminal. The isolation of the millionaire on the island makes it clear that by segregating the zombies—the infected—the problem is solved.

The film also understands the epidemic as a rich man's disease. The first cases in Brazil were associated with the "new" urban gay man, someone who travels abroad, then brings back the virus to innocent Brazilian people. In Brazil, there was speculation of the disease's arrival even before the first cases were officially documented. Such announcements fostered the notion of a foreign disease, almost as an ideology coming from the Cold War days. The first famous case reported in Brazil also helped "spread" this idea of a foreign epidemic. As Bastos (1999) writes, "[T]he first publicized case of AIDS in Brazil reinforced its stereotype as a disease of the rich and famous. The disease struck São Paulo's well-known gay designer Markito in 1983. Markito was seen as a cosmopolitan gay traveler who was believed to have contracted AIDS in New York. He was also portrayed as the irresponsible type who went back to the metropolis for fun and partying instead of getting treatment" (72).

The millionaire Ney, while denying being "a homosexual," is portrayed as a flamboyant man. In his silk robes and with his low voice, he resembles the classic image of the millionaire perpetrated by Brazilian telenovelas: refined and connected to international "savoirs." He, then, is the perfect target for the new international "plague" afflicting Brazil. He is a porn dandy, and based on the understanding of gender identities of the time, his sexual relationship with his transgender maid would have signaled his homosexuality to the audience.

In order to conduct his investigation, the detective must ask the suspects about their sexual history. However, since the four women he questions are not willing to

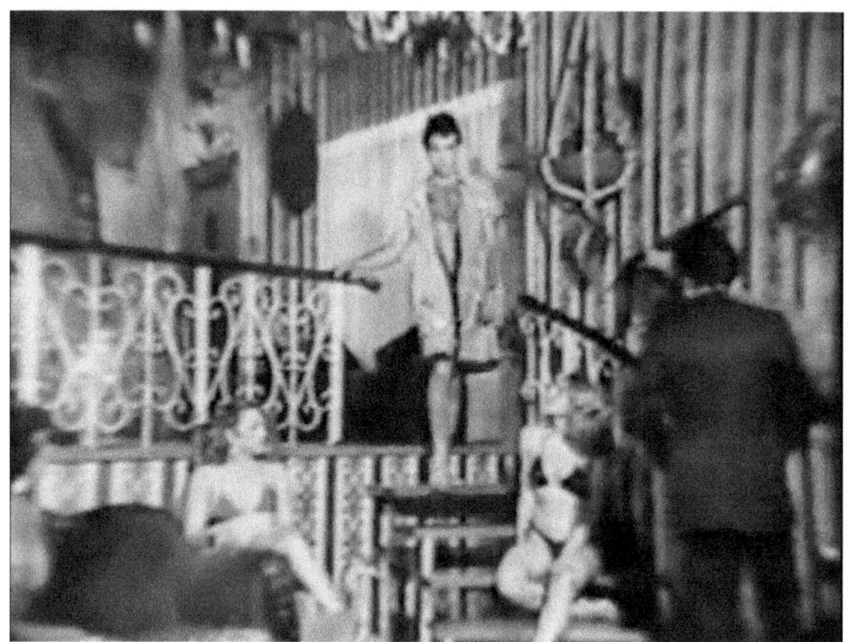

The main character in *AIDS, furor do sexo* enters the scene wearing a fancy silk robe.

disclose their sexual history, the detective must resort to torture. He burns the hands of one woman; another, he ties to a tree. Each woman is tortured while narrating her sex adventures. Torture represents both an erotic pleasure and also a form of punishment for the women's liberated behavior. Such interrogations give narrative space for the explicit sex scenes to happen. The last woman to be tortured/interrogated admits she has had sex with Rui, a transgender woman (the same actress who falls sick in the initial scene). Her story is enough for the detective to solve the case. He declares that "the spreader of the AIDS disease, must be gay. Her friend." His conclusion brings to light not only the prejudice against gay men but also trans women who, at the time, were always associated with homosexuality and gay identity. Not only in *AIDS, furor do sexo* but also in most pornographic films at the time, trans women and *travestis* were referred to with masculine pronouns and treated as "homosexuals." Their bodies were usually depicted with scorn or disgust.

Nevertheless, as in most detective stories, a plot twist must happen, and via a telephone conversation the detective finds out the Rui is not guilty. He proceeds with his investigation and overhears a conversation between the butler and the maid. Based on the tone of the butler's flamboyant voice, the detective learns the butler is gay. In the detective's conclusion, he is guilty. After all, he is the butler and gay. Another phone call confirms that the butler is infected and has been for two months. When the detective leaves the island with the four women who are deemed not infected, he "saves" them—or saves heterosexuality and female sexuality from the flamboyant and reckless life in the millionaire's island.

Homosexual panic, therefore, is in a sense the real subject of the movie. The first question the men on the island must answer is if they are homosexual, something they all vehemently deny. However, in true murder-mystery style, we find out they have been lying all along. In the end, the butler comes out as a flamboyant homosexual, declaring, "The butler is always guilty." The millionaire's maid, being transgender, is not deserving of leaving the island, and after the detective leaves the island, Ney and the maid engage in intercourse. The genitalia close-ups and "meatshots" are alternated with close-ups of dark spots on Rui's skin, presumably Kaposi sarcoma. "I've always known you'd be mine," Rui says in the final scene, ejaculating on the maid.

This closing scene is a repetition of the opening sequence, which shows a close-up of an ejaculating penis. It is what film scholar Linda Williams (1999) calls the "money shot" (233). The first money shot fades to an orgy where we see the first victim falling sick. In fact, in *AIDS, furor do sexo*, the money shots are medicalized; in both opening and ending sequences, the director uses an x-ray type of filter, portraying not the pleasure of an orgasm but rather a death sentence. The red filter approximates the shot with blood, mixing up all the bodily fluids as weapons of destruction.

That Mansur signed the film under a pseudonym hints at the shame of being associated with the genre of pornography. The pornographic wave was not necessarily celebrated by all Boca do Lixo directors. Following José Mojica Marins, some filmmakers from Boca do Lixo created their films as an exercise in self-conscious criticism on the state of cinema. It was quite common in the productions of the time to incorporate dialogues between characters that reflect on the end of cinema, the end of Boca do Lixo, and the lack of aesthetics concern in the films. It is as if the Boca do Lixo creators needed to make a moral statement about that "type" of cinema being made. They made money, but they also had to impose their artistic reservations on the films. AIDS, therefore, served as a handy metaphor for the embarrassment of making pornographic movies.

Thus, José Mojica Marins depicts what he considers the "ugly" in sexual representation, and Juan Bajon presents both an unsexy behind-the-scenes look at the porn industry (*Taras de colegiais* [High schooler's fantasies], 1984) as well as long dialogues on how industry exploited its actors (*Sexo de todas as formas* [Sex of all shapes], 1985).[14] Whereas these creators opt for a metacriticism, Mansur prefers to instill clear moral views in his film. Mansur's plot revolves around the AIDS epidemic and its attendant homosexual guilt. Isolating the infected characters ion the island makes it clear to the audience that flamboyancy is not a viable lifestyle choice. Medical science, according to media scholar Kylo-Patrick R. Hart (2000), is "presented as making committed attempts at finding a cure and saving individuals threatened by the other" (21). Mansur's film is bereft of such science. It is a detective who determines the victims' HIV status and decides on their future. His ludicrous investigation is even able to detect the exact date of infection. It is a morality tale that toys with the viewers' anticipation of pornographic pleasure, since all the explicit sex scenes are tinged by the possibility of infection, crime, and ultimately death. *AIDS, furor do sexo* is not shy on mixed messages. The poster of the film shows the picture of a sexy woman and an orgy.

The poster contains a warning to would-be viewers about the explicit sex scenes and audience age restrictions (the film is strictly forbidden for anyone younger than eighteen).

If in Bianchi's film the preoccupation with the aesthetics is detailed in order to present the characters' sense of loss and disillusionment, in Mansur's pornographic tale, there is no clearly articulated aesthetic agenda. It is a tale of morality that also reflects the complicated relationship between the filmmakers and the genre. In terms of aesthetics, the music is instrumental to Bianchi's film. However, Mansur's film simply borrows Vangelis's *Blade Runner* soundtrack. The unauthorized use of foreign soundtracks was not an uncommon occurrence in the pornographic genre in Brazil. The music of Vangelis, Kraftwerk, and others are co-opted without permission or credit. Vangelis's music lent itself as easily to the tale of a detective chasing nonhuman "replicants" as it did, in Mansur's view, to a group of HIV-infected abjects. It reinforces the detective narrative without necessarily creating a dialogue between image and sound. In another scene, the director uses the classic *Twilight Zone* theme music as a complement for the revelation of the perpetrator. Arguably, *AIDS, furor do sexo* is, like Bianchi's *Romance*, a tale of disillusionment. But whereas the latter offers artistic and political reflection on the state of 1980s Brazil, the former registers only feelings of panic, guilt, and shame.

Estou com AIDS

David Cardoso's 1985 *Estou com AIDS* is a documentary mixed with fiction. Cardoso's film blurs the definitions between docufiction and docudrama: some of the reenactments come from newspaper clippings, while others are fictional tales based on *pornochanchada* classic narratives. Cardoso is undoubtfully one of the most famous and prolific figures of the Boca do Lixo. He started his career behind the scenes in the

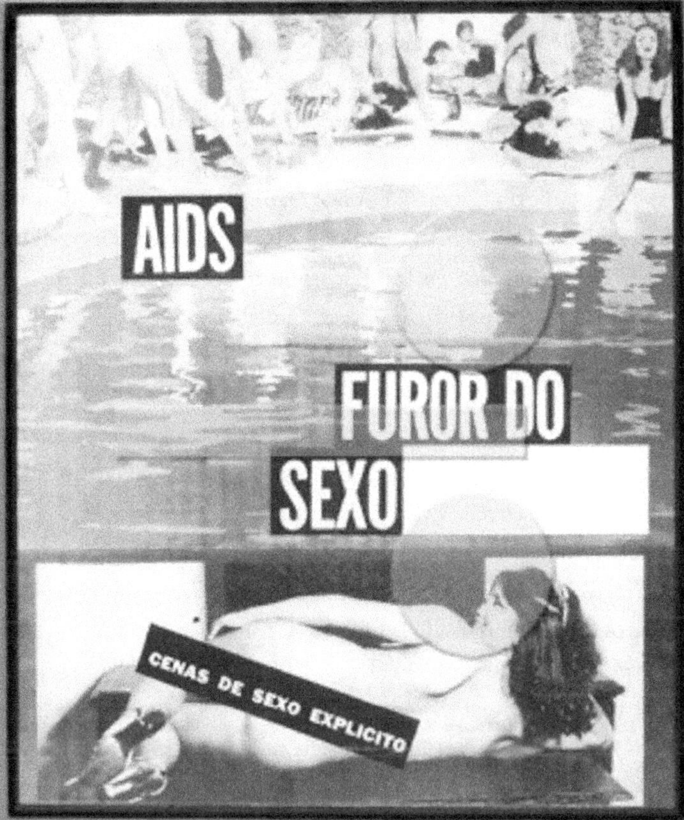

Poster for the release of *AIDS, furor do sexo*, 1985

1960s and became an actor in the 1970s and a producer/director in the 1980s. He is known as the *rei da pornochanchada* (king of *pornochanchada*). He produced, directed, and acted in dozens of films with major audiences. *Estou com AIDS* marks the end of his time as a producer, coinciding with the end of Boca do Lixo as a cinema production center.

In 2010, the Grupo pela Vidda (an HIV/AIDS nongovernmental organization in São Paulo) arranged a film festival about AIDS, and Cardoso's film was rediscovered by a whole new audience. At the time, he participated in several Q&As discussing the production of the film. He repeatedly mentioned that the film was ignored by critics and that it was one of his major failures. Cardoso explained that the campaigns against his film, together with the dissatisfaction of the audience members who were expecting to enjoy explicit sex (the trademark of Boca do Lixo), transformed the film into a commercial failure. Néstor Perlongher (1988), the Argentinian writer and AIDS activist, mentions the boycott imposed on Cardoso's film in his essay *El fantasma del SIDA* (The ghost of AIDS, 1988). Therefore, even though *Estou com AIDS* relied on the same distribution technique as any other film from Boca do Lixo, it was a commercial failure.

The film approaches AIDS in a quasi-documentary and scientific manner. Cardoso interweaves interviews with epidemiologists, scientists, politicians, actors, singers, athletes, and people on the streets with four highly dramatized stories of people infected with the virus. The film, however, also inherits some of the moral panic and sensationalism of the era. The poster proclaims: "The first realistic film in the world to show the disease whose only way out is death. Information, truth, lies, testimonials, and the real scenes of the plague of the century. HTLV3 = AIDS = DEATH."

The poster makes clear that there is no hope for the infected; death is their only outcome. The documentary, therefore, reinforces the idea also central in *AIDS, furor do sexo* and *Romance*: if you "get AIDS," you are going to die.

Cardoso's film has polished look that with specific investment in production. He hired Ronald Lark to create a similar-sounding musical track as that developed by the group Chance in *Romance*. The sound effect creates a sense of suspense and terror, an impression underscored by frequent, fast cuts, which resemble sequences of a horror movie. The first scenes are made up of short cuts of six people, men, women, and a child, saying, "I have AIDS." Their sad voices set the tone of the movie. The documentary reinforces the ideas of the disease as an affluent one, as depicted in *AIDS, furor do sexo*, and as an international urban affliction, as Bastos (1999) describes. Alcione, a famous singer from the north of the country, who calls herself "the queen of gays" in the film, claims that AIDS barely exists in the north of the country. To her, it is a

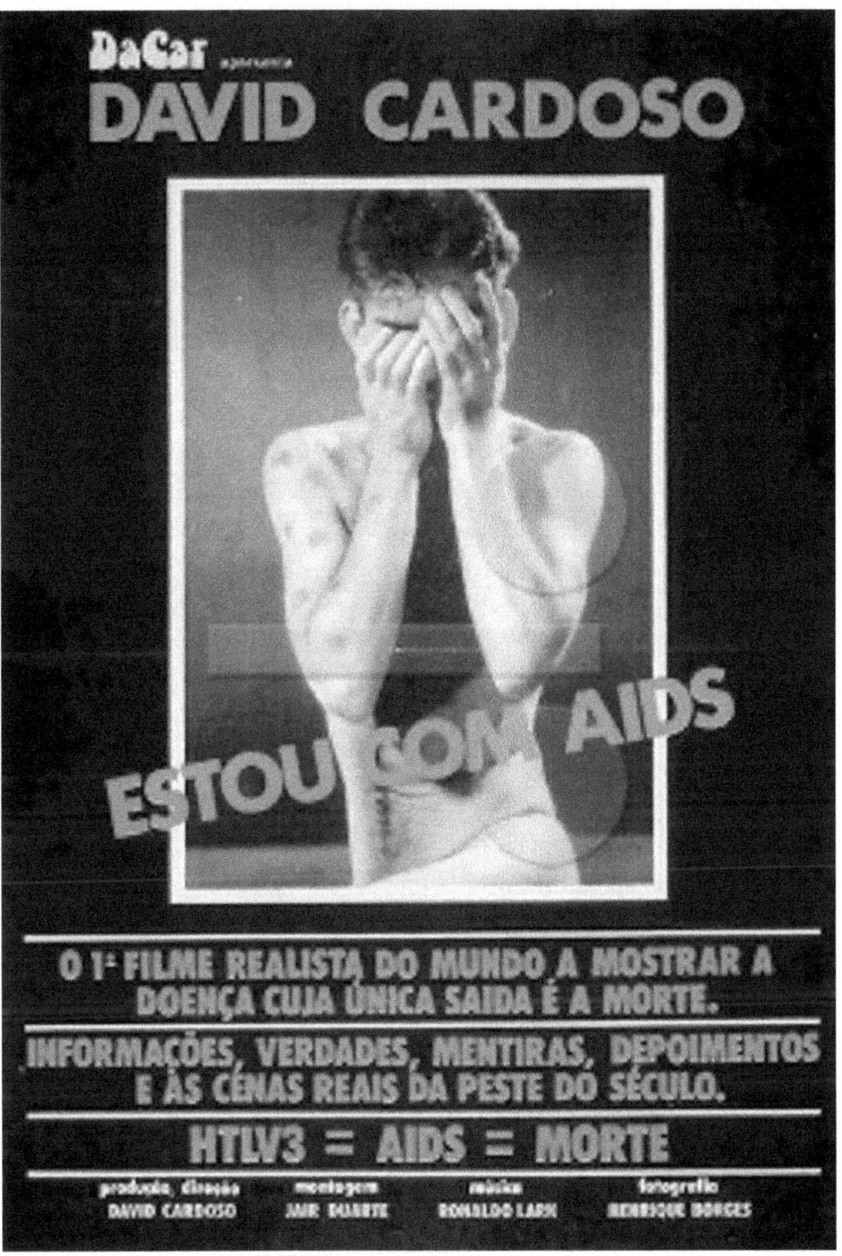

Poster for the release of *Estou com AIDS*, 1985

disease of the large urban centers like Rio de Janeiro and São Paulo (the most populated cities in the country). Tellingly, she implicates foreign gays for bringing AIDS to Brazil: she asks her public to be aware of those with "blue eyes." Eye color, in her usage, is an association with the foreigners who come to Brazil to celebrate carnival and spread the illness. Her response encapsulates a perception of the epidemic as a foreign disease and, more moralistically, as a punishment for those who privileged their sexual pleasures over the morals of society.

The interviews are interspersed with highly dramatized reenactments of real-life stories of people who became infected: A simple man from the countryside decides to try his life in the big city. Unemployed, he makes ends meet as a male prostitute. A woman (Débora Muniz)[15] who works as a maid participates in orgies with her boss. After contracting the virus, she returns home, but her family does not accept her. She goes back to the big city and commits suicide. A hairdresser is expelled from his town for being HIV-positive. A businessman finds out he is HIV-positive after a long business trip. The *pornochanchada* type of storytelling prevails in these short stories: nudity and sex scenes illustrate how the virus is spread; then, with a technique that alternates rapid cuts with dramatic music, the difference between fictionalization and the documentary is rendered subtly tenuous.

Notwithstanding the film's documentary angle, its formal devices (such as the sound montage and editing techniques) effectively resemble those of a horror movie, replacing the objective documentary tone with a rather sensationalist and fear-driven effect. Clearly, the film is a product of the moral panic of the decade. In addition, this documentary is overlaid with a classic terror narrative, blurring the line between reality and fiction. For instance, in the fourth story, the businessman is sitting naked on his couch while watching his wife perform a strip-tease for him. While she dances, he receives a phone call from his doctor, and by his reaction (we do not hear the doctor's voice) we understand he "has AIDS." From here, the image quickly cuts to a newspaper headline—"AIDS without Fear"—and then moves to an image of a lung x-ray. A female narrator explains the lung belongs to a person with AIDS. Then the camera cuts to a woman on the phone who explains the first symptoms of the disease. Clearly, the objective, informational aspect of the documentary is lost amid the fictional images and acting.

Yet unlike the other two films, *Estou com AIDS* occasionally attempts to cast a more hopeful message. In various interview segments, Brazilian politicians talk about the cure and ask the "afflicted" not to be hopeless. Hope is short lived, though. The positive messages are countered by comments colored with guilt, shame, and death. Pedro de Lara, a famous TV personality, for instance, declares that "AIDS is the plague sent

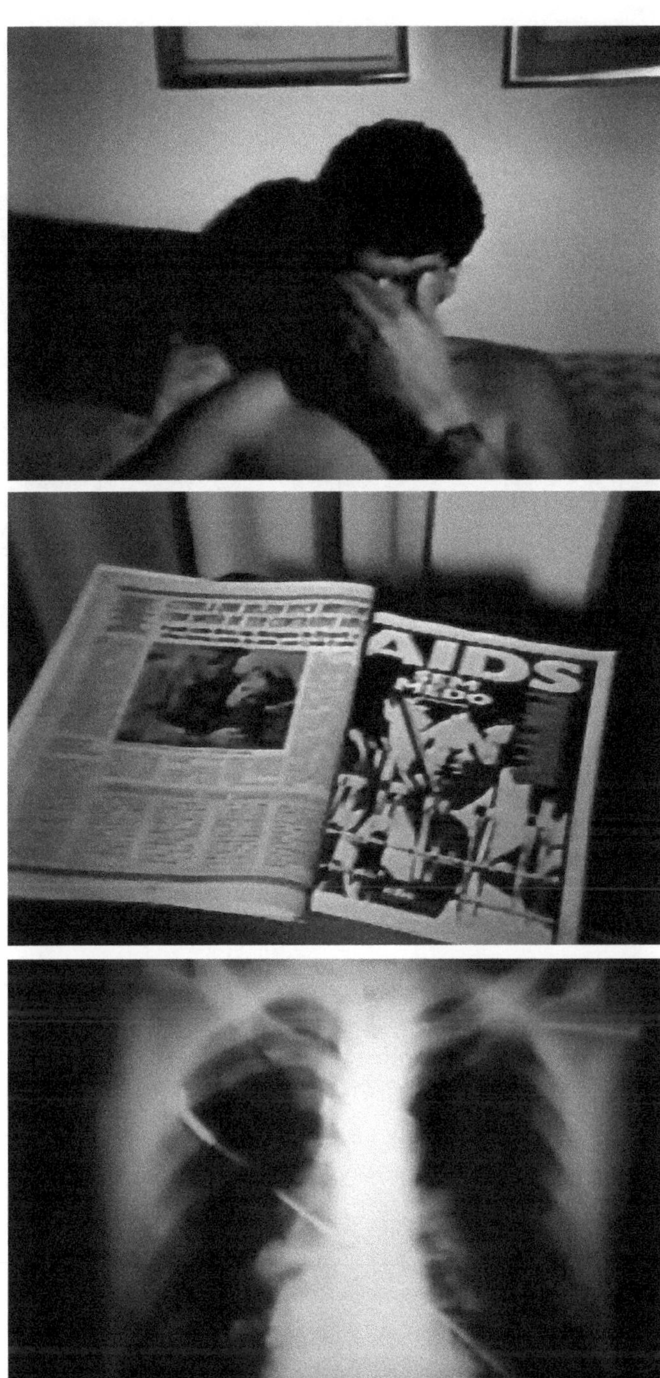

Stills from three sharp cuts. The images align with a soundtrack that instills a sense of horror in the audience.

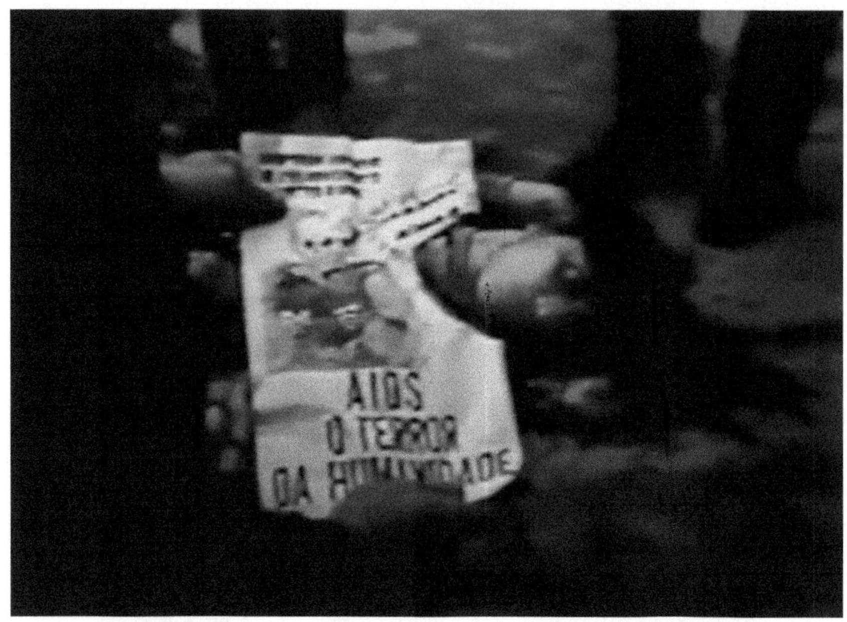

A man opens the newspaper with the headline "AIDS: The Terror of Humanity" below a picture of the maid who has committed suicide

by God to punish deviant sexual behaviors." Famed boxer Maguila voices his opinion that AIDS is for the unhealthy. According to the boxer, those who practice sports and stay healthy will not "get AIDS." Moreover, in the film's fictional overlays, all the characters either die from AIDS or commit suicide. As much as in the other two films, there is no restoration.

The final sequences revolve around the deaths of each the film's four characters. The last one depicts the maid whose family did not accept her. Following her suicide, the camera frames her face with a newspaper headline that reads "AIDS: The Terror of Humanity." Using the same sharp sounds and cuts, the film proceeds with a shot of Cardoso, the director, reading a newspaper story about Rock Hudson's death. It is a scene that reinforces the association of AIDS as a foreigner's disease and also with death. Rock Hudson's death, therefore, serves as a warning sign for the Brazilian population.

The film's final image consists of a billboard with a public service announcement created by the Brazilian government in 1985. The billboard reads "CUIDAIDS: Pense duas vezes" (CUIDAIDS: Think twice). CUIDAIDS is a play with the words *cuidado* (be careful) and *AIDS*. The film in its final scene, reveal its intention: it is a warning, a cautionary tale.

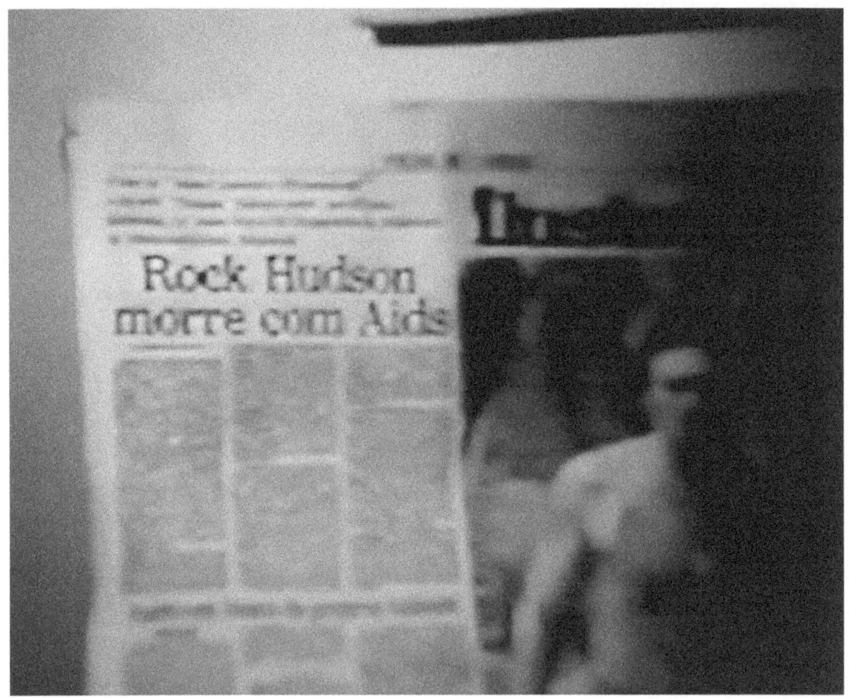

Close-up of a newspaper article headlined "Rock Hudson Dies of AIDS"

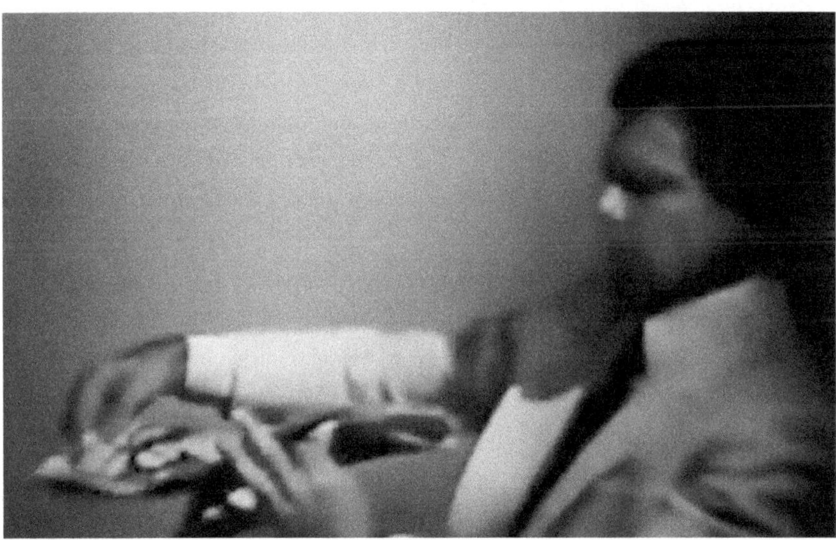

David Cardoso reading the newspaper article about Rock Hudson's death

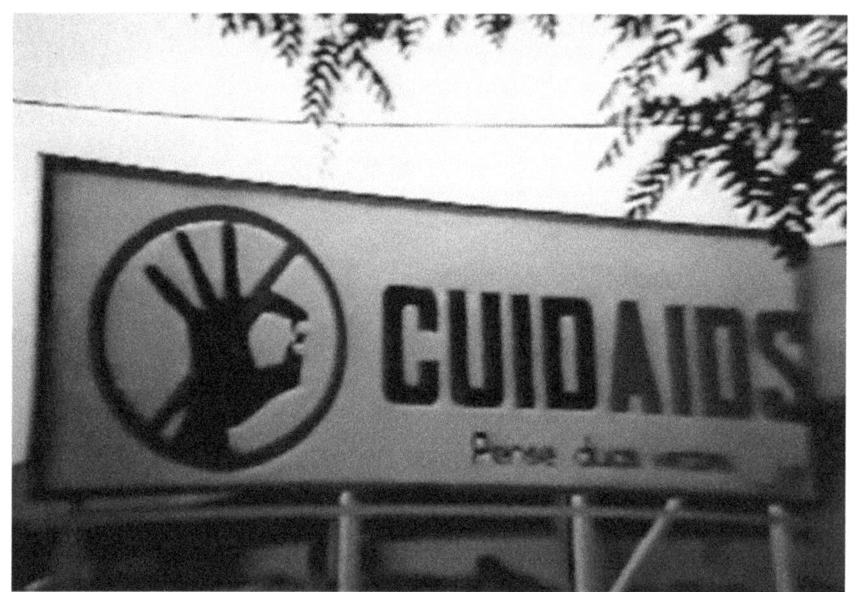

Panoramic shot: A public service announcement by the government reads "Be Careful with AIDS."

AIDS, furor do sexo and *Estou com AIDS* respond to the moral panic of the early stages of the epidemic in similar ways. Both rely heavily on fear and a sense of doom for deviants in a moral society. In *Romance,* however, AIDS is but one aspect of a decade of disillusionment. While both Mansur and Cardoso come from the *pornochanchada* tradition, Bianchi is a successor to the anthropophagic queer mode that João Silvério Trevisan inaugurated in Cinema Marginal. Like Trevisan, Bianchi deals with the lack of visibility and the space in-between that his characters occupy. The universe of both directors can be described as abject and hopeless. Trevisan is lost in amid a violent and brutal dictatorship, and Bianchi is coping with the aftermath of such violence. Bianchi relies on the Cinema Marginal tradition in his film in order to situate Trevisan's abjects almost twenty years later.

The movies highlighted in this chapter are also marked by the deterioration of Boca do Lixo as a film production center and the pause that the economic crisis will impose on local production. "[A]s the 1980s progress," explains Fernão Pessoa Ramos (2018b), "old existential dilemmas no longer work. Without having properly experienced the modernism of the 1920s, Brazilian cinema, especially the New Cinema, is in full modern ebullition when suddenly there is a shortage of fuel to burn in ruptures, challenges, manifestos" (378).[16]

The situation calls to mind the 1933 essay "The Theater and the Plague" in which Antonin Artaud (1994) invites us the think of the plague as a state of emergency that assembles a new body, a body with no boundaries, a collective body with no sense of communion. With Cardoso and Mansur, representations of bodies in decay operate as metaphors for struggling national cinema. The bodies in Cardoso and Mansur are collective in the sense that they represent a plagued body in isolation, just as on Mansur's island. Disillusioned bodies set the tone for the 1980s depiction of queerness.

TRAILER 2

Brazilian Cinematic Production and Effeminophobia

From its early beginnings, Brazilian cinema, like most Latin American national cinemas, faced competition with the American industry, notably Hollywood. As Randal Johnson and Robert Stam (1995) explain, "While American films are seen daily throughout Brazil, Brazilian films do not reach their potential audience in the United States or even within Brazil itself" (19). Nonetheless, throughout the twentieth century, Brazil produced a great number of movies. For example, the Atlântida Cinematográfica and Vera Cruz studios created a large national audience for Brazilian cinema in the 1940s and '50s, of which the Cinema Novo movement of the 1960s reaped the benefits and even received international recognition by critics.

According to David William Foster (1999), Cinema Novo "became probably the only truly international movement in Latin American filmmaking" (2). More recently, after the *redemocratização* (redemocratization), Brazilian cinema experienced another boost, the *retomada* (resurgence), of local productions, thanks to the 1993 Audiovisual Law, which "prompt[ed] a boom in film production" (Nagib 2003, xvii). In terms of audience, the *retomada* has so far successfully created new markets and found new viewers, and several recent productions obtained both critical and commercial success. For instance, *Cidade de Deus* (2002), *Central do Brasil* (1998), *O quatrilho* (Fábio Barreto, 1995), and *Tropa de Elite (Elite Squad, José Padilha, 2007)* and *Tropa de Elite 2* (Padilha, 2010) won both local and international awards.

Most recently, Globo Filmes (a sister company of the giant media and entertainment company Globo) has produced with tremendous commercial success films for a mass audience eager to watch local movies, mainly comedies and TV-related movies (movies that derive from telenovelas and TV series aired on TV Globo). The current list of the most watched movies in the country, excluding American productions, consists primarily of Globo Filmes movies, most of which have been drawn from the *pornochanchada* and *chanchada* traditions. Popular comedies such *Minha mãe é uma peça* (My mother is a character, 2013) and its two sequels (2016 and 2019) are among these record-breaking productions.[17]

Even though the current scenario does not seem propitious for independent filmmaking, functioning as it does in the shadow of Hollywood and Globo, some filmmakers have been able to release smaller budget movies to positive critical acclaim. In the past five years, numerous Brazilian productions have received awards, mentions, and recognition in international festivals. Among them: In 2012, Kléber Mendonça Filho's *Sons ao redor* (*Neighboring Sounds*) was on the *New York Times* list of best movies of the year; in 2013, Fernando Coimbra's *O lobo atrás da porta* (*A Wolf at the Door*) won more than five awards in different festivals; in 2014, Karim Aïnouz's *Praia do Futuro* (*Futuro Beach*) won the Horizons Awards at the San Sebastián Film Festival, and Daniel Ribeiro's gay-themed *Hoje eu quero voltar sozinho* (*The Way He Looks*) won the Teddy Bear at Berlin Film Festival; and in 2015, Anna Muylaert's *Que horas ela volta* (*The Second Mother*) received an award at Sundance Movie Festival and an audience award at the Berlin Festival. The 2018 film *Bixa travesty* also received acclaim in Berlin. Most notably, Juliano Dornelles and Kléber Mendonça Filho's *Bacurau* (2019) was recently awarded the Jury Prize at the Cannes Festival. Along with the rise in the movie production, there has been a gradual increase in scholarly attention. In particular, movies that focus on the country's complicated class and race issues (e.g., the favela movie genre, which deals with life in the slums of the country's big cities) have often been "big hits" on the international festival circuit and, generally speaking, have accordingly received the bulk of recent academic attention.

With respect to films dealing with the topics of gender and sexuality, however, criticism of national cinema appears to lag behind. This is unfortunate, especially since, as Antônio Márcio da Silva (2013) argues about Brazilian cinema, "many of the films repeat the gender roles and identities dictated by patriarchal society that have been reinforced since Portuguese colonialism, especially the ideal binary gender that propagate heteronormativity" (83). There has, however, been significant (though limited) work on the stereotypical image of the homosexual (e.g., Foster 2010; Subero 2016; Moreno 2002; Albuquerque 2004) in different artistic and media productions. These authors generally concur that in most cultural productions, LGBTQAI+ presence is either virtually absent (defined as "an embodiment of absence" by Albuquerque 2004, 60) or is expressed in crudely clichéd stereotypes. While I generally agree with their findings, I do question the overriding tendency to portray LGBTQAI+ visibility in a solely negative light. Gustavo Subero (2014), for instance, writes, "In the majority of gay Latin American fiction cinema that addresses homosexuality, although not necessarily made by gays for gays, the figure of the *maricón* as the ultimate form of gay typification is commonly employed whether to pathologise or demonise this sexual orientation or to demonstrate the perils of going against (hetero)normativity" (51).[18]

There is danger, I think, in perpetuating certain prejudices *against* the actual queer bodies that these critics believe to be defending. Stereotypical or not, it is important to keep in mind that some queer bodies, in movies and in real life, do not conform to normative (and in that sense, equally, stereotypical) representations of gender. These authors, in other words, seem often blind to their idealized notions of homosexual (and in that sense not "queer") identity, thus reinforcing what queer critics have started to call homonormativity.

In "The New Homonormativity: The Sexual Politics of Neoliberalism," Lisa Duggan (2002) bases her understanding of the term *homonormativity* on Michael Warner's (1993) term *heteronormativity*. According to Duggan, homonormativity "is a politics that does not contest dominant heteronormative assumptions and institutions but upholds and sustains them while promising the possibility of a demobilized gay constituency and a privatized, depoliticized gay culture anchored in domesticity and consumption" (179). Following Duggan, other scholars, such as J. Jack Halberstam (2012), Jasbir Puar (2007), and Roderick Ferguson (2005), have applied the notion of homonormativity to their criticisms of contemporary gay politics. I take my cue from these scholars as a way to show how critics like Subero (2014) tend to undermine the representation of effeminate and gay characters in favor of homosexual characters that fulfill normative images.

Antônio Moreno's 2002 pioneering study, *A personagem homossexual no cinema brasileiro*, perpetuates this idea of negative portrayal of homosexuality. Moreno's work is important because he presents a brief history of same-sex experience in Brazilian cinema. He gives an overview of all movies produced in Brazil in the twentieth century that portray same-sex desire and classifies them in three groups: "filmes com teor pejorativo" (movies with pejorative content), "filmes com teor não-pejorativo" (movies with nonpejorative content), and "filmes com teor dúbio" (movies with dubious content). The movies with pejorative content are precisely those whose characters are depicted with more effeminate ways. For example, while analyzing Arnaldo Jabor's *Toda nudez será castigada* (*All Nudity Shall Be Punished*, 1973), a movie with "teor não-pejorativo," Moreno writes, "*All Nudity Shall Be Punished* does not portray such characteristics, presenting the character Serginho as *a young man with normal features* as any other who, after prison, is involved with a gruesome Bolivian thief" (95, emphasis added).

The characters with "normal characteristics," in Moreno's schema, are listed under the nonpejorative category. Yet he separates "normal" from "abnormal" behavior according to the expressions and mannerisms of the characters. That effeminate characteristics are considered part of the negative expression of sexuality reinforces the normativity and homonormativity that LGBTQAI+ individuals face in their daily lives.

Homonormativity, of course, arguably is symptomatic of a country struggling with widespread homophobia when it must reckon with same-sex desire in the public sphere. As David William Foster (1999) notes, "[T]here should be little surprise that, in a country like Brazil where homophobia continues to be firmly entrenched, especially as regards the visibility of same-sex desire, there should be so few films in which homoeroticism is dealt with in any significant measure" (7).

Nonetheless, there have been a significant number of recent movies that portray same-sex desire in Brazilian cinema. Some of these include queer characters who do not represent or conform to the heteronormative roles of sexuality and as such present a different perspective on queer lives in Brazil. The final two chapters of this book discuss selected examples of such queer-themed recent audiovisual media from the anthropophagic queer perspective proposed here. The movies selected for these two chapters illustrate that certain silences and bodies can be both productive and disruptive, even when they do not adhere to expectations of an assimilationist, liberal white politics of "homonormativity."[19] Ironically, in some of these movies, the silent queer lives at the margin are not necessarily silenced at all but instead propose another form of queer (anthropophagite) visibility or, as Brazilian gay activist Herbert Daniel (1982) has described, a model of productive silence. These characters do not necessarily "come out" (in the way of the US model of identity politics), yet neither are they invisible. Their productive silence can actually be seen as a political statement of resistance. After all, in the critical context of these movies, not saying "Eu sou gay" (I am gay) does not mean being "in the closet" but rather not subscribing to either a certain political status quo or to a ready-made (American) model of homosexual visibility that some artists and scholars have discussed.[20]

Silence and abjection, in the specific sense I have applied in the preceding chapters, are two sides of the same conflict for homosexual bodies in the films analyzed in this book. It is worthwhile to recall that in the first chapter I presented an analysis of an anthropophagic queer sensibility that I then used in the second and third chapters to explore a number of cinematic perspectives on the politics of queer visibility. In these final chapters, I rely on both the theoretical issues and historical landscape I have mapped out so far to therein situate the particular characters and issues my selection of films raise. Their stories and concerns resonate with some of the central ideas I have touched on so far. The films analyzed in these chapters portray effeminate men, *travestis*, trans people, and queer people who live beyond any gay/lesbian fixed classification. Far from being "negative" or a "disservice" to the gay community, such characters can help us understand how instead of denying their abjection or silencing their being, they have found ways to express their sexuality in a more liberated way.

The characters in these films claim alternative possibilities; on the one hand, they seem silenced and have their rights violated, but on the other hand, they find in their very silenced abjection a productive mode of sexual authority. If in chapters 2 and 3, I presented three perspectives in relation to abjection and visibility, now I will present not different perspectives but alternative modes of experience that support Daniel's (1982) positions in terms of abjected productive silence. "Queer" in that sense thus "enables a productive intervention into the visual representation of same-sex desire and the history of cinema. 'Queer' encapsulates 'perverse' sexualities without fixing them into specific identities and can therefore capture different configurations of cinematic representation and non-normative desire" (Mennel 2012, 3).

The following chapters take up real representations that try to break this normative depiction of masculinity and the anxieties over the effeminate body among gay men.

DZI CROQUETTES AND THE QUEER DOCUMENTARY TRADITION

4

In this chapter, I propose that the cultural logic of the anthropophagic queer continues into the last decades of the twentieth century and the beginning of the twenty-first century in a different manner. As I argued in the previous chapter, after João Silvério Trevisan and Cinema Marginal, anthropophagic queer cinema seemed to come to a standstill. During the period when *pornochanchada* and erotic dramas dominated the theaters, queer visibility mostly disappeared from the screen. However, I contend that it is in theater and in music that an anthropophagic and queer mode of cultural production will reappear. This chapter analyzes the celebrated 2010 documentary *Dzi Croquettes*, which centers on a 1970s Brazilian theater troupe that despite all the adversities—government dictatorship, lack of sponsorship, and conservatism—gained national and international success. At a time when dissident sexuality was meant to be hidden from public view, Dzi Croquettes reclaimed queer bodies for performance, redefining a genealogy in Brazilian queer images in a similar way that Antropofagia had done forty years before. Documentary makers Tatiana Issa and Raphael Alvarez in turn found in this icon of queer performance a national archive to devour for a burgeoning tradition in national documentary.

The choice to yet again discuss documentary in this book is no coincidence. As Amir Labaki (2003) explains, Brazil "boasts a rigorous tradition of documentary filmmaking, proof of which can be seen in the excursions made into this medium by every great Brazilian filmmaker" (97). These "excursions" explore, and sometimes blur, the wavering line between fact and fiction. As early as 1929, the film *São Paulo, a sinfonia da metrópole* combines the style of an objective, informative documentary with fictional frames. Another example is the work of Helena Solberg, the only female director to be recognized as part of the Cinema Novo movement. Her 1966 documentary, *A entrevista* (The interview), offers a feminist take on documentary, and her use of the then new Nagra technology for voice-overs often creates a striking juxtaposition. The interviews conducted with twenty-seven women from Rio de Janeiro do not always match the images, and the critical, distancing effect of this technique soon became a major influence in documentary filmmaking. Solberg also made *Carmen*

Miranda: Bananas Is My Business (1995), an awarded documentary about the life of perhaps the most famous Brazilian personality in Hollywood. Miranda achieved legendary status in Brazil and became a queer symbol for future generations (analogous to Judy Garland). In the documentary on her life, Solberg alternates historical footage of Carmen Miranda with images of drag queen Erick Barreto, who became famous in Brazil as a Miranda impersonator.

Solberg's techniques clearly influenced Issa and Alvarez in *Dzi Croquettes*, not only because of its interest in documenting and reconstructing queer lives but also in terms of the film's structure. At the heart of *Dzi Croquettes* are personal stories that the directors present to create a national archive of queer memory that gives visible proof of lives otherwise silenced. They do this, I argue, in a manner that incorporates an anthropophagic queer perspective and that inaugurates a particular form and style of queer documentary.

The film portrays the theater group Dzi Croquettes, which performed from 1972 to 1976[1] amid the dictatorial regime in Brazil. The group was originally formed by thirteen men who created a show that challenged the normative gender and social barriers of the time. The name Dzi Croquettes comes from the combination of the word *croquete* in Portuguese, a salty snack made of meat, and the Brazilian pronunciation of the English definite article *the*. As Wagner Ribeiro (one of the group's original members) explained, "I have always enjoyed the English article 'the'; it could also be the Portuguese *zê*. Since we were eating croquettes, why not baptize the group Dzi Croquettes"[2] (qtd. in Lobert, 1979, 3). And even though it is not clear from their interviews, one might also trace a genealogy to "The Cockettes," the San Francisco–based drag queen group of the same era.

Through a series of interviews and footage from the only remaining show of the group, the documentary reconstructs the theater troupe's trajectory and argues for its importance to Brazilian performance history. Interestingly, Issa and Alvarez also cite conventions and techniques from other Brazilian documentaries to tell the story of Dzi Croquettes. They use archival material in ways that call to mind other 1990s productions, such as Aurélio Michiles's *O cineasta da selva* (The filmmaker from the jungle, 1997) and Paul Caldas and Lírio Ferreira's *Baile perfumado* (Perfumed ball, 1996).

In his well-known *Introduction to Documentary*, Bill Nichols (2010) proposes six different categories, or "modes," for analyzing the documentary genre, depending on how the movie is made. Issa and Alvarez's feature fits in more than one of those categories. For example, *Dzi Croquettes* calls to mind the "poetic mode" since the film "emphasizes visual associations, tonal or rhythmic qualities, descriptive passages, and formal organization" (32). The film adopts the "expository mode" because it "emphasizes verbal commentary and an argumentative logic" (33) through a series of interviews in which we only hear the interviewee's voice. Finally, the film fits in the "participatory mode" category because it "emphasizes the interaction between filmmaker and subject" (33). It is the blending of these aspects that makes *Dzi Croquettes* a compelling and innovative documentary that sheds light on an important episode in Brazilian (and queer) performance history.

In addition, *Dzi Croquettes* portrays the search of coproducer Tatiana Issa for her father, who was a member of the theater group. (In that sense, this documentary brings to mind—and extends—Paul Julian Smith's [2011] observation in a review about Daniela Thomas and Walter Salles's 2008 Brazilian movie *Linha de passe* [Line-breaking pass] that "Brazilian boys just can't seem to hold on to their fathers.") Besides an attempt to rescue footage and the history of a cultural moment that *revolucionou o Brasil*, as many interviewees affirm, the film is a poetic search for personal belonging. As Issa explains in the beginning of the documentary, "I was born in January of 1974. When I was born, I could not imagine that the movement that had started two years before would change my life and revolutionize Brazil."[3] A quest for private and public history, the documentary thus reflects both on the importance of this theater group and on the political and cultural changes in Brazil since the 1970s.

In its double search for the father and for the revitalization of the cultural heritage of this theater group, *Dzi Croquettes* blends the personal and the historical, the fictional, and the nonfictional in unusual ways. In "The Scene and the Inscription of the Real," César Guimarães (2013) suggests that "the relations between documentary and fiction have taken on a configuration in which several things stand out: [among these are] the use of theatrical proceedings in the composition of the filmed scene . . . [and] the staging of lived events and experiences" (87). *Dzi Croquettes* complicates this view in that it proposes two forms of staging. On the one hand, "the staging of lived events" consists entirely of real (historical) footage from the group. On the other hand, the director's daughter "plays the director" as a child in the scenes where she (Issa) narrates her past experiences with the theater group as a child. Jean-Claude Bernardet (2007), a Brazilian film critic and professor, calls this a "voz do saber" (voice of God). To the scholar, it means "the voice of experts or voice-over commentators that gives 'technical' or 'official' information, in conflict with the 'voice of experience' of the ones directly involved in the facts" (112). *Dzi Croquettes* thus overlaps and associates Issa's personal search with an argument about the cultural importance of the group.

Unlike many other documentaries in which the interviewees look at the camera as if speaking "directly to the spectator, without interference from the cinematic mechanism" (Smith, 1996, 60), in *Dzi Croquettes* the interviewees do not look straight at the camera; instead, they speak indirectly to a third person, Issa, who can be briefly seen three times throughout the film. Suggestively, the directors thus create proximity between the (implied) audience and the interviewees.

The film opens with Issa's narration (through her voice and subtitles) as she presents a historical overview of Brazil in the 1960s and '70s and her personal relationship with the theme. After this brief introduction, her voice disappears from the film giving space to the "voice of experience." At this point, the viewer learns about Dzi Croquettes. The director's voice is heard again only toward the end, when she narrates her past experience as a child with the group and her relationship with the father. The *voz do saber* plays an interesting role in this documentary since the shared knowledge in this film is her personal experience: "My father made me sleep between the theater chairs. I saw the show in the dark. It was like a fantasy, a dream."[4] Toward the end of the film, for the first and only time, the viewer sees the documentary crew— cameramen, directors, assistants, and others—through a crane shot. "Since the crew is visible and they talk about their documentary, the film artifice is revealed" (Dias 2003, 112). Hence, both perspectives—personal and political—are intertwined based on the directors' final editing. Issa's personal search is also the viewer's discovery of a forgotten moment of Brazilian recent history. Henceforth, these perspectives confirm Bill Nichols's definitions and how the directors blend these categories into one film. Issa's search relates to the "participatory mode," and the political aspect of the documentary merges the "expository mode" and the "poetic mode," as we shall see in the following paragraphs.

The film's opening sequences signal a clear intention to associate the body and politics. The film alternates images of Caco Barcelos (one of the troupe's original members) dancing on a stage with images of citizens being arrested; subtitles explain key moments of the dictatorial government, especially the AIs, or *atos institucionais*, the government measures that restricted individual liberties.

Along with the crosscuts between Barcelos and archive footage, sound plays an important role here as well. While Barcelos dances to Lou Reed's "Goodnight Ladies," the footage from the 1960s anti–military regime protests is accompanied by sirens, screams, and bombs. If at first such an editing technique seems to give a sense of alienation, since the sexy dance does not match with the violent images seen, once the film turns to Dzi Croquettes' real footage, the violent sounds continue, mixed now with lively music while the actors apply makeup. In this moment, both sirens and music are juxtaposed in crosscutting images. Hence, from the beginning of the film, all the images from the group are permanently associated with politics.

Following the initial historical background, Issa and Alvarez work with superposition of images of the artists (in color) and political historical footage (in black and white). The succession of images foreshows what most of the commentaries will say. At first, the testimonies explain the dictatorship and the AI-5,[5] as viewed through the eyes of the artistic class; this is followed by the testimony about the importance of the theater group. As the first full footage of the group is shown, Ney Matogrosso intones, "Paradoxalmente foi o momento em que surgiram os Dzi Croquettes" (Paradoxically it was the moment Dzi Croquettes arose).

Dzi Croquettes "brought to Brazil the most contemporary and questioning elements of the international homosexual movement, especially the American movement,"[6] affirms João Silvério Trevisan (2004, 288). The group is the epitome of the anthropophagic queer, since through parody, mockery, and music and dance, they exposed the boundaries of sexuality, gender identity(ies), and sexual orientation, without leaving aside the political aspect of the country at the moment they performed. If there is one point on which most interviewees agree, it is the transgressive nature of the group. As journalist and songwriter Nelson Motta says in the film, "[I]t was a way to contest dictatorship through mockery, sarcasm."[7] They were masculine, feminine, and androgynous, all in one body. Finally, the interviewees note that the troupe expressed a positive sexuality on stage, an "absolute exercise of our sexuality."

Like *Madame Satã* (which I discuss in chapter 5), the documentary *Dzi Croquettes* has a clear intention of associating the group with neither masculinity nor femininity but instead with the possibility of a queer imagining for repressed bodies beyond Anglo-American definitions. In one short excerpt from their show, the actors say on stage:

> Not ladies, not even gentlemen. Not even.
>
> Sorry people, we are not men. Got the wrong show. We are not men (laughs)
>
> Ah e nós não somos mulheres também, não.
>
> Exactly, if you are looking for a girlie show we are not women either, so you got the wrong show.
>
> Outro papo. Nós somos gente.
>
> Exactly.
>
> We put it together. We become just one thing. People. Just like you. You are people too.[8]

Dzi Croquettes thus made clear their notion of sexuality. Although dressing in what are traditionally women's clothes, they were not performing as drag queens or *transformistas*; rather, they were breaking with the notions of gender binaries—man/woman, *macho/bicha*. Their muscular bodies in tiny thongs were not intended to depict a feminine body but instead an artistic rendition of sexuality generally. Dzi Croquettes thus made a strategic appeal to universal humanism while transgressing gender norms. Because their act did not necessarily relate to homosexual bodies but to sexual bodies (in the words of one of the actors: "sexualidade gostosa, nem homossexual, nem heterossexual" [nice sexuality, neither homosexual, nor heterosexual]). Similarly, Peter Fry, Edward MacRae, and Jose W. S. Moraes (1985) describe the show as an "apotheosis of debauchery," neither masculine nor feminine but both (10).

This idea of breaking with normativity refers us back, once again, to *Madame Satã*. Issa and Alvarez's documentary, like Aïnouz's fiction feature, is thus able to play with the male/female dichotomy but in this case through the alliance of image and testimony. All the artists interviewed in the documentary agree that Dzi Croquettes portrayed a new way of experiencing sexuality. "There was good sexuality," actor Pedro Cardoso observes. "Masculine. Feminine, homosexual. There was an absolute possibility of the exercise of sexuality."[9]

Dzi Croquettes, through their dance and performance, showed the audience that the boundaries of the body (not to mention our abjected homosexual bodies) can be much more fluid and fruitful than one could expect and pointed to queer possibilities of imagining bodies and lives, as evidenced by "Borboleta" (Butterfly), just one emblematic performance of the group. Rosemary Lobert, in her 1979 thesis about the group, describes this dance as follows: "Opening their wings, rag wings, striped, flowered, evoking all colors, in the middle of the stage, the butterflies dance" (46).[10] To the sounds of Richard Strauss's *Also sprach Zarathustra*, the actors dance the part of butterflies (*borboleta*—a feminine noun in Portuguese). To the group, the butterfly signifies the rebirth of a new time, neither male nor female. "A new rebirth comes and with it, a new being with all the strength of the male and the female grace. It is easy to live with it, I am just not sure how to explain it, so I do it with a scream" (Lobert 1979, 46).[11]

The group's performance seemed to incorporate a post–identity politics in which bodies are not marked by masculinity or femininity but both. Dzi Croquettes, then, refers us back to the discussion I presented in the first chapter. Their activism was not an identitarian type but rather a post–identity engagement similar to the modes the academy has been recently proposing in Brazil.

This exercise of sexuality also represents the troupe's own family arrangements. According to the documentary, Dzi Croquettes formed a family among themselves in which each of them had a specific role: the father, the mother, the aunt, and even the fans were part of this family. Tatiana Issa, in restoring the image of her father, also reconstructs a queer, familiar arrangement that she previously belonged to, an arrangement that evokes Trevisan's notion of accumulation—that is, a family that surges around the necessity of proximity and queer alliance.

Moreover, the documentary plays an interesting role in creating and activating memories. Actors, singers, and directors are invited to talk about the group, and among those people, Liza Minnelli, Miguel Falabella, Pedro Cardoso, Betty Faria, Ney Matogrosso all share their memories of Dzi Croquettes. Issa and Alvarez intersperse their informants' remarks with the remaining images of the group from the 1970s. This crosscutting between the interviews and the group's footage proves a powerful technique because it gives the viewer the impression that the commentary and the footage are both occurring in the present moment and reinforces the continuing cultural relevance the group has for current actors, directors, and musicians in Brazil. The memories that surface in the interviews reaffirm that the group has left an indelible mark on Brazilian popular culture. "Foi um trabalho único, avant-garde" (It was a unique work, avant-garde) is a typical sentiment. Moreover, since Issa and Alvarez's editing technique highlights the repetition of what is being said (in a succession of shots, different interviewees repeat the same statement, thus creating a list of keywords that refer to the group), the interviews also reinforce this idea of veracity and of stimulating memories.

The interviews also create a chronological narrative that aligns Issa's personal search with the objective of reconstructing collective memory. The film is implicitly divided into several blocks of interviews, each focusing on one specific topic that was likely prompted by a question (although we do not hear the director posing these questions). Broadly, these topics include (1) the historical period in which the group is inserted; (2) the sexual revolution that the group initiated in Brazil; (3) Dzi Croquettes as a family ("Uma comunidade que deu certo" [a community that worked]); (4) the fan base and the relationship with public; (5) censorship; (6) the European "tour"; (7) the dissolution; (8) the story of Issa's father and herself; (9) AIDS and the death of eight of the members, and, finally, (10) the death of Issa's father.

Even though this structure is entirely implicit, it nonetheless provides a progressive coherence to the documentary: for Issa to discover what happened to her father, she must first uncover the lost history of the group in which he performed.

Ernest Hardy (2011) takes a somewhat different view, arguing that the documentary loses its power when it stops superimposing images of "grim-faced soldiers marching down the street, serving as muscle for the dictatorship then running Brazil" and the "half-nude androgynous men dancing up a storm onstage—faces slathered in makeup" and turns instead to repetitive interviews with famous actors, singers, dancers, and theater directors who have witnessed the group's work. However, my position remains that the way in which the directors structured the interviews alongside the documentary material in this repetitious way in fact serves to highlight the group's social and political importance.

On political and social levels, the documentary rescues the Dzi Croquettes' performance and shows how influential the group has become to a great deal of the political and artistic work produced in Brazil. It was, according to Issa, the "movimento que iria revolucionar o Brasil" (movement that would revolutionize Brazil). José Possi Neto, a renowned theater director, says that he witnessed the revolution in the theater Dzi Croquettes developed in Brazil. Issa and Possi Neto's comments are backed up by the other interviewees who say, among other things, that the group helped launch the gay movement liberation in Brazil. In a magazine review for the film, Julia Moreira (2010) explains the influence of the group, saying that with time, the troupe members paved a path for other artists, including those in a new genre of theater known as "Besteirol" (debauchery theater). The genre would further influence a number of television shows and artists in the decades that followed. In addition, As Frenéticas, created in the image of Dzi Croquettes, was probably one of the most successful all-female musical groups in Brazil during the 1970s and 1980s releasing a number of singles that reached peak position on the local charts. Some of the former members say that they even released songs written by the Dzi Croquettes in the documentary.

Dzi Croquettes also brings to light Oswald de Andrade and the *Manifesto antropófago*. When discussing the modernist movement, one aspect that seems a common among various critics and scholars is Antropofagia's notions of mockery and debauchery. Kenneth David Jackson (1999), borrowing Richard Morse's words, describes the manifesto as "brincadeira séria" (279), or a serious joke, meaning that even though the manifesto is full of humor and jokes, there is a serious project underneath it that tries to reconcile the Brazilian experience with the inherited tradition (Luís Costa Lima qtd. in Jackson 1999, 278). Using the *brincaderia séria* technique, Dzi Croquettes' theater was able to criticize the patriarchal institutions through scorn.

Finally, Dzi Croquettes helps us imagine different family arrangements and different possibilities of identity beyond the binary male/female, and Issa's opening up about her father's sexuality gives voice and form to different queer arrangements in Brazilian society. Such arrangements take the form of fiction in the next chapter, which features Aïnouz's *Madame Satã* and Lacerda's *Tatuagem*.

CONTEMPORARY TRENDS IN ANTHROPOPHAGIC QUEER

Challenging Effeminophobia

This final chapter analyzes two contemporary films that continue and, in a sense, rescue and reinvent the sensibility of what I have been calling the anthropophagic and queer mode of cultural production in Brazilian cinema. Both Karim Aïnouz's 2003 *Madame Satã* and Hilton Lacerda's 2013 *Tatuagem* offer queer reflection on traditional gender dichotomies that remain vigorously intact in Brazilian society today. Both films bring to the fore multiple queer characters and sensibilities, steering away from negative or pejorative conclusions. They represent a new style in Brazilian queer cinema that is attentive to a queer past but decidedly gesturing toward future possibilities informed by a queer and anthropophagic outlook on culture. Brazilian sociality is expanded with a new cast of characters: the homosexual rogue in 1920, the homosexual (and passive) soldier, the queer artist, the effeminate actor, the accepting mother, the young boy whose father is a performer, the philosophy professor—all can join in a queer family arrangement of new possibilities.

Crucial for the timeline of this study is how these films look to specific moments in the past to pave the way to the future; *Madame Satã* looks to the 1920s to depict the lives of the marginalized in Rio de Janeiro, then the country's capital; *Tatuagem*, set in the 1970s under the oppressive dictatorship, follows a group of militant social outcasts plotting a queer liberation. Both films highlight critical moments in Brazilian history: modernism and Andrade's avant-gardist longings in the 1920s and Cinema Marginal and Trevisan's film, *Orgia*, in the 1970s. By devouring past historical moments in an anthropophagic queer mode, *Madame Satã* and *Tatuagem* investigate the historical constraints imposed on queer bodies in the past and propose alternative modes to relate to the present and the future.

Madame Satã and the Fictionalized Reality

Madame Satã, or João Francisco dos Santos (1900–1976), was born to former Black slaves in the northeastern part of Brazil. When he was eight, his mother sold him to a commerce trader. He eventually ran away to Rio de Janeiro, where he lived until his death. He was famously known for being a rogue (*malandro*), a performer, and a street fighter. He was arrested more than ten times and over the course of his life spent more than twenty years in prison. He was also a known homosexual (in a 1971 interview with Sérgio Cabral [Altman 1995] and others for the famed Brazilian magazine *Pasquim*, when asked if he was a homosexual, he said he had always been and would always be). The nickname Madame Satã stemmed from a carnival costume competition in which he won first place.

Madame Satã lived among prostitutes and other lower-class workers in tenement slums in the bohemian neighborhood of Lapa in Rio de Janeiro. In Brazil, homosexual men have found ways of affirming their identities among different social groups. According to Silviano Santiago (2002), "[T]he conceit of privacy made patently visible how gay and lesbian marginality did not exist among the lower classes, since lesbians and gays were there accepted as they were by their social peers" (16). And, indeed, I argue that the film affirms Madame Satã's identity as a "homosexual" along various axes: gender, social class, and both racial and sexual categories. As B. Ruby Rich (2013) observes with regard to *Madame Satã*, "Race and class are often too incidental to queer narratives. In this tale of Brazil's unlikely hero/heroine, such omissions were impossible, for they are the core of Madame Satã's life and narrative" (176). His flamboyant lifestyle can help us understand the prejudice against effeminate men that has been so prevalent in Brazilian social and academic life. Gustavo Subero (2014), following Oscar Montero, notes that "Latino society does not punish the attraction to people from one's own sex, but punishes effeminate behaviour in men or masculine behaviour in women; in other words, it punishes any deviation from traditional male/female sexual roles" (57).

Madame Satã, in his performances and public persona, challenges this traditional view of the dichotomy *homem/bicha* (man/homosexual). As Satã himself explained in a 1970s *Pasquim* interview, he had decided to be a *bicha* by age thirteen, when he and other local kids were invited by prostitutes to participate in orgies. He experimented with both homosexuality and heterosexuality. As Rogério Durst (1985) explains, "He tried to have sex as a man and as a homosexual, preferring the latter" (30).[1]

As a street fighter and performer, Madame Satã consciously complicated the meanings traditionally ascribed to effeminacy, in particular by adapting the attitude of a *malandro*. As James Green (1999) points out, "He was proud of his ability with the knife and fighting, two signs of bravery and virility" (155). He was a violent man who was repeatedly arrested for crimes, including murder. He was also considered a deviant, because he performed in feminine (or feminized) attire (at the time, and maybe still, an indelible sign of homosexuality); his adoption of an exaggerated version of the traditional macho role can perhaps be seen as overcompensation. Albuquerque (2004) explains that "the performative nature of Satã's life could be read as a critique of traditional gendered behavior in Brazil. This is apparent in his sometimes exaggeratedly macho behavior and his close ties with the underworld of crime, on the one hand, and his patently camp ways and enjoyment of homosexuality, on the other. Satã's ability to combine macho bravado and uninhibited campiness reveals much about cultural definitions of masculinity in Brazil" (23–24).

Madame Satã precisely captures this dichotomy that dos Santos / Madame Satã represented in his life and, I argue, defies the logic of sexuality and normativity as much as Satã himself did at his time. Aïnouz understands how Satã's persona took on mythic proportions that exceeded even his outsized personality as a public figure. The film, then, plays with both the history and the myth of João dos Santos.

To Geisa Rodrigues (2013), the "multiple faces of Madame Satã" are not merely the various characteristics that João dos Santos displayed but are also, in a sense, the "mythological" images that made Madame Satã into a legend. Any contemporary political strategy, according to Rodrigues, must be situated within a double commitment. It is important to identify "deterritorializations" and to articulate "masks" of the time (191).

Because João dos Santos consists of both person and myth, Aïnouz realizes the story cannot be approached as a simple biopic but must inevitably involve a re-creation and reinterpretation of Madame Satã's legend. Toward this end, the film follows Madame Satã's life during adulthood in Lapa in the 1930s and relies on actual police records, interviews with João dos Santos, and other historical sources to re-create a possible chronology and narrative that depicts his life.

Aïnouz explains in an interview that he wanted to "capture, through an intimate cinematography, the enthusiasm and contradictions of the experiences of a *malandro* hustler, a black and a homosexual in Brazil at the beginning of the last century" (qtd. in Shaw, 2007a, 88). And thanks to his frequent use of close-ups and the constantly vigilant presence of the camera in the small spaces of the *cortiços* (slum tenements), bars, and clubs where the characters' lives play out, he succeeds. Aïnouz also takes advantage of dark, light, and shadowy settings that resemble the atmosphere and aesthetic of 1940s and '50s noir movies. The close-ups in turn, according to Lisa Shaw, present the body as "strategy of resistance to authority and social conventions" (98).

The film's opening and closing sequences are the same, both showing a close-up of Madame Satã's beaten face while a voice-over reads his prison sentence (these are actual police records); however, in the last sequence, the police officer's voice is interposed with Madame Satã's voice telling a fictional story of an imprisoned princess who is

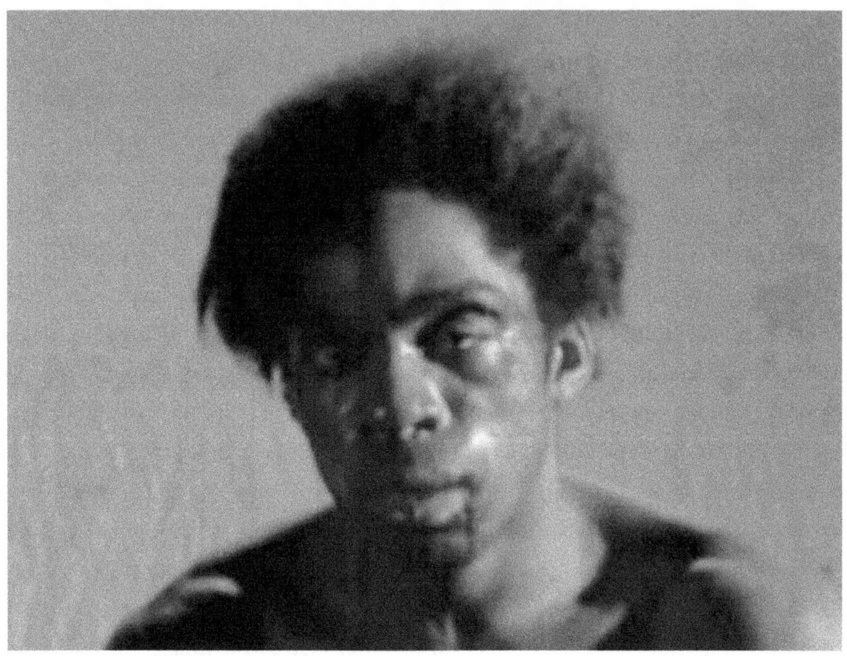

Still from *Madame Satã*. In the opening sequence, Madame Satã is in prison.

released during Carnival. These sequences further reveal parts of Satã's life. He spent more than twenty years in prison for multiple crimes, and his famous persona made him a police target, not only for his *malandragem* but also for his homosexuality.

Satã's voice at the end imbues the film with his own persona (or the voice of the myth). In the beginning, João dos Santos is arrested; in the end, Madame Satã has already become a legend, and his voice, even in prison, will not be silenced any longer.

As if with the intent of contextualizing the legend around Madame Satã, it is no coincidence that at the start of the film we see Madame Satã watching a performance by a female artist reciting excerpts from *A Thousand and One Nights*. We see Satã for the first time in a close-up behind a curtain of sequins, where he dubs the artist for whom he works as a helper. At this point, we are not sure if it is his show, and consequently this visual technique establishes a game among Satã's desire, the film, and the play in the film (Rodrigues 2013, 194). As the camera moves around Satã, we see he is behind the scenes watching the performance. The next sequence presents Satã in a suit and a panama hat—the traditional image of the *malandro carioca*—and then we see the streetcar that was made famous the Lapa region, where the film is set.

The opening sequences of the film help the audience understand that Madame Satã incorporates multiple sides, or faces: the artist, the homosexual, the feminine, the masculine, and, most important, the *malandro*. This image of the *malandro* has been perpetuated in music, television, and cinema as a virile, womanizer, uneducated but smart and philander man, and Madame Satã embodied this in a way few other men were able to do in Brazil. He then combined all these characteristics with his desire for people of the same sex, complicating, then, the traditional macho role portrayal. In the Aïnouz film, Lázaro Ramos, who plays Madame Satã, manages to harness all these features in his portrayal of the actor, capturing the feminine/masculine dichotomy. As Satã himself explains, society could not grasp his bravery because he was a known homosexual. People wanted to beat him up all the time (qtd. in Green 1999, 155).

Madame Satã, despite his love for feminizing dress, nonetheless refused to be labeled as a passive object of erotic pursuance; that is, he did not conform to the dichotomy of the top/bottom and *homem/bicha* tradition. When asked in an interview for *Pasquim* (Altman 1995) if he was the "caça" (hunter) or "caçador" (hunted), he categorically answered "caçador." In the film, this conflict between sexual behavior and ascribed gender roles manifests itself in combative ways. For instance, Madame Satã aggressively pursues Renatinho, a much younger man (in that sense, someone who can more easily be forced into the passive role) in a public restroom, grabbing him tightly, groping him all over, and domineeringly slapping him in the face. Later in the film, when they finally meet in Satã's room, Satã says: "Sit down. Are you looking for a girl like me, my height, dark skin? Feel the dark, big thighs."[2]

It is clear from the start that Renatinho will be penetrated. The extreme close-up of the camera, while involving the audience, also initially obscures the two bodies; but then the camera retracts, and we see Satã penetrating Renatinho. After Satã's orgasm, the camera focuses on Renatinho licking Satã's hand. Following the transition from the audience participative close-ups to a voyeuristic gaze once climax has been reached, the scene ends with viewers witnessing the action through open doors (a recurring technique in the film), which reinforces the sense of a lack of privacy in such accommodations.

In a critique of *Madame Satã*, Subero (2014) writes that the film fails to show Satã's femininity. However, I would contend that this depiction of hypermasculinity and *travestismo* would fit Satã's modes of operation. He saw himself as a *bicha*, the only label available at the time that expressed his desires. Subero's critique reduces Satã's performativity and the importance of his behavior to the expression of sexuality outside the standards of normativity. Moreover, I find that the film *does* show the character's femininity, exploring it in many different ways, through transvestism, his performances, and his use of feminine pronouns when speaking of himself. For instance, in the sex scene between Satã and Renatinho, a white male lover, even though

Satã is not penetrated and therefore does not act as a *bicha*, defying the expectations of the binary top and bottom, he starts the conversation with "A girl like me?" As Aïnouz explained, he wanted to depict an "enigmatic figure that plays with both masculinity and femininity" (Shaw 2007a, 96).

The main problem with such Subero's criticism is that it reinforces the prejudice against the effeminate man and sexual passivity, as I demonstrated in the previous trailer. The fact that Madame Satã identified himself as a *bicha* does not necessarily link his sexual practices to passivity; self-describing with feminine pronouns and adjectives does not make him—her—a passive sexual object. Aïnouz intended to depict a character whose "identity could not be defined in conventional terms" (Shaw 2007a, 96), and this is precisely what such scenes do—they complicate our normative views of sexuality and identity, something that Madame Satã did at his time. The final scenes show with clarity the director's view for the film. Satã presents a show in which he dances and sings for a large audience. In his chosen outfit, from the waist down, he mimics Carmen Miranda and Josephine Baker. However, his naked torso speaks to his virility.

While singing, he alternates between low and high pitches, and he dances in a way that calls to mind Josephine Baker in Edmond T. Gréville's 1935 *Princesse Tam-Tam* (the movie he had watched prior to his show) and Candomblé rhythms. Also, he sings a samba that, according to biographers, Noel Rosa[3] wrote for Madame Satã: "When a samba appears, it is news / in the slums or in the city / He was always famous / Women are always lamenting / because they know he won't fall in love with a woman."[4]

Madame Satã's image and portrayal in the film would thus precisely break with the *bicha/macho*, active/passive dichotomy that I presented in the first chapter. Satã at the same time plays the roles of the *mulato forte*, *malandro*, and the *bicha*. The either/or possibility that such binaries allow is restructured by the idea of either/or/and/both in Madame Satã's persona. Antônio Márcio da Silva (2014) presents Madame Satã as a femme fatale in the modes of the noir films. Even though Madame Satã is a man, his role in the film fits the femme fatale category since it "is a construct that causes anxieties because of her challenges to hegemonic gender and sexual roles" (16). Da Silva's analysis is noteworthy because he sees the femme fatale as "independent of the biological body" (61). Both male and female (and nonidentifying gender individuals) could play this role and therefore represent "challenges to patriarchy" (61). Through the representation of Madame Satã in the film, the creators incorporated not only noir aesthetics but also the femme fatale imagery in order to compose the character.

Satã's nickname comes from a 1930 Cecil B. DeMille motion picture named *Madame Satan*. The American movie tells the story of a woman played by Kay Johnson who disguises herself as Madame Satan in a costume ball in order to revenge her cheating husband. As Aïnouz's film shows, João dos Santos was fascinated by movie stars. In one scene, we see him watching Josephine Baker in an iconic scene in which she takes her shoes off and eloquently dances. The choice of Baker was not accidental in the film. Baker's career (like Carmen Miranda's) was punctuated by the New World exoticism and challenge to normative practices. As Madame Satã says in the film, "Eu sou filho de Iansã e Ogum e de Josephine Baker, sou devoto" (I am the son of Iansã and Ogum and a devotee to Josephine Baker). Watching Baker, João dos Santos is inspired to perform as the Mulata do Balacoxê.

Right before his final performance, Madame Satã tells a story about a creature named Janaci and a furious shark. In Andrade's anthropophagic mode, Satã re-creates a story, mixing in local and international elements, in order to recount his own story, as an entity with both animal and human, male and female, passivity and aggression:

> A brutal and cruel shark lived in the wonderful China / It bit everything and transformed everything in coal / To calm the best down, the Chinese man sacrificed seven cats every day / that it bit before sunset/ In order to end such barbarities / Janaci, an entity from the Tijuca Forest arrived / She ran through the woods and flew over the hills / Then Janaci became a golden jaguar / with soft ways and delicious taste / and started to fight the shark for a thousand and one nights / in the end glorious Janacy and the furious shark / were so hurt that nobody knew who each one was / and then, they turned into one thing.[5]

I quote in full because it brings together many of the elements that make this film and this character/individual such an important person for our anthropophagic queer perspective. The story references *One Thousand and One Nights* but transforms it using the local, natural, and mystical elements of Brazil: Janaci, forests, and also queer elements of both male and female, animal and human in one body. "E assim viraram uma coisa só" (And then they became one thing). Satã's narration brings us back to the initial moments of the film when he watched mesmerized an actress narrating Scheherazade's story. But at the end of the film, Janaci replaces Scheherazade. Madame Satã's version of the story is his own queer narrative.

By alternating these notions of fantasy and reality, his crimes and his homosexuality, in a complementary way, the film helps us understand not necessarily who the person João dos Santos was but rather the persona and the image that has been created around him. Madame Satã thus portrays an alternative mode of life that resists normativity and homonormativity. At the very least, an anthropophagic queer perspective helps us understand that sexuality cannot be represented as a fixed model, and this is exactly what the film does. Criticism (like Subero's) that implicitly defines the film as one-dimensional or takes an unrealistic view of Satã's sexuality simplifies the importance of such portrayal.

Most analyses of Madame Satã[6]—both the persona and the film—focus on the multiple facades of the character and on his transitioning between two worlds, male and female. In a country whose definition of sexuality has been simplified into dichotomous views of what and how one must be—passive/active, homosexual/heterosexual, aggressive/passive—*Madame Satã* tries to inject nuance into possible modes of our understanding of sexual experiences. In the end, Satã cannot be defined by any one side, for his sexuality, his whole persona, impossible to pin down, rests entirely within the contradiction. As with the story of the shark and Janaci that he recites in the film, Madame Satã does not transition between sides but *anthropophagically queerly* (mis) represents all those aspects in one body.

Aïnouz's *Madame Satã* revisits Trevisan's characters, and as with the ending of the magical narrative, Satã tells the audience, he lives as one: as the bandit, the *travesti*, the homosexual, the Black God, the prostitutes. All the characters in *Orgia ou o homem que deu cria* come together as one in Madame Satã. He is the contemporary representation of an anthropophagic queer body.

Tatuagem and the Uses of Naturalism

Tatuagem is Hilton Lacerda's directorial debut. Prior to his first full-length film, he worked as a scriptwriter for several award-winning movies, including *Amarelo manga* (*Mango Yellow*, 2002), *Baixio das bestas* (Bog of beasts, 2006), *A festa da menina morta* (The dead girl's feast, 2008), and *A febre do rato* (Rat fever, 2011). *Tatuagem* tells the story of a short-lived, romantic entanglement between Clécio (Irandhir Santos), an exuberant queer performer and theater director, and Arlindo Araújo (Jesuíta Barbosa), an eighteen-year-old cadet in the military, an encounter set in 1978 in Recife. Clécio is the director of a theater group in the mode of Dzi Croquettes and runs an avant-garde queer theater/bar called Chão de Estrelas (Floor of stars),[7] where one night he meets the young Arlindo. Chão de Estrelas is a place of creative and artistic resistance against the government and its support for a rigid (implicitly middle-class and hetero-) normativity. "Soldado Araújo" (also called "Fininha"[8] in the film) serves the regime as a "soldier." The film is set during the final years of the dictatorship. The film thus attempts to re-create the creative and political resistance of queer communities against the dictatorship at a time before the AIDS epidemic took hold. In addition, by situating in Recife a (fictional) theater troupe modeled on the tradition of Dzi Croquettes, *Tatuagem* moves the "revolution" out of the traditional urban and political centers (Rio de Janeiro and São Paulo) and brings visibility to regions that have often been culturally isolated.[9]

Right at the beginning of the film, the first thing we hear, even before we see the actors, is a voice announcing "A nossa arma é o deboche" (Debauchery is our weapon). Mockery is thus the way the characters have found to fight the system or to pursue alternatives modes of sexuality and life. *Deboche* is also a common word found in interviews with Dzi Croquettes. Thus, by creating a theater group that focuses on mockery, Hilton Lacerda borrows Dzi Croquettes' technique in order to tell this story. Another important reference point for Lacerda is a 1970s experimental theater group from Recife whose work draws directly from Dzi Croquettes. João Silvério Trevisan (2004) explains that Vivencial could have been directly related to Dzi Croquettes had it not been the middle-class aspiration of the group from Rio de Janeiro. Most of the members from Vivencial were young people from the outskirts of Recife.

The film begins with a 360-degree pan from the camera still, showing only the image of an empty Chão de Estrelas; Clécio's voice-over introduces the show. The camera then cuts to Soldado Arlindo Araújo at the military base, sitting in bed, waiting for the morning bell. Immediately, the viewer is struck by the contrast between the two worlds of these characters: Clécio's is loud and lively; Arlindo's, quiet. The visual imagery further highlights the difference. Chão de Estrelas is a colorful scene, whereas Arlindo's military surroundings are subdued and monochromatic. For instance, all the soldiers in the scene wear the same white briefs.

During the first twenty minutes of the film, the director continues crosscutting between Chão de Estrelas and the military, reinforcing the dissimilarity of the two characters' lives. While at Chão de Estrelas, the artists stage a sarcastic and orgiastic performance with songs like this: "Dad, I want to get married / Oh, my daughter, tell me with whom / I want to marry the *travesti* / with the *travesti*, you can marry / Why? / The *travesti* can serve as a man and then she serves as a woman too."[10] Arlindo also "sings," though his song is performed as a chant with his fellow soldiers, which sheds light on the life of a soldier: "I've seen soldiers die in the jungle / and they never returned home."[11]

The characters' sexuality is also revealed in the film's early minutes. Arlindo's colleagues call him "queridinho do sargento" (sergeant's darling), implying that he is having an affair with the sergeant. Arlindo does not respond (though later the relationship is confirmed by Arlindo himself). When Clécio and his best friend, Paulete (Rodrigo García), are at the beach and a vendor calls them "homosexual," they defiantly ask the vendor if he is really trying to offend them. While Clécio seems both assertive and combative with his sexuality, Arlindo is more discreet.

Still through crosscutting, we watch as the characters take turns presenting their families, their jobs, their routine, and their lifestyle. We learn that Arlindo has a girlfriend and a pregnant sister and that Clécio has a son and a good relationship with the boy's mother. *Tatuagem* (like *Madame Satã* and *Dzi Croquettes*) thus considers the possibility of queer family arrangements at the margins. *Tatuagem*, like *Orgia ou o homem que deu cria*, creates a possible family arrangement. In *Tatuagem*, however, the idea of accumulation is less intense than in Orgia since the "family" in *Tatuagem* is already set and has found a home. Nevertheless, the arrival of Arlindo creates tension in the family arrangements: as a soldier, he represents the repressive state.

This alternation between Clécio and Soldado Araújo continues until the moment they meet at Chão de Estrelas. Arlindo goes to the theater/bar to meet his girlfriend's brother, Paulete, and decides to stay to watch the performance. The camera first focuses on Arlindo's face as he curiously takes in the surroundings and then comes to rest on the stage where we see Clécio, who begins singing Caetano Veloso's "Esse cara" (This man). At this point, the camera focuses on Clécio's point of view. Looking into the audience, he has his eyes fixed on someone in the crowd. As the song's lyrics describe a man "com seus olhinhos infantis, com os olhos de um bandido" (with childish eyes, eyes of a bandit)—a kind of man, in other words, like Arlindo. The camera, never losing sight of Clécio, moves through the audience till it pauses behind Arlindo. At this point, our view of Clécio lines up with Arlindo's view of the performer (in fact, in this "eye line match," as it is called, it almost feels as if Clécio were looking straight at us). Crosscutting between these different points of view, the camera thus re-creates the cabaret's seductive atmosphere of song and spectacle and encourages the spectator to adopt the perspective of the characters.

After Clécio's song, a documentary-style handheld camera is used in some scenes, as if to follow the two characters more easily. This moving camera also follows Clécio and Arlindo later while they dance together. Arlindo seems at ease with the situation even though it is the first time he has ever danced with a man. He says: "Nunca tinha dançado assim com outro homem" (I had never danced with another man like that). Clécio responds, saying that he had never danced like that with a soldier. The distinction for both of them is important: while Arlindo is taking pleasure in his first dance with a man, Clécio enjoys the novelty of dancing with an "agente da ditadura" (dictatorship agent), as he calls his companion.

In terms of sexuality, this film, like *Madame Satã*, tries to break with the rigid boundaries of feminine/masculine, top/bottom. Arlindo is in the army and thus supposedly virile. Clécio is the artistic type, singing with a female voice and dressed in colorful and feminine ways (during his performance, he sings, "Eu sou apenas uma mulher" [I am just a woman]). Yet, as with *Madame Satã*, the characters in *Tatuagem* do not conform to the stereotypical gender norms that people might expect. When Clécio and Arlindo have sexual intercourse, Arlindo is penetrated by Clécio. If scholars have been concerned about the image or the portrayal of homosexual characters in the films, *Tatuagem* is then an important example of alternative possibilities for the depiction of queer lives. As much as *Madame Satã*, *Tatuagem* goes beyond traditional views of sexuality and images of the queer male body. The dichotomy between the passive and the active has been one point of ongoing discussion among scholars. Both films explore the possibility of a masculine-identified man who adopts the so-called passive role in sex, reverting traditional roles associated with femininity and passivity.

This unconventional relationship between a soldier and a performer aims to highlight an important issue that we have already seen in *Dzi Croquettes*—namely, how does one reconcile private and public lives? In *Tatuagem*, Deusa (Sylvia Prado), Clécio's coparent, says she saw Arlindo with his army unit during a repressive police act and that she does not want to see her son with people who work for the military regime. Arlindo is part of the military, but now he is also part of the theater and counterculture group. While not in action with his military brigade, his life does not seem to be in conflict with his new milieu. However, how does one reconcile the repressive regime and the liberationists?

The film answers that question definitively: Arlindo leaves the army. In the end of the film, as the army prepares to break into the theater, we see Arlindo dancing with the group. Under the dictatorship, there is no possible alternative life inside the army. To resist the regime, one needs to be outside of it.

The final show at Chão de Estrelas is the summation of the revolutionary perspective of the group. Significantly, the group's idea of transcending norms is explained by the song "Ode ao cu" (Ode to the asshole). Following the 1970s liberationist movements and utopias discussed by authors like Caio Fernando Abreu (2017) and João Silvério Trevisan (2019) himself, Chão de Estrelas proposes a view of the "asshole" as the one part of the body that signifies liberation for everybody—men and women. If the phallocentric society (in the film represented by the army and its guns) creates a hierarchy in social relations, a society in which the asshole is the center would redefine all our social relations. The song and the performance thus intend to socialize the anus. As Hocquenghem argued, if the phallus is essentially social, the asshole is essentially private. (72). Therefore, Chão de Estrelas proposes the total liberation and revision of the sublimated and marginalized status of the anus. The theater troupe's performance proposes "el uso deseoso del ano" (the desirable use of the anus [Hocquenghem 2009, 74]), not only for the homosexual body but also for everybody.

If the erotic dramas and *pornochanchadas* exploited the female body under a male gaze in order to satisfy a mostly male audience, *Tatuagem* uses the Brazilian erotic tradition in cinema to depict, in an attempt at equality, all bodies. In *Tatuagem*, the body, when nude, is collective. The "Ode ao cu" is the group's effort to unify desire as a *human* desire, even though the love story focuses on two cis men. Classic camera movements adopted from female-centered erotic dramas, as I discussed in chapter 3 in the context of *pornochanchadas* and erotic dramas, are used in the sexual close-ups of the two men's bodies. The gaze here is toward two male bodies, which had been (for the most part) traditionally ignored in classic erotic dramas.

The performance space thus becomes part of the utopian project of the theater group since it is there that the audience and the performers become one in their elegy to the anus. Clécio, with a phallic crucifix inserted in his anus, opens the "Ode ao cu" with a monologue in which he asks if democracy and liberty are equated. He concludes: "The symbol of liberty is the asshole. It is democratic and everybody has one."[12] Clécio's performance is crosscut with images of military trucks making their way to the theater. Again, the camera insists on highlighting the contrast between the happy, vibrant energy of the audience in the theater and the apprehensive faces of the young men inside the approaching trucks, who serve the brutal dictatorship.

Cutting from the truck to the theater, the camera focuses on the naked actors who are entering the stage to perform "Ode ao cu." One of the last is Arlindo, who has left the army and joined the group. The actors dance with the audience in a total celebration of the *cu*. The crosscutting between the theater and the military trucks continues until the moment we hear glasses breaking. There is a fade to black and for several seconds the sound of people screaming. Silence takes over as the camera cut to and holds a long shot of the theater during sunrise. At this point, the film returns to parallel shots of Clécio and Arlindo. The latter is now back in the same scene where we first saw him, sitting on his military bed but this time with a bag next to him. Clécio is with his son and Deusa; they are in a car, heading to the theater. Once again, the contrast of both lives is clear.

The opposition between queer possibility and impossibility is reinforced by the dialogue in the car: Clécio's son says that he has received a letter from Arlindo who is now in São Paulo trying to find work. In the letter, Arlindo says that he has not been able to find a job owing to the fact that he has a tattoo. This leads us back to a point in the film where we see Arlindo being tattooed by his fellow soldiers. Scenes of Chão de Estrelas and the military base once again alternate. The theater audience are loud and boisterous; Arlindo's space is dark and quiet. The title of the film, *Tatuagem* (Tattoo), is probably a reference to Chico Buarque's song of the same name: "Quero ficar no seu corpo feito tatuagem / que é pra te dar coragem pra seguir viagem quando a noite vem" (I want to stay on your body like a tattoo, so that you'll have courage to go away when the night comes).

In an earlier sequence, Arlindo had tattooed the letter *C* surrounded by a heart on his chest. The moment Clécio sees it, he cries and they kiss. The body is, then, permanently marked by their relationship. As a visible mark of their relationship, Arlindo's tattoo also serves to remind him of the impossibility of life in a normative society since the tattoo is the reason he cannot find a job in São Paulo.

Another important element of *Tatuagem* that deserves attention is the filming of a documentary that occurs within the film. Professor Joubert (Silvio Restiffe), a Chão de Estrelas enthusiast, is making a movie about the theater troupe. Professor Joubert's character nods to Jomard Muniz de Britto, a filmmaker, pedagogue, and poet from Recife whose work spanned over five decades. He is arguably one of the most important figures of Brazilian counterculture. Professor Joubert recites texts that resemble Jomard's own texts. Jomard also filmed the group Vivencial in the 1970s.[13]

Throughout *Tatuagem*, the digital camera used for the greater film is alternated with a Super 8mm—a motion picture camera that was used throughout the 1970s—for Professor Joubert's documentary within the film. Thus, Professor Joubert's shots are made with a traditional technique that contrasts with the modern filming. In home-video-style, Professor Joubert shoots scenes of the day-to-day life of Chão de Estrela's theater troupe for his own piece, titled *Ficção e filosofia* (Fiction and philosophy), a Tropicalist rendition that incorporates Indians, Carmen Miranda, robots, and music. *Ficção e filosofia* is an avant-garde film that tries to portray the possibility of a future with no sexual boundaries, a new "paradise"[14] in which all humans are free to express their libido.

Although we do not have the chance to see Professor Joubert's whole film, *Tatuagem* ends with a part of his documentary, in which he predicts a future with no gender. Joubert's film contrasts with the conventionality of *Tatuagem* in terms of technique and linearity, and even though *Tatuagem* does not "blur the barrier between art cinema and popular film," as Paul Julian Smith (2014, 2) has suggested about the recent films by young Mexican directors, Lacerda's film portrays same-sex desire with a naturalistic perspective that helps the audience see a love affair between two men, and its social and political connotations, without imposing on it a traditional story line of a failed and tragic relationship. The conventionality of Larceda's movie serves as a way to portray this naturalistic perspective of the same-sex desire without putting aside the possibility of freedom represented by Professor Joubert's unconventional piece.

When Jomard Muniz de Britto (2013), the inspiration for Professor Joubert, published his 1968 the *Manifesto Tropicalista* with Aristides Guimarães and Celso Marconi (2013), they wrote: "We attest: 'Desacralizing and corrupting the festive left, Tropicalismo invades and breaks, explodes and exploits its supporters as well as its attackers.' (Ha, ha, ha, for those who 'don't understand us.')" (108).[15]

For the *entendidos* (those who understand), the queerness of Tropicalismo is obvious; *Tatuagem* devours Brazilian queer history in the same manner that Madame Satã is "discovered" by a new generation of writers, journalists, and artists in the late 1960s and '70s. Both forge a queer past to understand an anthropophagic queer future.

CONCLUSION

When João Silvério Trevisan released *Orgia ou o homem que deu cria*, in his *Manifesto entendido* he made it clear he had made a queer film, a film for those who "understood," on the one hand, the references to Cinema Novo but also, on the other hand, the queer and anthropophagic perspective on a country desperately in search of itself. Trevisan's film set the tone of this study, in which I've presented a selection of contemporary Brazilian films that project a queer and anthropophagic mode of viewing (and being in) the world. While these films stand as reminders of historical friction (Madame Satã gets arrested multiple times both in real life and on the screen, Dzi Croquettes are censored, André and Antônio César in *Romance* die, Arlindo and Clécio in *Tatuagem* do not remain together, and Trevisan's own important film is censored for over a decade), their (his)stories are crucial for considering a genealogy in queer filmmaking in the Brazilian context.

For Julio Bezerra (2010), cinema narrates a state of being "à flor da pele" (under the skin) and allows the spectator to take in a privileged position in the sphere of intimacy (3). This makes cinema a particularly appealing genre for queer art practices: the use of close-ups invites the audience to take a closer look at the body, allowing them to inhabit and experience personal intimacies that are otherwise accessible. Cinema has the specific capacity to turn the spectator's attention to queer bodies and invest them with affect, emotion, cathexis, and desire. Bezerra contends that cinema's hallmark invention lies in its ability to almost touch "the skin, in the experience and a physical relationship with the camera" (2). The body—or rather the skin—is closer to the camera and hence to the audience's field of vision. The naked, hairy bodies of the *Dzi Croquettes*, the naked bodies and their "Ode ao cu" in *Tatuagem*, the sculpted body in a Carmen Miranda outfit in *Madame Satã*, the meat and money shots in *AIDS, furor do sexo* and in *Orgia ou o homem que deu cria*, and the body in pain in *Romance*—these are corporeal expressions drawn into the sensorial eye of the camera.

This study has suggested that an anthropophagic and queer mode of reading can shed critical light on the marginal position of queer bodies in Brazilian contemporary cinema. In all the films I have discussed, queer subjects seem caught up in state of abjection—in a social, cultural, and personal sense. Yet I do not think that abjection and marginality in the films should be equated with despair. Rather, the films use "[a]bjection or transvestism" as "two techniques (strategies) to render the invisible

visible" (Smith 1996, 34). From within the margins, these characters manage to plot and live alternative forms of existence. Each film features a set of characters who defy straightforward categorization—a thematic concern that is also extended formally, for instance by inserting metahistorical commentary and self-referential techniques. *Madame Satã* is a docudrama, *Tatuagem* weaves (fictional) performance footage through its story, *Romance* explicitly alternates self-referential storytelling with archival footage and Brechtian-like didactic voice-overs, and *Estou com AIDS* develops fictional characters whose narratives are intertwined with documentary commentary. Trevisan appropriates the Cinema Novo technique in order to queer it and make the characters' bodies visible. Fiction, in all the cases, blurs the boundaries with documentary. In *Dzi Croquettes*, Tatiana Issa observes that "tudo era uma fantasia, um sonho" (everything was a fantasy, a dream). If fantasy and dreams are part of the fictional realm, the documentary not only builds a forgotten collective memory but also appeals to our emotions with elements that constitute the fruition of fiction, as Fernão Pessoa Ramos (2018a) says. The fictional films, on the other hand, besides the *faz-de-conta ficcional* (fictional fairytale), deploy documentary elements in order to convey their stories.

J. Jack Halberstam (2011) in *The Queer Art of Failure* argues that "before queer representation can offer a view of queer culture it must first repudiate the charge of inauthenticity and inappropriateness" (95). He goes on to criticize the American TV show *The L Word* because of its attempt to "clean up" the lesbian image. To Halberstam, the series repudiates the butch (manly looking lesbian) in order to "represent lesbian as successful" (95). As I have shown in the second trailer of this book, Antônio Moreno's 2002 book falls into a similar "repudiation trap" by deeming the effeminate man (the *bicha*) as a merely stereotypical image of gay men and hence as irrevocably demeaning. The films I have analyzed, rather than overtly denouncing effeminacy as "bad," take an inquisitive, at times even celebratory, stance to gender plasticity and sexual diversity. The effeminate man is not *merely* a stereotype; he is also a citizen who, by necessity, creatively exercises pleasure in an often hostile cultural environment. The daily struggles and ways of being of these films' characters suggest subtle forms of activism that are similar to Silviano Santiago's 2002 proposals in "The Wily Homosexual":

> I ask whether the homosexual couldn't and shouldn't be more wily. Whether subtler forms of activism are not more profitable than aggressive ones. Whether subversion through the courageous anonymity of subjectivities in play—a slower process of consciousness-raising, I admit—doesn't provide better conditions for future dialogue between homosexuals and heterosexuals

> than the open confrontation on the part of a group that marginalizes itself, proposed by North American culture as more rapid and efficient. More rapid and efficient, yes, but certainly less wily. (18)

The Travesti Poeta, Madame Satã, Dzi Croquettes, Clécio, Arlindo, and even André Antônio César are in that sense "wily." They do not fully conform to normativity or to what Santiago describes as an "aggressive" Anglo-American model of coming out. Strictly speaking, they do not even conform to the idea of "being gay," since the term *gay* is not explicitly proposed in any of the films to express same-sex desire.

More than a form a resistance, the abject, then, comes to the center of the discussion, and pleasure. Bodies become centers and sources of pleasure; orgasm can be manipulated, created, and invented. Orgasm, as Paul Preciado (2011a) in *Manifesto contrasexual* describes, "será parodiado sistemáticamente gracias a diversas disciplinas de simulación y repeticiones en serie" (29) (will systematically be parodied through several disciplines of simulation and serial repetition). Preciado organizes his manifesto in terms of total freedom of the body, with no control by the state and political organizations. If "queer studies offer us one method for imagining, not some fantasy of an elsewhere, but existing alternatives to hegemonic systems," as Halberstam (2011, 89) proposes, and if the homosexual body has been historically associated with "failure, impossibility, and loss" (Love 2007, 21), Preciado (2011a) is exactly showing alternative modes of living, just as the *antropófagos* did in the 1920s. Erasing failure (whether in the past or in the present) and what I call abjection in order to create a rainbow-colored scenario for queer bodies can also be violent.

The difference between the abject and the normative is the presence of the surveillance of the state. By becoming part of society, gay men enter the state, and their practices become regulated by the political instances that control their bodies: marriage, divorce, adoption, assisted fertilization, grants, insurance, and all the rights that different groups have been advocating for. The abject (and their abjected practices) are, then, redefined as those who are not participating in these institutions. The discourse that praises abject practices is, therefore, a discourse that praises the possibility of not conforming. The discourse of normality in terms of acceptance is complicated since one must question which parts of same-sex sexuality we have normalized. Preciado (2011a) proposes the "desnormalización" (denormalization) of all sexual practices—that is, the idea that as long as there is a contract ("toda relación contrasexual será el resultado de un contrato consensual firmado por todos los participantes," 29), there is a possibility of sexual expression. Romanticizing aside, such ideas can become powerful tools for questioning in which ways our bodies have been denied visibility.

Finally, it is perhaps not accidental that *Romance* is the only fictional film that does not portray a possibility for queer lives (interestingly enough, it is a film that Moreno [2002] classifies as "nonderogatory," 138); it was produced in 1988, in the midst of one of the worst economic and social crises of Brazil. In contrast, the more recently produced films (*Madame Satã, Dzi Croquettes*, and *Tatuagem*) show that queer lives in the past—even in dire circumstances—have always been possible, and perhaps "subtler forms of activism" can be more "profitable than aggressive ones" (Santiago 2002, 18). In agreement with Halberstam's 2012 argument, I have thus argued in this book that the anthropophagic queer offers us methods for "imagining, not some fantasy of an elsewhere, but existing alternatives to hegemonic systems" (89) in the form of critical "spaces in-between."

While preparing this conclusion, I looked through a number of news items from mainstream media, which I had been collecting over the years, that highlight the prejudice against effeminate men. Some examples: In 2015, Russell Tovey, an openly gay actor who performed in a gay-themed US premium cable TV series, said in an interview that he is "thankful he is not an effeminate man" (Rivas 2015). In 2016, Brazilian scholar Luiz Mott affirmed that there is a misrepresentation of homosexual characters in Brazilian telenovelas because "em realidade" (in reality) most gay men are masculine looking, whereas the majority of characters on television are exaggeratedly effeminate (Lima 2014). In 2019, Maluma, a famed Colombian singer, faced backlash for posting a picture on Instagram that viewers said made him look "gay." While it is important to acknowledge the specific (melodramatic) genre expectations of Brazilian telenovelas with respect to gender representation or with the popular appeal of stock characters vis-à-vis the (high-brow) expectations of literary texts and "serious" author-centered cinema (or indeed the "quality TV" of HBO), these comments reveal the explicit prejudice against effeminate men and propagate the cultural visibility of what I call homonormative plots and persons more generally.

One can easily find fault with such statements, which present a number of problematic assumptions. First, they project with certainty that one can somehow "measure" masculinity and assert without evidence that most homosexual men "in reality" are masculine looking. Second, this masculine-looking man becomes an ideal to be emulated, so that third, by extension, the effeminate character necessarily *misrepresents* "reality." Finally, the statements conclude that for gay men (not surprisingly, as it is indeed for all men) being/acting masculine is better than being/acting effeminate (as much as it is frowned upon, I might add, when a woman acts "masculine"). Hence, the seduction (i.e., social pressure) to behave and be perceived as "normal" (and normative) by society at large operates with full force even inside the LGBTQAI+ community. The statement by Mott (who is otherwise a pioneer scholar in his demands for visibility) lacks self-conscious interrogation into what that desired visibility might mean for a diverse "queer" (and not merely "gay" or "homonormative") community. His unquestioned desire for gay men to be read as masculine (i.e., as masculine is defined by a normative majority) easily merges with old-fashioned *machismo* and insidious forms of intracommunal homophobia. Moreover, by discarding representations of effeminate man as inaccurate and negative, Mott denies visibility to effeminate queers, relegating them once more to the margins.

Mott and Tovey's remarks are contemporary examples of what Eve Sedgwick (1993) calls "effeminophobia" (20). Their comments also confirm Thomas Piontek's (2006) argument that "this preoccupation with the image of the masculine gay man left gay theory and gay politics ill-equipped to intervene in the war 'against effeminate boys'" (54). The examples of Maluma, Mott, and Tovey illustrate the kind of stigma I described in chapters 4 and 5 and reassert the supremacy of an idealized masculine looking and probably middle-class gay man—a point Trevisan had already alerted us in his *Manifesto entendido*. Giacarlo Cornejo (2013) calls attention to the phenomenon of effeminophobia in the context of the noticeable presence that the term *gay* has gained in Latin America: "Nos dicen 'pero no eres marica, eres gay' o no te pongas en la posición de víctima" (92; Say "you are not a 'sissy boy,' you are gay" and do not put yourself in the victim position). The combination of the denial of effeminate queer people with the denial of local vernacular creates a sense of displacement for those who do not conform to the "ideal" (middle-class Anglo-American) masculine view.

The Brazilian films I have analyzed, however, show configurations of same-sex desire and queer experience that extend beyond the narrow mold of "gay." While these works are not themselves completely free of a deep-seated cultural effeminophobia, they do at least show forms of resistance to such phobias and prejudice: first, these films showcase a great diversity of queer bodies, and second, they shift various forms of social and psychic abjection—exemplified in a sense of passivity, promiscuity, and effeminacy, for instance—from the margins to a specific place of visibility, which I call the "never innocent" space in-between.

In my view, abjection offers a unique model of self-understanding that is less reliant on (or even defined against) majority normativity. The films I analyzed in the preceding chapters reflect queer modes of living that do not conform to an Anglo-American model of identity politics. They show an alternative to the American way of coming out and are thus "wily" (Santiago 2002).

It is important to mention at the close of this book the tremendous setbacks that the LGBTQAI+ community in Brazil has recently faced in the country's current political climate. The 2016 elections put in power an openly homophobic and misogynistic president,[1] who, among other things, said in 2011 (and reiterated multiple times later) that he'd rather have a dead son than a gay heir.[2] The current government cabinet has been paying lip service to right-wing religious conservatives who are relentlessly trying to undermine queer lives by positing conspiracy theories that left-wing politicians, activists, and academics intend to "turn" every child who enters the public school system "gay" (most religious conservatives tend to use *gay* as an identity for the whole LGBTQAI+ spectrum). The present minister of human rights—currently the only woman in the cabinet—has claimed that she intends to end so-called gender ideology and that she will strive to make mandatory for "boys to wear blue and girls pink."[3] The impact of such hate speech on public life has already become sadly apparent. In September 2018, an exhibition titled *Queermuseu* at a museum in Porto Alegre in the south of Brazil was abruptly canceled following local protests that deemed the theme of sexual diversity offensive. Shortly after, the mayor of Rio de Janeiro vetoed the transfer of the exhibition to the city, exclaiming in an apocalyptic manner that such an event would be possible in Rio only if the city were under the sea.[4] Unfortunately, it is hard to keep track of the countless examples of anti-gay and anti-queer rhetoric that continue to be spewed by the current presidential cabinet.

On a brighter note, cinema (and television, visual arts, theater, literature, etc.) has flourished with queer images that present new forms of being, often in direct response to the current political and social climate, and a number of these fictional features and documentaries have made their way to international festivals. Films such as Leal's *Divinas divas* (2017), Alice Riff's *Meu corpo é politico* (My body is political, 2017), Priscilla and Goifman's *Bixa travesti* (2018), Filipe Matzembacher and Marcio Reolon's *Tinta bruta* (*Hard Paint*, 2018), and Rodrigo Carneiro and Gustavo Vinagre's *A rosa azul de Novalis* (The blue rose of Novalis, 2019) suggest that independent cinema continues to offer a vital opportunity to bring visibility to queer identities in Brazil. One must hope that this trend will persist, even if at the margins, since the current government continues to cut funding for the arts, human rights, reproductive rights, and racial inclusion and to promote a speech based on hate and violence.

The commercial success of one romantic drama is worth noting here: Daniel Ribeiro's 2014 *Hoje eu quero voltar sozinho* is probably the first film of its kind in Brazil to present queer identities in a nonabject way, which reflects a noticeable change in cultural attitudes. In this coming-of-age story, a blind boy, Leonardo (Guilherme Lobo), falls in love with his classmate Gabriel (Fabio Audi) in a fairly uncomplicated and reciprocated manner. What is striking is that neither Leonardo nor Gabriel express their feelings for each other through fixed-identity categories, not even when they become a couple at the end of the movie. When in the last scene some other students try to bully them, they simply hold hands and keep walking, leaving behind the bullies who wear defeated looks on their faces. This exemplifies Santiago's (2002) silent affirmation of being a homosexual; it does not necessarily align with the Anglo-American model's announcement of coming out is an other, perhaps more productive way of affirming one's identity.

The story of a blind boy falling in love with a person he cannot see—when social representation of gay identity is in large part dependent on the visual realm—troubles a great deal more than I can analyze here. Crucial, however, is that unlike the cinematic story lines analyzed in the preceding chapters, Ribeiro's movie imagines an unproblematic resolution. Both boys are white, middle-class teenagers who reside in a major urban center. The abjection and "shame" that are central to my readings of the films in this book are partially removed from the boys' bodies and steer toward a positive conclusion.

The happy ending of *Hoje eu quero voltar sozinho* is a narrative resolution that reflects recent progressive LGBTQAI+ legal reforms that have been celebrated in many places around the world (even, partially, in Brazil), including rights to marry and adopt children; it invites queers to gradually embrace a newfound (and decidedly less abject) identity as respectable national subjects. Although the films analyzed in this book do not end on such an affirmative note, they do, however, provide alternative modes of existence at the margins or, as I call it, the anthropophagic queer space in-between. If for some, the lack of a happy ending is deemed as failure, to the anthropophagic queer, failure might be seen as a distinct form of representation, as we saw in the chapter 4.

I would like to conclude by briefly mentioning Kléber Mendonça and Juliano Dornelles's important 2019 film, *Bacurau*, which in my opinion clearly illuminates a tradition of queer anthropophagic filmmaking. Drawing on trope of both Brazilian and American cinema, their film tells the story of a queer community in the north of Brazil. Of particular interest is one of the main characters, Lunga (Silvero Pereira), who seems to fluently transition between genders. They (I have deliberately chosen the neutral singular *they* pronoun) are a violent character crucial to the survival of a local community besieged by corrupted politicians, foreign invaders, and the destruction of natural resources. Is there a happy ending to this movie? It seems more productive to consider its conclusion from the point of view of queer failure, as an unconventional mode of living that helps a marginalized community to survive. Failure in this case, as elsewhere in this book, need not be understood merely in a negative manner; rather, it is simply part of the trial-and-error of anthropophagic queer world-making. As Quentin Crisp once said, "[F]ailure might be your style" (qtd. in Halberstam 2012,

110). This goes to the heart of the queer anthropophagic mode: like queer theory, it was born in and out of adverse and limited conditions, yet it has made the best of this adversity. Halberstam holds that "failure presents an opportunity rather than a dead end; in a true camp fashion, the queer artist works with rather than against failure" (96). Antropofagia, as the films in the book suggest, can also resonate with queer theory in this sense.

I have argued that Antropofagia and queer are mutually relatable concepts, and I have used both ideas to investigate Brazilian culture as an inherently dynamic process that comes into being by way of tense and often violent social negation over the meaning of gender, sexuality, culture, and the nation itself. In this fraught in-between space, failure is not merely a problem but also enacts a necessary disturbance of settled expectations, hence creating opportunity. Certainly, in the films discussed herein, queer experience "fails" in the view of homonormativity, but this failure can also be deployed a "style" (in Crisp's terms) for those who "understand" (as in Trevisan's manifesto). Failure viewed as such is also a paradoxical confirmation of existence and of a queer visibility that can be retraced in the history of Brazilian queer cinema, as I have canvassed in this book.

APPENDIX

Interview with João Silvério Trevisan in São Paulo, Brazil, October 2018 and June 2019

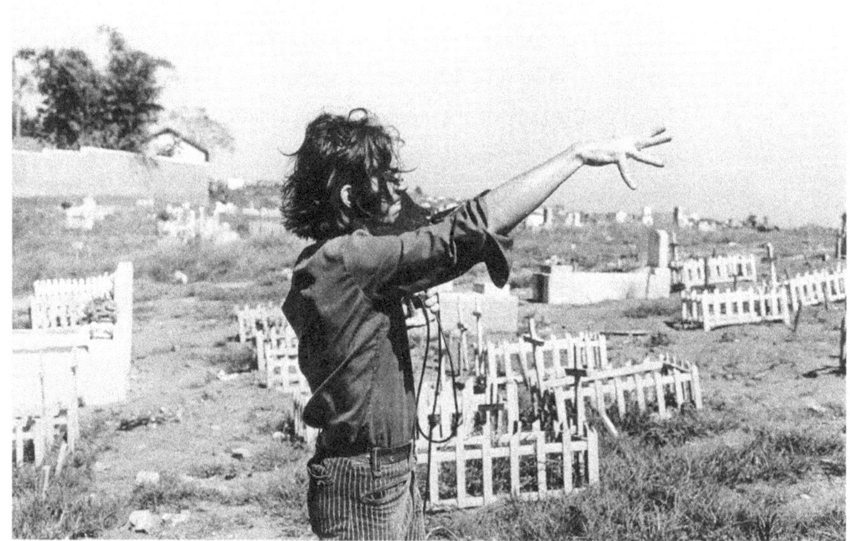

João Silvério Trevisan directing *Orgia ou o homem que deu cria*, 1970

João Silvério Trevisan, now in his seventies, is arguably one of the most important LGBTQAI+ activists in Brazil. Since his first novel in the 1960s, he has addressed same-sex desire and discussed important questions for the queer community. He created, alongside other prominent figures, the first gay newspaper in 1978, *Lampião da esquina* (all the issues are available online). He was also a member of Somos, one of the very first gay organizations. Consequently, he was at the forefront of the first responses to the AIDS crisis in Brazil in the early 1980s. His career spans throughout the past five decades in literature, essay, cinema, activism, and journalism.

João Silvério Trevisan sat for two interviews with me between the release of his two latest books, *Pai, Pai* (Father, Father, 2018) and *A idade do ouro* (The golden age, 2019).

This interview has been translated and condensed from the original Portuguese.

Q: Let's start talking about your most recent book, *Pai, Pai* . . .

João Silvério Trevisan: In my book, in the autobiographical novel, *Pai, Pai*, I approach the death and devouring of the father. It is a book with many essays. It is an autobiographical book, my trajectory from my father, and I work a lot on the issue of devouring the father, dialoguing not only with Freud but with a lot of Jung as well. Face-to-face with Freud, Dostoievski, parricide, Freud's essay, and, curiously, I finished a script last semester in which I fictionalize part of the story. There is a banquet in which the father's body is served as the main dish inside a cemetery. The whole story takes place inside a cemetery, which becomes a neighborhood in the city, and ends with this banquet . . . it's a kind of *feijoada* [pork and bean stew], but it is at Easter, at the Easter banquet, the father of the main character is served. He will take revenge on that father. And revenge is to serve you as a banquet. I really, really, really like the subject of anthropophagy. Do you know what the first title of the film was? *Foi assim que matei meu pai* [This is how I killed my father].

In fact, when I was in the seminary, there was a book, a little cheap book in the most rigorous period of the seminar. . . . I had two phases, right, at the seminar. The first phase was very authoritarian, and then with the Second Vatican Ecumenical Council, young priests opened up and I ended up studying at a more progressive seminary in Latin America. But in this first period . . . it is the face of Brazil today. If you take this minister of citizenship,[1] it is her mentality, the 1940s and 1950s. And then there was a little silly book called *Foi assim que eu matei meu filho* [That was how I killed my son], [about] a boy who wanted to be a priest, and the family did not allow it, so the boy died. I don't remember under what circumstances. I left the seminary feeling very critical of the Catholic Church. And one of my ironies, in this film, was precisely the idea of making a reference to the Catholic Church, and my most specific reference was, precisely, *that is how I killed my son*, through this kind of reelaboration to kill the father. The producer, the coproducer, was very stupid, as Boca do Lixo was a very current thing, without any aim, really, other than making a commercial success, which was its great obsession. . . . In fact, he was furious and he said no to that title. So I put up a very provocative title, which was the face of Boca. I put up *Orgia ou o homem que deu cria*, which was really something against the machismo of Boca.

Q: The film, in its way, foreshadows the criticism against Boca do Lixo and its overtly machismo.

JST: Boca's attitude was unbearable. I was coming out of the closet at that time. It was a crucial moment for me and I felt like a guy completely out of orbit. I was the different one there. In many ways. Then when I made *Orgia*, I remember, I was wearing a wool coat that I had bought at a thrift store because I had come from a trip abroad, my first trip, in the winter. It was winter in Brazil, and one little monkey on the shoulder, and long hair. So everybody was, "Look at the different guy." Nobody called me a fag directly. So this idea of "how I killed my father" is actually a reference to the seminary and my own father. The father is the whole genesis of *Orgia*; it is the most direct reference I made to my father at a crucial moment because it was the moment I was coming out of the closet. All the drama with my father was about the son not being the male he expected. He was the family sissy because I didn't like to play with the boys, etc. etc. So all this is intensely analyzed in *Pai*, as is the suffering I experienced as a child—bullying and being beaten by my father because of I was the family sissy. And I was the oldest son, so it was a disaster for my father, who was an alcoholic. So alcoholism is present in the film, including the various attempts to kill the father, because I could not solve the problem. So I equated it fictionally.

In the film, not by chance, the father's death is all related to the son's transgressions. And not by chance, censorship realized that there was something very, very bad in the film because it was, indirectly, a criticism of this whole patriarchal and sexist system, and I directly used some references that I had to make that criticism. The first poem that appears is a poem by Rimbaud.

Q: There are other poems in the film, aren't there?

JST: The idea is that the boy kills his father, he is in distress, and then he finds freaks along the way. I introduce the character of the *travesti*, who is a Carmen Miranda completely resignified with the potty in her head. It is a reinterpretation of anthropophagy in a way that was transgressive for the '60s. . . . Of course, Tropicalismo goes into this a lot, only that I radicalized Tropicalism itself, which stepped on some toes in relation to the homosexual issue, homosexual transgression. She [the *travesti*] next recites Oswald de Andrade. . . .

I think there are two poems that she recites, and then at the end, the anarchist, who is a clown-anarchist but not so serious, he is a comic book anarchist, with those big juggling balls that appear in comic stories, arrives in São Paulo and recites a beautiful poem by Oswald de Andrade: "O português chegou e conclamou ao negro da fornalha, sois cristão? Não. Sou cristão pela graça de Deus" (The Portuguese man arrived and asked the Black man from the furnace, Are you a Christian? No. I am a Christian by the grace of God).[2] Anyway, he recites from the top of a hill, in front of the city of São Paulo, with all those city noises. So it is the celebration of arriving in a city, which is also a country, absolutely enigmatic. So much so that when they [the troupe of outcasts or freaks] arrive in São Paulo, the city is empty. I live in this enigmatic city. That kid who appears in white, if you remember . . .

Q: Is that you?

JST: Yes! Because I didn't know how to work the ending of the film. I wanted to crucify myself on the roof of the truck, the truck we used, but I thought that would be very centered on me. Also, the making of the film was very happy. We fucked a lot, it was fun. Brigite, the *travesti* . . . Sérgio, in fact, had sex with the driver, everything was very free. But as the film was being made, and, above all, when I reached the end, I didn't know how that joy was going to unfold in an atmosphere that was not at all happy. And the film comes to a very hard end, in the cemetery. It is as if the city, the only space that existed in the city, was the cemetery. And it is there in the cemetery that the child is devoured. It is devoured not only anthropophagically but also in a celebratory way, but a celebration inside out. It is a celebration of syphilis. You could say that the celebration of syphilis would be AIDS later.

Q: The characters do not make it into the city . . .

JST: In fact, the city is not the city that they expected because when they arrive on its main road, they say, "Let's go to the city." . . . They were looking for an inhabited space. And when they arrive in the city, the city is nothing.

Q: It is a cemetery.

JST: It is not real. The film ends in the cemetery. I think that all this is related to the figure of my father. You will understand very well, much better, *Orgia ou o homem que deu cria* if you read *Pai, Pai.* The first sentence is: "All my father gave me was a spermatozoon," which is full of resentment. When I presented the publisher with a good part of the book already written, they went crazy, so much that they asked me—I have a trilogy of pain, with two books already under way—to continue. It has nothing to do with Father, but the problem is very similar, and as I was writing the book, I was discovering my father's presence, thanks to his absence, permeating my entire trajectory, including intellectual. In this bulge, my homosexuality as a problem facing my father. How do I face my father being a homosexual? Being what I am? And being what I am implied forgiving me for being a transgressor and I was very punished for that.

Q: Let's talk about Cinema Novo. Is there some criticism regarding Cinema Novo in the film?

JST: In 2012, I went to Rotterdam to participate in a festival on Boca do Lixo cinema, organized by [Brazilian director and writer] Gabriel Klinger. He didn't know what I had experienced, which was very painful when it came to [the film's] criticism. Not even Jean-Claude Bernardet, who, nonetheless, worked on the film dared to write a review about my film. The only criticism that was made—when I say criticism, I mean, review—was Paulo Emílio Salles Gomes, who had helped create the cinema studies major at the Universidade de Brasília, and who was hunted by the regime. He wrote a review addressed to the censors that came out in *Jornal da tarde*.[3] While I was out of Brazil, my brother sent me the review. I have a copy there in my files, and in it Salles Gomes mentioned exactly that: "What is it about this film that bothered you so much?" But all this to tell you that the critics didn't give a damn. When I arrived in Berkeley, which for me was the great melting pot of what was happening in the world at that moment . . . I, the Brazilian Leftist, was horrified because I couldn't understand what was happening in the world through the eyes of the Brazilian Left, and I went, I didn't go to the USA, I went to Berkeley, that was my project. And I went on foot, I say, by land. I took a copy of *Orgia* with English subtitles. I had spent time in Argentina, among those absolutely fanatical Peronists, who criticized me because Brazilians were not in my film. It started there, and I spoke in Spanish in the way I could, saying: "Quién son ustedes? I am Brazilian, and I understand what it is to be Brazilian. You don't." It was an extremely imperialist position.

All the criticism of Cinema Novo, including the acting marks for Othon Bastos in *Deus e o diabo na terra do sol* that I gave to my bandit. It is the same Brechtian mark, that whole thing that Brazilian theater at the time thought was Brecht, which I think was not quite like that. But anyway, then there are all these, say, negative stories surrounding *Orgia*. I showed it to an Italian critic, in a Boca booth. I showed it to a guy who was taking it, I don't know to which Italian festival. He wanted to present Brazilian films and he came to see them. Do you know what he said? "This is a copy of [Pier Paolo] Pasolini's cinema. I do not care." And I didn't know anything about Pasolini except *Teorema* (*Theorem*, 1968), at the time. I saw it at Paulista [São Paulo]. I left the theater and I saw my boyfriend at the time. I walked hand in hand with my boyfriend. I'll never forget that. I was so enchanted by the film. *Orgia* has nothing to do with *Teorema*. So, I don't know if he had seen any other Pasolini's films.

NOTES

Introduction

1 The bibliography on Cinema Novo is vast and diverse. For a more detailed list of books and authors, see chapter 2.

2 Abraccine, the Brazilian Association of Cinema Critics, released its list of the best one hundred Brazilian films of all time in 2016. See abraccine.org/2016/09/04/abraccine-lanca-100-melhores-filmes-brasileiros-no-festival-de-gramado/.

3 A significant body of scholarship has observed the limitations of Anglo-American terminology (gay, queer, LGBTQAI+, etc.) in describing and analyzing sexual identities in Latin America. For reasons of focus and internal coherence, this book will refer to scholarly work in the Spanish-language context only briefly, and explicitly only where it is directly relevant to cinema and cultural studies. Readers interested in the sociological and political aspects of recently emerging rights movements based on sexual identity in Latin America may turn to Raphael de la Dehesa's 2010 Queering the Public Sphere in Mexico and Brazil: Sexual Rights Movements in Emerging Democracies, which provides a useful backdrop to my reading and understanding of the more contemporary films in my selected corpus. The comparative focus of de la Dehesa's work is laudable, pointing the way to productive insights that can be gleaned from bringing into conversation Spanish-speaking and Lusophone contexts without either reducing local specifics or denying productive overlaps. While anthropophagic queer occasionally places its discussions of queer national cinema in Brazil in a zone of influence, resonance, and confluence with Spanish-speaking Latin America, this study, for reasons of space and thematic coherence, makes no qualms about predominantly focusing on what it holds to be a still largely untold history of queer Brazilian cinema.

4 "Epps, citando a Oscar Montero, afirma que si gay circula en el mundo hispanoparlante de manera que 'las complejidades de su estatus importado son imposibles de editar, y algo de su carga originariamente celebratoria se pierde en la traducción' los 'usos de queer están aún más circunscritos a la metrópoli imperial.'" (Unless otherwise stated, all translations are my own.)

5 Edward Said (1983) formulates the idea of "traveling theories" in *The World, the Text, and the Critic* (Harvard University Press, 1983). According to Said,

"One should go on to specify kinds of movement that are possible, in order to ask whether by virtue of having moved from one place and time to another an idea or a theory gains or loses in strength, and whether a theory in one historical period and national culture becomes altogether different for another period or situation" (226).

6 "Traduzir de maneira imediata o termo queer da sociedade central para a sociedade da periferia é trair a própria antropofagia que nos confere identidade."

7 See Héctor Dominguéz Ruvalcaba's 2016 *Translating the Queer: Body Politics and Transnational Conversations* for a cogent exploration of the transnational bartering and transcultural processes that inform the various recent meanings that "queer acquire[s] in its translation into Latin American codes" (1) more generally.

8 If one were to translate these words, it would be "dyke" (*sapatão*) and "faggot" (*bicha/veado*). The origin of these vernaculars is up for debate. We can trace the use of the three examples mentioned to the beginning of the twentieth century. For most part, they are used pejoratively. Only recently can one hear these words as identity nouns. *Bicha*, for instance, has become "bee"—a short version approximating a possible English pronunciation of the syllable "bi" (bi-cha). For example, Canal das Bee is one of the biggest LGBTQAI+ YouTube channels in Brazil today. As I write this book, it is noticeable how *veado* and its phonetic variation *viado* are becoming mainstream. Multishow, a cable network, added the word *veado* as one of the catchphrases of 2019.

9 *Bicha*, *veado*, *travesti*, *marica*, and *afeminado* are words currently used in Brazil to refer to different identitarian expressions. These terms are hard to translate, because their meanings shift with political and social changes over time. However, these words are of special interest since they are used both as an affirming identity and as an insult.

10 There are a number of scholars who focus their studies on the Luso-Hispanic (or Hispanic-Luso) perspective, including, to name a few, David William Foster (1997, 2003), Gustavo Subero (2014), Paul A. Schroeder (2016), and Lisa Shaw and Stephanie Dennison (2005). Robert Patrick Newcomb and Richard A. Gordon's 2017 edited volume is relevant for its comparative approach to Latin American cultures.

11 Sophia McClennen (2011) smartly uses the concept of "cosmetics of hunger in her article 'From the Aesthetics of Hunger to the Cosmetics of Hunger in Brazilian Cinema: Meirelles' *City of God*." To the author, there is a shift from the Glauber Rocha's manifesto Aesthetics of Hunger to later films that

appropriate misery as a trope in order to produce Hollywood-style films for larger audiences.

12 *Bacurau* (Kléber Mençonda, 2019), also from Recife, won the Jury Prize at the 2019 Cannes Festival.

Chapter 1. Devouring Cinema

1 Unfortunately, only less than 10 percent of films produced in the first decades of past century still exist according to statistics and research on the topic (see, e.g., Bernadet and Galvão 1983).

2 Maite Conde (2018) analyzes Machado's book in detail.

3 In "The Rule of Anthropophagy: Europe under the Sign of Devoration," Haroldo de Campos (1986) shows that some of the anthropophagic principles also appear in authors such as José Lezema Lima and Severo Sarduy (334).

4 Among the texts that I will present here, the journal *Nuevo texto crítico* published an entire issue on Antropofagia in 1999, followed in 2011 by *Antropofagia Hoje? Oswald de Andrade em cena.*

5 Self-aware attention for the stakes and risks involved in the translatability and application of Anglo-American terminologies meant to "out" dissident sexualities in the context of Latin American cinema studies is also at the heart of Venkatesh's 2016 *New Maricón Cinema: Outing Latin American Film.* Predominantly Hispanophone in scope and more exclusively focused on recent cinema than anthropophagic queer, Venkatesh's revindication of the "new" *maricón* (a term close in meaning to "faggot" or "queer") as a descriptor for a recognizably queer and Spanish-American style in cinema is in this regard confluent with this book's critical project to articulate a Brazilian queer visibility in film through the paradigm of Antropofagia.

6 "Para uma cultura que verdadeiramente nunca coube num espaço único, as identificações culturais que daí derivam tendem a autocanibalizar-se."

7 The concept of *mestiçagem* has been widely discussed in Brazil and abroad in terms of the formation of the Brazilian people(s). The idea of *mestiçagem* (miscegenation) creates a false sense of racial democracy in Brazil. An idea that forms stereotypes of race perpetuating racism in the country. Fundamental texts for this discussion include Gilberto Freyre's 1933 *Casa-Grande e senzala (The Masters and the Slaves)*, Sérgio Buarque de Hollanda's 1936 *Raízes do Brasil* (*Roots of Brazil*), and Paulo Prado's 1928 *Retratro do Brasil—Ensaio sobre a tristeza do Brasil* (Portrait of Brazil: An essay on Brazilian sadness). By pointing it out, though, I do not intend to accept the notion of racial democracy as

proposed by so many in the country. *Mestiçagem* has served a political purpose of maintaining white privilege as a form of oppression in the country. Queering such ideas would be beneficial for understanding the oppressive racial politics in the country.

8 Andrade uses *deglutir* instead of *engolir*. Both mean "swallow" in English. However, *deglutir* brings a slightly more vivid expression of swallowing than *engolir* does. Andrade writes in the first issue of *Revista de Antropofagia*: "Piratininga Ano 374 da Deglutição do Bispo Sardinha" (Andrade 2000a, 74).

9 The choice of the verb "to eat" is not accidental. In Portuguese, *comer* has also a sexual meaning. *Comer algúem* means to penetrate someone. As Claude Lévi-Strauss (1955) says in *Tristes tropiques*, all societies conceive an analogy between eating and sexual practices.

10 "En cuanto a la producción cultural una lectura queer es una lectura que trata de entender cómo esa producción reproduce y al mismo tiempo cuestiona los sistemas sociales."

11 Teresa de Lauretis's work (in particular her 1991 "Queer Theory: Lesbian and Gay Sexualities: An Introduction") has been widely recognized as a queer theory foundational text (see, among others, Jagose 1996 and Ceballos Muñoz 2009). However, Nikki Sullivan (2003) in *A Critical Introduction to Queer Theory* argues that Gloria Anzaldúa mentions the word queer as early as 1987 in *Borderlands/La Frontera: The New Mestizo*.

12 Ben Sifuentes-Jauregui (2014) makes a similar case about the existence of various modes of non-Western-centric, non-Anglophone modes of queer identification and (self-)representation in his broad-ranging discussion of Spanish-American and Latino literary texts in *The Avowal of Difference: Queer Latino American Narratives*.

13 Later, when I present and discuss the *Manifesto antropófago* and the *Revista de antropofagia*, I will situate the Caraíba revolution in the context of Antropofagia. *Caraíba* refers to the "orginal" populations prior to the arrival of the European settlers.

14 "A alegria é a prova dos Nove / No matriarcado de Pindorama."

15 Jorge Schwartz has mapped out the vanguards in Latin America in his 2008 *Vanguardas Latino-Americana*. A Spanish edition was published in 1991.

16 In 1922, the year of the Semana de Arte Moderna, Brazil also celebrated its one hundredth anniversary of independence.

17 "Apenas brasileiros de nossa época. O necessário de química, de mecânica, de economia e de balística. Tudo digerido."

18 In 2000, Maria Eugênia Boaventura published a collection of articles of that era, bringing to light the view of the critics during that famous February week of 1922 and its outcomes. "[T]he favorable articles were signed by the two Andrades—Oswald and Mário—by Menotti del Picchia, Sérgio Milliet (writing for French newspapers), Sérgio Buarque and by a half dozen that preferred anonymity. Among the adversaries, Mário Pinto Serva, responsible for acute attack against the modernists, the journalists Galvão Muniz, Oscar Guanabarino and the yet-to-be *Integralista* leader, the novelist Plínio Salgado'" (19).

19 *Dentição* means "dentition" in English. The artists are playing with the words *edição* (edition) and *dentição*. The use of *dentição* besides giving the idea of a first phase and a more mature phase (*segunda dentição*) also gives us the ideas of eating, devouring and *degultição*.

20 "Oswald embaralha os dados cronológicos, propondo antecedências liberadoras e procedências castradoras. Liberação e castração se dão num idêntico compasso."

21 The modernist movement was also active in other Latin American countries, as Schwartz (2008) describes: "[O]s movimentos de vanguarda na América Latina—à diferença dos europeus—em algum momento depararam com a questão: quem somos?" (42) ("The vanguard movements in Latin America—unlike the European ones—at some point questioned: who are we?"). However, according to the author, the Brazilian vanguard stands out due to its intensity and originality.

22 For more on the influence of cinematic language and literature, see João Manuel dos Santos Cunha's 2011 *A lição aproveitada: Modernismo e cinema em Mário de Andrade* Maite Conde's 2018 *Foundational Films: Early Cinema and Modernity in Brazil.*

23 "distribuídas na proporção necessária, as substâncias mais adequadas para o alimento do próprio homem"

24 "Cet événement, à notre avis, manifeste l'une des plus nobles tendances de l'espirit humain, sa propension à s'assimiler ce qu'il trouve bon."

25 "Yo confio en que, para bien de la humanidad, llegará pronto el día de la libertad de antropofagia!"

26 "[A] operação metafísica que se liga ao rito antropofágico é a da transformação do tabu em totem."

27 In Bastide's words: "C'est alors que Oswald de Andrade invente l'anthropophagie, forme moderne de l'indianism, non plus la glorification du bon sauvage de l'époque romantique mais du mauvais sauvage, tueur des blancs,

anthropophage, polygame, communiste. Une apologie de l'ogre indigene. Mais bien vite le caractère international occidental, modern de São Paulo passe dans cet indianisme renouvelé, le colore de freudisme ou de marxisme selon les époques. Oswald dévore les théories étrangères, comme sa ville dévore les inmigrants pour en faire de la chair et du sang brésiliens."

28 Braham (2015) gives a detailed analysis of the sixteenth-century accounts on cannibalism and female voracity. The author describes the narratives of Amerigo Vespuccci, Dr. Chanca, Jean de Léry, Father José de Anchieta, and Hans Staden and observes how Indigenous women were seen as more cannibal-like than men. For instance: "The Jesuit Father José de Anchieta . . . reported on a Tupi cannibal incident in 1554, describing how women defiled their male victims' bodies before devouring them" (60).

29 Giuliana Martins Simões's 2017 *Veto ao modernismo no teatro brasileiro* presents a remarkable work on Flávio de Carvalho and Oswald de Andrade's 1930 theater productions, discussing both the censorship and prohibition of their plays.

30 "Ordem e progresso," which appears on Brazil's flag, is the national motto.

31 Clark's full video can be seen at www.youtube.com/watch?v=ynq7JMXvWvA. In 2014, New York's Museum of Modern Art presented a retrospective of Lygia Clark's work, including the original 1970s video.

Chapter 2. João Silvério Trevisan's *Orgia ou o homem que deu cria*

1 After the creation of Embrafilme, of the ten most watched Brazilian films to this day (2020), three were produced in the 1970s. The other seven films were all produced in the 2010s.

2 José Mojica Marins, also known as Coffin Joe, is undoubtedly one of the most important Cinema Marginal filmmakers in Brazil. Celebrated as a genius, his productions have achieved cult status. I will return to his work in chapter 3, where I discuss his pornographic film production against the 1980s backdrop of the HIV/AIDS epidemic.

3 Until today, the movement has shown its remanences in contemporary Brazilian cinema. For instance, the most recent internationally acclaimed films draw on the idea of Brazil's misery; two examples are *Central do Brasil* (*Central Station*, Walter Salles, 1998) and *Cidade de Deus* (*City of God*, Fernando Meirelles and Kátia Lund, 2002).

4 Among many others who have discussed the dichotomy between *desbunde* and

luta armada, José Celso Martinez Corrêa, whose importance to Antropofagia I have already discussed, notes in an interview in *Sala Preta* magazine (Corrêa 2012) that part of his generation was part of *desbunde* in revolutionary arts.

5 Between 2015 and 2018, HBO Latin America produced a TV series titled *Magnífica 70*. The show recounts the story of Boca do Lixo through the lenses of the producers, directors, actors, and censors.

6 Cinema de Invenção was the name coined by Jairo Ferreira in his critical work and in his 1986 (repr. 2000) seminal book, *Cinema de Invenção*, in which he analyzes a group of filmmakers he considers important for the generation. However, during the 1970s, most of his newspaper articles still discuss Cinema Marginal as a movement. For instance, in 1971, he writes, "[O] udigrúdi ou cinema marginal (no caos é difícil distinguir) poderia ser aplaudido na praça e onde é que os exibidores tem que meter a cara?" (The udigrudi or Marginal Cinema [amid chaos, it is hard to distinguish between them] should be lauded in public and everywhere cinema operators exhibit the films.) (Ferreira 2000, 249).

7 Cinema cafajeste é cinema de comunicação direta. É o cinema que aproveita a tradição de 50 anos de exibição do "mau" cinema americano, devidamente absorvido pelo espectador e que não se perde em pesquisas estetizantes, elocubrações intelectuais, típicas de uma classe média semi-analfabeta.

É a estética do teatro de revistas, das conversas de salão de barbeiro, das revistinhas pornográficas. É a linguagem do "Notícias Populares," do "Combate Democrático" e das revistinhas "especializadas" (leia-se Carlos Zéfiro). É Oswald de Andrade e Líbero Rípoli Filho; é "Santeiro do Mangue" e "Viúva, Porém Honesta": obras primas.

É cinema tipicamente brasileiro, portanto é o cinema cafajeste paulista, sem bairrismos, porém com uma visão lúcida da fauna paulistana.

Preparem-se cinéfilos frustrados, adoradores dos Cahiers e de Godard, pois o cinema cafajeste já é uma realidade. É o cinema de Rogério Sganzerla, o cinema de Roberto Santos (de "O Grande Momento" e o genial episódio de "As Cariocas"), de Mojica Marins; é o verdadeiro cinema paulista.

E o seu valor será contado em cifras, em borderôs, em semanas de exibição: em público. E os filmes serão geniais.

(The original brochure for the film release is available at the Museum of Modern Art, Rio de Janeiro.)

8 "Trata-se da descoberta intertextual atraída pelo verniz clássico que incorpora numa inspiração nouvelle vague, desde o filme autoral hollywoodiano mais precário (ou cafajeste), o western, o musical, o policial noir, até as próprias

chanchadas, agora glorificadas exatamente na precariedade que antes incomodova e no deboche, que lhes é inerente."

9 A similar nuanced meaning occurs in Spanish. *¿Entiendes?* (Do you understand?) refers to a hidden question with the same subtle meaning as in Portuguese. See Paul Julian Smith and and Emilie L. Bergmann (1995) for a collection of essays that map out same-sex desire and gender identities across the Hispanic world.

10 "In rapporto alla cultura erudita brasiliana, troviamo nei più significativi artisti posteriori al movimento modernista, alcuni elementi che hanno servito di base al 'cinema novo'. Molto vicini all'idea di un 'modo di dire cinematograficamente le cose del Brasile' sono Mario e Oswald de Andrade: una nuova lingua brasiliana parlata agli angoli delle strade e dei paesi, tanto diversa da quella dei salotti e dei discorsi ufficiali."

11 In 1992, Sganzerla produced and directed *Perigo negro* (Dark danger), a film based on Oswald de Andrade's book, *Marco Zero*. The persistence of Antropofagia into the final decades of the twentieth century is seen by other works produced in Brazil. Besides Sganzerla's film, for instance, one can mention "O homem do pau-Brasil" by Joaquim Pedro Andrade (Macunaíma, 1969) in 1982.

12 The *chapéu de cangaceiro* (*cangaceiro*'s hat) has also been traditionally associated with the northeastern region of Brazil (the only region where the current president did not win with a vast majority of the vote). The president is constantly photographed with such a hat in his visits to the region. His macho image is reinforced with the hat as a way to bring him closer to the population. A recent image (from August 2020) can be seen here: istoe.com.br/bolsonaro-desembarca-em-sergipe-para-inaugurar-usina-termoeletrica/.

13 In the 1970s, for the first time in Brazilian history, the majority of the population (56 percent) lived in the cities and/or urban centers (today that population has increased to 84 percent). In Brazil, as in many other regions of the world, industrialization and large-scale urbanization not coincidentally form the backdrop of many queer narratives. Venkatesh (2016) discusses a movement from urban to rural in contemporary Hispanic Latin American cinema.

14 "Apertado à direita e à esquerda, em dúvida quanto à sua própria validade, chocado com os acontecimentos que não controla, o Cinema Novo começa a decretar a sua própria morte, assinando o óbito preenchido pelas novas gerações. Acho que fui o primeiro a falar disso, numa entrevista aos Cahiers du Cinéma, em fins de 69."

15 I choose to keep the Portuguese word *travesti*, for which there is no equivalent in English, for describing the character in the movie because it is the word Trevisan uses to talk about the character and also because it is a gender identity widely recognized in Brazil. Some LGBTQAI+ associations in Brazil maintain two *T*s as a way to give recognition to transgender people and *travestis*. Therefore, *travestis* represent a category of people in the trans world who do not conform to any other existing trans classification. More recent understandings from the *travesti* community in Brazil have been acute on the respect for their identity. Between Trevisan's film and today, a lot has changed and our understandings of gender identity and sexual orientation has also evolved. Today, *travestis* in Brazil still claim their identity as individuals. In 2018, Renata Carvalho created and acted in *Manifesto transpofágico* (directed by Luiz Gernando Marques), a clear reference to the *Manifesto antropofágico*. In her play, she traces a genealogy of trans lives in Brazil. For more on this play, see mitsp.org/2019/manifesto-transpofagico/.

16 "Não permita Deus que eu morra / Sem que volte para São Paulo / Sem que veja a Rua 15 / E o progresso de São Paulo."

17 Moreover, the idea of a man being penetrated, or "passive," in sexual relations presents a case of double abjection; first, because of the notion of penetration itself and, second, because of the anus's association with being a source of diseases. Such notions are still evident in the rhetoric of groups such as "G0ys" (G—zero—ys), men who do not identify as homosexual or gay but who take pleasure in being with another man as long as there is no anal intercourse.

18 Even though one can find parallels between Santiago's formulation and Victor Turner's idea of liminality, the translation of the term *entre-lugar* was proposed in a collection of Santiago's (2001) essays edited by Ana Lúcia Gazzola. In the *Encyclopedia of Latin American Literature*, edited by Verity Smith (1997), the term *inBetweenness* is proposed as a translation for Santiago's *entre-lugar*.

19 ". . . no era impulsar una política de identidad homosexual sino promover lo que después llamarían de queer."

20 "También es a partir del entre-lugar que podemos incluir la experiencia gay en este redimensionamineto de la nación, tratando su invisibilidad histórica no solo como represión sino también de ambigua Resistencia a partir de una afectividad entre hombres como lugar del habla sobre el mundo."

21 Even today, such perspective seems important. A recent cover of the now defunct Brazilian magazine, *Momento Inesquecível*, wholly dedicated to gay weddings, parties, celebrations, and fashion, showed two white males getting

married. Marketed for the wealthy, Santiago's ideas of a democratic socialism seemed to fade away with such a magazine. The only homosexual person rendered visible was a white gay man who could afford such luxuries as getting married. See www.doistercos.com.br/segunda-edicao-da-revista-momento-inesquecivel-destaca-casamento-gay/. Moreover, the magazine's website as a whole was a celebration of white male couples, who formed the majority of couples depicted.

Chapter 3. HIV/AIDS in 1980s Brazilian Cinema

1 A quick note must be made about one of the major successes from the 1970s to 1990s: Os Trapalhões. This group of four comedians was responsible for sixteen of the top twenty-five box offices in Brazilian history between 1970 and 1990. The group had a TV show than ran for decades on national television, and every year (sometimes twice a year), it released a film for children that drew millions of spectators to the cinema. Following this tradition, Xuxa, the "queen of the children," also produced extremely popular films in Brazil during the 1980s and '90s.

2 The film has also appeared with the titles *Furor, do sexo explícito* (Furor of explicit sex), *AIDS, a fúria do sexo* (AIDS, the fury of sex), and *AIDS, o furor do sexo* (AIDS, the furor of sex). I have opted to keep the title as it appears on the original poster during the release of the film in 1985.

3 In line with the self-avowedly Brazilian orientation of the book, this chapter does not discuss *Via Appia* (1989), a German production on AIDS by director Jochen Hick that is set in Rio de Janeiro's Via Appia district, known as a zone for male prostitution. For a discussion of this film, see Gustavo Subero (2014).

4 During the 2014 electoral debates for Brazilian presidency, Levy Fidelix, one of the candidates, condemned homosexuality, stating that "aparelho excretor não reproduz" ("the excretory apparatus does not procreate"). See noticias.uol.com.br/ultimas-noticias/redacao/2014/10/03/aparelho-excretor-nao-reproduz-veja-frases-da-semana.htm. In the aftermath of the 2016 elections, which were won by far-right religious conservatives, such statements became the norm among the politicians, and a clear and daily attack on LGBTQAI+ lives has been visible since in the country. The murder of human rights activist Marielle Franco by the militia in Rio de Janeiro is, unfortunately, the most tragic example of the devastation that this type of conservative agenda and rhetoric can cause. Brazil is the country with the highest murder rate against LGBTQAI+ people in the world.

5 "[O] abjeto é algo pelo que alguém sente horror ou repulsa como se fosse poluidor ou impuro, a ponto de ser o contato com isso temido como contaminador e nauseante."

6 "Rocha não poupou insultos ao gênero: vulgar (1981: 146), colonizada (1981: 199), miserável (1981: 290), cínica em seu tratamento da miséria (1981: 291), imoral (2003: 170), fundada sobre o pitoresco miserabilista (1981: 100), câncer conformista do sub-desenvolvimento (1981: 321), pornografia a baixo preço (2003: 171)."

7 Patti Smith's "Birdland" and Kate Bush's "Cloudbusting" are two songs from the 1970s and 1980s inspired by the works of Wilhelm Reich.

8 Robert Mulligan directed *Kiss Me Goodbye*, a 1982 American version of the Brazilian film, with Sally Field, James Caan, and Jeff Bridges on the title roles.

9 It is important to note that *pornochanchada* is still relevant today. Canal Brasil, a cable network devoted to Brazilian cinema includes daily screenings of the genre, and for over a decade, it is still among the most watched programs in the channel. In 2016, MIS—Museu da Imagem e do Som—presented an exhibition by the artist Fernando Pessoa using censored scenes from classic *pornochanchada* films. Also, a series of documentaries have been recently produced in an effort to understand and document the Boca do Lixo in São Paulo.

10 In 2019, André Canto released a documentary about AIDS and HIV in Brazil over the past forty years. He named the documentary *Carta para além dos muros* in a clear reference to Abreu's texts. See agenciaaids.com.br/noticia/pre-estreia-do-filme-carta-para-alem-dos-muros-reune-em-sao-paulo-ativistas-gestores-politicos-e-jornalistas/.

11 "Embaralhando as trajetórias desses quarto protagonistas—um, Antônio César, morto desde o início do filme, três, vivos—, Bianchi toca em três preocupações básicas do momento: a degeneração moral, da qual a corrupção política é o sintoma mais explícito na área política, a degradação da qualidade de vida (isto é, a sistemática violação da ecologia) e o verdadeiro 'macartismo' sexual que se fortaleceu na esteira da Aids."

12 In 2012, an evangelical priest used referred to AIDS as "gay cancer" (see Charles Nisz, "Marco Feliciano: A Aids é o câncer gay," Yahoo! Notícias, September 21, 2012, br.noticias.yahoo.com/blogs/vi-na-internet/marco-feliciano-aids-é-o-câncer-gay-213329908.html). After almost four decades of the first cases of HIV in Brazil, misinformation and prejudice still abound.

13 Canto's *Carta para além dos muros* discusses how shame and social stigma persist today.

14 Most pornographic films from that era are available today on sites such as PornHub.com and XVideos.com. Some have been restored by Canal Brasil, a TV Globo affiliate in Brazil, while others are simply uploads of VHS tapes.

15 There is no record of the other actors who appeared in this film.

16 "Conforme a década de 1980 avança, não fazem mais efeito velhos dilemas existenciais. Sem ter vivenciado propriamente o modernismo dos anos 1920, o cinema brasileiro, em especial o Cinema Novo, encontra-se em plena ebulição moderna quando, de súbito, começa a faltar combustível para queimar em rupturas, desafios, manifestos."

17 It is relevant for this book to mention that for the third installment of the franchise, Paulo Gustavo, the creator and main actor (he plays the mother in the main title) decided not to include a kiss between two men in the film, believing the audience would not accept it. Despite all the criticism from the LGBTQAI+ fans, he kept his decision in the final cut. As of 2020, it is the most watched Brazilian film (oca.ancine.gov.br/paineis-interativos?painel=viz1558970268340) and already among the top five most watched movies historically.

18 For an overview of current critical debates on the representation of nonheteronormative sexual identities in Spanish-language Latin American cinema specifically, see Venkatesh (2016) and Subero (2014).

19 The term "homonormativity" is Lisa Duggan's (2002), who in "The New Homonormativity: The Sexual Politics of Neoliberalism" critically analyzes an Anglo-American gay (mostly male, white, and middle class) neoliberal striving to be fully assimilated into mainstream culture, this at the expense of ideological and social diversity. To the extent that homonormativity coincides with globally marketed definitions of *gay*, Duggan's work is fundamental to query contemporary understandings of sexual identity politics in Brazil and Latin America, particularly as these have crystallized in recent cultural expressions.

20 This point is resonant with Ben Sifuentes-Jarégui's (2014) that queer (self-)representation in Spanish-American and Latino literatures often resists, circumvents, and complicates convential (Anglo-American) expectations of "coming out."

Chapter 4. Dzi Croquettes and the Queer Documentary Tradition

1 After the group's 1976 breakup due to creative divergences (as documented in the film), they staged a comeback in the early 1980s with similar success and did so again, more recently, in 2011, after the release of the film. Their

last reunion was less successful, however, and after a few performances in São Paulo and Rio de Janeiro, the show was canceled.

2 "Eu sempre curti muito o pronome inglês *the*, também poderia ser o *zê* português. E como a gente no bar comia croquetes, porque não batizar o grupo Dzi Croquettes."

3 "Eu nasci em janeiro de 1974, quando eu nasci não poderia imaginar que o movimento que havia começado dois anos antes iria mudar minha vida e revolucionar o Brasil."

4 "Meu pai me colocava pra dormir entre as cadeiras do teatro, eu ficava ali olhando o espetáculo no escuro. Tudo era como uma fantasia, um sonho."

5 Among other restrictive acts, AI-5 shut down the Senate, and initiated the *anos de chumbo*, the most trying and painful period of the Brazilian dictatorship.

6 "Dzi Croquettes trouxeram para o Brasil o que de mais contemporâneo e questionador havia no movimento homossexual internacional, sobretudo americano."

7 "[E]ntão era uma forma de você contestar a ditadura pelo escracho, pelo sarcasmo."

8 The dialogue directed to the audience is originally in English and Portuguese. Lennie Dale, the creator and choreographer of the group, was an American expatriate who adopted Brazil as his homeland in the 1960s.

9 "Havia uma sexualidade boa. Masculina, feminino, homossexual. Havia uma possibilidade absoluta do exercício da sexualidade."

10 "Abrindo as suas asas, asas de retalhos, listadas, estampadas, floridas, evocando todas as cores, na plataforma do meio, dançam as 'borboletas.'" After the release of the documentary, Lobert's thesis was published in 2010 under the same title and so far remains the only monograph written about the group.

11 "E eis que surge o novo renascimento, e com ele um novo ser trazendo toda a força do macho e toda a graça da fêmea. É fácil com ele viver e atendê-lo, eu só não sei explicá-lo e o faço com um grito."

Chapter 5. Contemporary Trends in Anthropophagic Queer

1 "Ele contava que, quando tinha seus 13 anos e era moleque de rua da Lapa, as putas chamavam a ele e a outros guris para bacanais nas pensões. Ele, então, experimentara transar como homem e como bicha gostou mais como bicha e resolveu continuar assim."

2 "Senta. Tu também tá querendo uma moça assim como eu, da minha altura, escurinha? Sente aqui os coxões da preta, sente."

3 Noel Rosa (1910–37) was one of the most important singers in Brazil. He is considered one of the founders of samba, and his compositions are considered fundamental for one's understanding of samba.

4 "E quando tira um samba é novidade / Quer no morro ou na cidade / Ele sempre foi o bamba / As morenas do lugar vivem a se lamentar / Por saber que ele não quer se apaixonar por mulher." The song is recorded as "Mulato Bamba" (1932).

5 Vivia na maravilhosa China um bicho tubarão bruto e cruel / que mordia tudo e virava tudo em carvão / pra acalmar a fera, o Chinês fazia todo dia uma oferenda com sete gatos maracajá / que ele mordia antes do pôr-do-sol / no intento de por fim em tal ciclo de barbaridades / chegou Janaci uma entidade da floresta da Tijuca / Ela corria pelos mato e avoava pelos morro / E Janaci virou uma onça dourada / de jeito macio e de gosto delicioso / e começou a brigar com o tubarão por mil e uma noites / no final a gloriosa Janaci e o furioso tubarão / já estavam tão machucados que ninguém mais sabia quem era um e quem era outro / e assim, eles viraram uma coisa só.

6 João Silvério Trevisan (2018) and Rogério Durst (1985) are two authors who concur with the analysis above.

7 The name of the theater/bar is not accidental. Chão de Estrelas refers to a 1937 song composed by Silvio Caldas (1908–98), which has since been recorded by a great number of artists. Caldas is one of the artists who was revitalized and rediscovered during the Tropicália movement. Hence, this choice for the name places the group in the movie inside this anthropophagic and *tropicalista* tradition as a form of resistance through mockery.

8 Fininha can be translated as "skinny"; however, it is important to note that his name takes the feminine form (*fininha*) rather than the masculine (*fininho*).

9 Recife has recently been nominated as the current capital of cinema in Brazil, with many local directors producing Brazilian movies there. In addition to *Tatuagem*, a number of other movies that have traveled the international festival circuit were produced in the region. For more on the topic, see cultura.estadao.com.br/noticias/cinema,o-cinema-fertil-do-recife-em-novas-producoes,553972 and https://revistaforum.com.br/?s=recife-e-a-reinvencao-do-cinema-politico.

10 "O pai eu quero me casar / Oh minha filha diga com quem / Eu quero me casar com o travesti / Com o travesti você se casa bem/ Por quê? / O travesti pode servir como homem e depois serve como mulher também."

11 "Vi guerrilheiros na selva tombar / E para casa nunca mais voltar."

12 “O símbolo da liberdade é o cu que é democrático e todo mundo tem.”

13 Jomard Muniz de Britto was also the coauthor of the *Manifesto Tropicalista* written in 1968.

14 “E só restará um símbolo que representará a igualdade: Paraíso.”

15 “Afirmamos: ‘Dessacralizando e corrompendo a esquerda festiva, o Tropicalismo investe e arrebenta, explode e explora os seus adeptos tanto quanto os seus atacantes.’ (Qua, qua, qua, para os que ‘não nos entendem.’).”

Conclusion

1 As part of a documentary series about queer lives around the world, Elliot Page interviewed then congressman Michel Temer, confronting him on homophobia. Among other things, he told Page that he has nothing against him and that when he was young, there weren't so many gay people, but now, thanks to liberal tendencies, drugs, and women working, the number of homosexuals has increased.

2 His comments were part of an interview published by *Playboy* magazine in its June 2011 issue. The full comment reads: “Seria incapaz de amar um filho homossexual. Não vou dar uma de hipócrita aqui: prefiro que um filho meu morra num acidente do que apareça com um ‘bigodudo’ por aí. Para mim ele vai ter morrido mesmo” (I would be unable to love a homosexual son. I am not going to be a hypocrite: I'd rather see a son dying in a car accident than showing up with a “mustache”). In the same interview, he said he was against violence but would make an exception in order to “fix” an effeminate son.

3 Right after Damares Alves took office in 2019, she posted a video online stating that Brazil had entered a new era, one in which boys wear blue and girls wear pink (“O Brasil entra em ‘nova era’ em que ‘meninos vestem azul e meninas vestem rosa’”).

4 In the words of Marcelo Crivella, Rio de Janeiro's mayor: “Só se for no fundo do mar.” For a detailed account of the events, see https://www.bbc.com/portuguese/brasil-45191250.

Appendix

1 João Silvério Trevisan refers to Damares Alves, the current minister of citizenship in Brazil who sparked a number of controversies with a conservative agenda. At the time of the interview she stated that in the new government (Jair Bolsonaro's presidency), boys would wear only blue and girls, pink.

2 The poem (Andrade 2017) is actually as follows: "O Zé Pereira chegou de caravela/ E perguntou pro guarani da mata virgem / Sois cristão? / Não. Sou braco, sou forte, sou filho da morte . . ." (Zé Pereira arrived in a caravel / asked the Guarani from the virgin forest / Are you a Christian? / No. I am white, I am strong, I am the son of death . . .)

3 Paulo Emílio Salles Gomes's review was published in English in 2018.

WORKS CITED AND SUPPLEMENTAL READINGS

Abreu, Caio Fernando. 2006. *Pequenas epifanias*. Rio de Janeiro: Agir.

———. 2017. *O essencial da década de 70*. São Paulo: Nova Fronteira.

Aguilar, Gonzalo. 2005. *Poesia concreta brasileira: As vanguardas na encruzilhada modernista*. São Paulo: Edusp.

Albuquerque, Severino J. 2004. *Tentative Transgressions: Homosexuality, AIDS and the Theater in Brazil*. Madison: University of Wisconsin Press.

Almeida, Maria Cândida Ferreira de. 2002. *Tornar-se outro—O topos canibal na literatura brasileira*. São Paulo: Annablume.

Altman, Dennis. 2001. *Global Sex*. Chicago: University of Chicago Press.

Altman, Fábio. 1995. *A arte da entrevista*. São Paulo: Scritta.

Andrade, Oswald de. 1928a. "Esquema para Tristão de Athayde." *Revista de antropofagia* 5:3.

———. 1928b. "Manifesto antropófago." *Revista de antropofagia* 1:7.

———. 1978. *Marco Zero I—A revolução melancólica*. Rio de Janeiro: Editora Civilazação Brasileira.

———. 1991. *Estética e política*. São Paulo: Editora Globo.

———. 2000a. *A utopia antropofágica*. São Paulo: Editora Globo.

———. 2000b. *Os dentes do dragão*. São Paulo: Editora Globo.

———. 2017. *Poesias reunidas*. São Paulo: Companhia das Letras.

Anzaldúa, Glória. 1987. *Borderlands / La Frontera: The New Mestiza*. San Francisco: Aunt Lute Books.

Araújo, Vicente de Paula. 1985. *A bela época do cinema brasileiro*. São Paulo: Editora Perspectiva.

Archer, Neil. 2013. *The French Road Movie*. New York: Berghahn Books.

Artaud, Antonin. 1994. *The Theater and Its Double*. New York: Groove Press.

Bastos, Cristina. 1999. *Global Responses to AIDS: Science in Emergency*. Bloomington: Indiana University Press.

Bayman, Louis, and Natália Pinazza, eds. 2013. *Directory of World Cinema: Brazil*. Bristol: Intellect Books.

Berlant, Lauren, and Michael Warner. 1995. "What Does Queer Theory Teach Us about X?" *PMLA* 110 (3): 343–49. JSTOR. www.jstor.org/stable/462930.

Bernardet, Jean-Claude. 2007. *Brasil em tempo de cinema: Ensaio sobre o cinema brasileiro de 1958 a 1966*. São Paulo: Companhia das Letras.

Bernardet, Jean-Claude, and Maria Rita Galvão. 1983. *Cinema: Repercussões em Caixa de eco ideológica. As ideias do nacional e popular no pensamento cinematográfico brasileiro*. São Paulo: Editora Brasiliense.

Bersani, Leo. 1987. "Is the Rectum a Grave?" *October* 43:197–222.

———. 1996. *Homos*. Cambridge, MA: Harvard University Press.

———. 2010. *Is the Rectum a Grave? And Other Essays*. Chicago: University of Chicago Press.

Bezerra, Julio. 2010. "O corpo como cogito: Um cinema contemporâneo à luz de Merleau-Ponty." *E-Compós* 13 (1): 1–12. doi.org/10.30962/ec.476.

Bitarães Neto, Adriano. 2004. *Antropofagia oswaldiana: um receituário estético e científico*. São Paulo: Anablume Editora.

Boaventura, Maria Eugênia. 1985. *A vanguarda antropofágica*. São Paulo: Editora Ática.

———. 2000. *A semana de arte moderna vista pelos seus contemporâneos*. São Paulo: Edusp.

Bopp, Raul. 1956. *Cobra Norato*. Rio de Janeiro: Livraria São José.

———. 1966. *Movimentos modernistas no Brasil, 1922–1928*. Rio de Janeiro: Livraria São José.

———. 1977. *Vida e morte da antropofagia*. Rio de Janeiro: Editora Civilização Brasileira.

Bosi, Alfredo. 1994. *História concisa da literatura brasileira*. São Paulo: Cultrix.

Braham, Persephone. 2015. *From Amazons to Zombies: Monsters in Latin America*. Lewisburg, PA: Bucknell University Press.

Britto, Jomard Muniz de. 2013. *Jomar Muniz de Britto*. Rio de Janeiro: Azougue.

Butler, Judith. 1999. *Gender Trouble*. New York: Routledge.

———. 2004. *Undoing Gender*. New York: Routledge.

———. 2011. *Bodies That Matter: On the Discursive Limits of "Sex."* New York: Routledge.

Callegari, Jeanne. 2008. *Caio Fernando Abreu: Inventário de um escritor irremediável*. São Paulo: Seoman.

Campos, Augusto de. 1975. "Revistas Re-revistas: Os antropófagos." *Revista de antropofagia*. São Paulo: Editora Abril.

Cândido, Antônio. 1970. *Vários escritos*. São Paulo: Livraria Duas Cidades.

Conde, Maite. 2011. *Consuming Visions: Cinema, Writing and Modernity in Rio de Janeiro*. Charlottesville: University of Virginia Press.

———. 2018. *Foundational Films: Early Cinema and Modernity in Brazil*. Oakland: University of California Press.

Conde, Maite, and Stephanie Dennison, eds. 2018. *Paulo Emílio Salles Gomes: On Brazil and Global Cinema*. Cardiff: University of Wales Press.

Córdoba Garcia, David. 2005. "Teoría queer: Reflexiones sobre sexo, sexualidad e identidad. Hacia una politización de la sexualidad." In *Teoría queer: Políticas bolleras, maricas, trans, mestizas*, edited by David Córdoba, Javier Sáez, and Paco Vidarte, 21–63. Madrid: Egales Editorial.

Cornejo, Giancarlo. 2013. "La guerra declarada contra el niño afeminado: Una autoetnografía 'queer.'" *Íconos—Revista de ciencias sociales* 39:79–95. doi.org/10.17141/iconos.39.2011.747.

Corrêa, José Celso Martinez. 2012. "O terreiro eletrônico e a cidade: O olhar do mestre antropófago." *Sala Preta* 12 (1): 209–23. doi.org/10.11606/issn.2238-3867.v12i1p209-233.

Cortanze, Gérard de. 2005. *Le monde du surréalisme*. Paris: Éditions Complexe.

Costa, Lara Valentina Pozzobon da. 1999. "Na boca do estômago, conversa com J. C. Martinez Corrêa." *Nuevo texto crítico* 23/24:49–60.

Costa, Patrícia Anzini. 2011. "Pra não dizer que não falei de Antropofagia: A tropical devoração oswaldiana." *Revista darandina* 4 (1): 1–22. www.ufjf.br/darandina/files/2011/06/Pra-n%C3%A3o-dizer-que-n%C3%A3o-falei-de-Antropofagia-A-tropical-devora%C3%A7%C3%A3o-oswaldiana.pdf.

Couto de Barros, Antônio Carlos. 1922. "Livros e revistas." *Klaxon* 6:12–13.

Cowan, Benjamin A. 2016. *Securing Sex: Morality and Repression in the Making of Cold War Brazil.* Chapel Hill: University of North Carolina Press.

Cunha, João Manual dos Santos. 2011. *A lição aproveitada – Modernismo e cinema em Mário de Andrade*. São Paulo: Ateliê Editorial.

D'Alessandro, Stephanie, and Luis Pérez-Oramas. 2017. *Tarsila Do Amaral: Inventing Modern Art in Brazil.* New Haven, CT: Yale University Press.

Daniel, Herbert. 1982. *Passagem para o sonho*. Rio de Janeiro: Codecri.

Davis, Adrienne D. 2011. "Bad Girls of Art and Law: Abjection, Power, and Sexuality Exceptionalism in (Kara Waler's) Art and (Janet Halley's) Law." Legal Studies Research Paper Series 10-06-09, Washington University School of Law, St. Louis, MO, June, 100–154. papers.ssrn.com/sol3/papers.cfm?abstract_id=1628726.

De la Dehesa, Rafael. 2010. *Queering the Public Sphere in Mexico and Brazil. Sexual Rights Movements in Emerging Democracies*. Durham, NC: Duke University Press.

de Lauretis, Teresa, ed. 1991, Summer. "Queer Theory: Lesbian and Gay Sexualities." Special issue, *differences* 3 (2).

D'Emilio, John. 1983. "Capitalism and Gay Identity." In *Powers of Desire: The Politics of Sexuality*, edited by Ann Snitow, Christine Stansell, and Sharan Thompson, 100–116. New York: Monthly Review Press.

Dennison, Stephanie, and Lisa Shaw. 2004. *Popular Cinema in Brazil.* Manchester: Manchester University Press.

Dias, Verônica Ferreira. 2003. "A Cinema of Conversation—Eduardo Coutinho's *Santo Forte* and *Babilônia 2000.*" In *The New Brazilian Cinema*, edited by Lúcia Nagib, 105–17. London: I. B. Taurus.

Duggan, Lisa. 2002. "The New Homonormativity: The Sexual Politics of Neoliberalism." In *Materializing Democracy: Toward a Revitalized Cultural Politics,* edited by Russ Castronovo and Dana D. Nelson, 175–94. Durham, NC: Duke University Press.

Durst, Rogério. 1985. *Madame Satã: com o diabo no corpo*. São Paulo: Editora Brasiliense.

Eco, Umberto. 1989. "How to Recognize a Porn Movie." In *How to Travel with a Salmon and Other Essays.* Translated by William Weaver. London: Vintage.

Eng, David L., Jack Halberstam, and José Esteban Muñoz. 2005. "What's Queer about Queer Studies Now?" *Social Text 84–85* 23 (3–4): 1–17.

Epps, Brad. 2007. "Retos y riesgos, pautas y promesas de la teoría queer." *Debate feminista* 36:219–72. JSTOR. www.jstor.org/stable/42625014.

Fédida, Pierre. 1972. "Le cannibale mélancolique." In "Destins du cannibalisme." Special issue, *Nouvelle revue de psychanalyse* 6 (Autumn): 123–28.

Ferguson, Roderick A. 2005. "Race-ing Homonormativity Citizenship, Sociology, and Gay Identity." In *Black Queer Studies: A Critical Anthology*, edited by Patrick Johnson and Mae G. Henderson, 52–67. Durham, NC: Duke University Press.

Ferreira, Jairo. 2000. *Cinema de invenção*. São Paulo: Ed. Limiar.

Foster, David William. 1984. "Latin American Documentary Narrative." *PMLA* 99 (1): 41–55. doi.org/10.2307/462034.

———, ed. 1995. *Latin American Writers on Gay and Lesbian Themes: A Bio-Critical Sourcebook*. Westport, CT: Greenwood Press.

———. 1997. *Sexual Textualities: Essays on Queer/ing Latin American Writing.* Austin: University of Texas Press.

———. 1999. *Gender & Society in Contemporary Brazilian Cinema*. Austin: University of Texas Press.

———. 2003. *Queer Issues in Contemporary Latin American Cinema*. Austin: University of Texas Press.

———. 2010. "Documenting Queer, Queer Documentary." *Revista canadiense de estudios hispánicos* 35 (1): 105–19. JSTOR. www.jstor.org/stable/23055670.

Freccero, Carla. 2011. "Queer Times." In *After Sex? On Writing since Queer Theory*, edited by Janet Halley and Andrew Parker, 17–26. Durham, NC: Duke University Press.

Freud, Sigmund. 1918. *Totem and Taboo: Resemblances between the Psychic Lives of Savages and Neurotics*. Moffat, Yard. archive.org/details/totemtabooresembr00freu/page/106/mode/2up.

Freyre, Gilberto. 2006. *Casa-grande & senzala*. São Paulo: Global Editora.

Fry, Peter, Edward MacRae, Silvana I. Afram, and José W. S. Moraes. 1985. *O que é homossexualidade*. São Paulo: Abril Cultural/Brasiliense.

Galvão, Jane. 2000. *AIDS no Brasil: A agenda de construção de uma epidemia*. São Paulo: Editora 34.

Gerace, Rodrigo. 2015. *Cinema explícito: Representações cinematográficas do sexo*. São Paulo: Edições SESC / Editora Perspectiva.

Godinho, Denise, and Hugo Moura. 2012. *Coisas eróticas: A história jamais contada da primeira vez do cinema nacional*. São Paulo: Panda Books.

Gomes, Paulo Emílio Salles. 1980. *Cinema: Trajetória no subdesenvolvimento*. Rio de Janeiro: Paz e Terra.

Green, James. 1999. *Além do carnaval: A homossexualidade masculina no Brasil do século XX*. São Paulo: Editora da UNESP.

———. 2000. "Mais amor e mais tesão. A construção de um movimento de gays, lésbicas e travestis." *Cadernos Pagu* 15:271–95.

———. 2003. "A luta pela igualdade: Desejos, homossexualidade e esquerda na América Latina." *Cadernos AEL* 10 (18/19): 19–39. https://www.ifch.unicamp.br/ojs/index.php/ael/article/view/2508/1918.

———. 2004. "Madame Satã (Satan): The Black 'Queen' of Rio's Bohemia." In *The Human Tradition in Modern Brazil*, edited by Peter M. Beattie, 267–85. Wilmington, DE: SR Books.

———. 2010. *We Cannot Remain Silent: Opposition to the Brazilian Military Dictatorship in the United States*. Durham, NC: Duke University Press.

Guattari, Félix, and Suely Rolnik. 2008. *Molecular Revolution in Brazil*. Translated by Karel Clapshow and Brian Holmes. Los Angeles: Semiotext(e).

Guimarães, Carmen Dona, Herbert Daniel, and Jane Galvão. 1988. "A questão do preconceito." *Boletim ABIA* 3:2–3.

Guimarães, César. 2013. "The Scene and the Inscription of the Real." In *New*

Argentine and Brazilian Cinema. Reality Effects, edited by Jens Andermann and Álvaro Férnandez Bravo, 87–102. New York: Palgrave Macmillan.

Gumbrecht, Hans Ulrich. 2011. "Mordendo você suavemente: Um comentário sobre o Manifesto antropófago." In *Antropofagia hoje? Oswald de Andrade em Cena*, edited by João Cezar de Castro Rocha and Jorge Ruffinelli, 289–97. São Paulo: Realizações Editora.

Halberstam, J. Jack. 2005. *In a Queer Time & Place: Transgender Bodies, Subcultural Lives*. New York: New York University Press.

———. 2011. *The Queer Art of Failure*. Durham, NC: Duke University Press.

———. 2012. *Gaga Feminism: Sex, Gender and the End of Normal*. Boston: Beacon Press.

Halperin, David. 2007. *What Do Gay Men Want? An Essay on Sex, Risk, and Subjectivity*. Ann Arbor: University of Michigan Press.

———. 2011. "The Normalization of Queer Theory." In *After Sex? On Writing Since Queer Theory*, edited by Janet Halley and Andrew Parker. Durham, NC: Duke University Press, 339–45.

———. 2012. *How to Be Gay*. Cambridge, MA: Belknap Press.

Hardy, Ernest. 2011, November 16. "DZI Croquettes." *Village Voice*. www.villagevoice.com/2011/11/16/dzi-croquettes/.

Hart, Kylo-Patrick R. 2000. *The AIDS Movie: Representing a Pandemic in Film and Television*. New York: Routledge.

Helena, Lúcia. 1983. *Uma literatura antropofágica*. Fortaleza: Edições Universidade Federal do Ceará.

Hocquenghem, Guy. 2009. *El deseo homosexual*. Barcelona: Melusina.

Holanda, Sérgio Buarque de. 2015. *Raízes do Brasil*. São Paulo: Companhia das Letras.

Holcombe, W. Daniel. 2012. "Desarrollando una óptica queer: Coloquio con David William Foster." *Studies in Latin American Popular Culture* 30:199–214.

Jackson, Kenneth David. 1999. "Novas receitas da cozinha canníbal. O manifesto antropófago nos anos 90." *Nuevo texto crítico* 12 (23–24): 273–80. doi.org/10.1353/ntc.199.0020.

Jagose, Annamarie. 1996. *Queer Theory*. New York: New York University Press.

Jarry, Alfred. 1902. "Antropophagie." Translated by Marcelo Rodrigues Souza. *Sopro: Panfletos político-culturais*. culturaebarbarie.org/sopro/verbetes/antropofagia.html.

Jarry, Alfred, and Décaudin Michel. 2004. *Œuvres*. Paris: Laffont.

Jáuregui, Carlos A. 2008. *Canibalia—Canibalismo, calibalismo, antropofagia cultural y consumo en América Latina*. Madrid: Iberoamericana.

———. 2016. "La otra antropofagia: Oswaldo costa y la crítica de la cuestión colonial." *Revista iberoamericana* 82 (349): 255–56. doi.org/10.5195/reviberoamer.2016.7393.

Johnson, Randal. 1982. *Literatura e cinema. Macunaíma: Do modernismo na literatura ao Cinema Novo*. São Paulo: Editora Tao.

———. 1984. *Cinema Novo X 5: Masters of Contemporary Brazilian Film*. Austin: University of Texas Press.

———. 1993. "Ascensão e queda do cinema brasileiro, 1960–1990." *Revista USP* 19 (November): 31–49. https://doi.org/10.11606/issn.2316-9036.v0i19p31-49.

———. 1995. "The rise and fall of Brazilian cinema 1960 1990." In *Brazilian Cinema*, edited by Randal Johnson and Robert Stam. New York: Columbia University Press.

———. n.d. "Cinema Novo." *Encyclopedia of Latin American History and Culture*. Encyclopedia.com. Accessed May 4, 2021. www.encyclopedia.com/humanities/encyclopedias-almanacs-transcripts-and-maps/cinema-novo.

Johnson, Randal, and Robert Stam. 1995. *Brazilian Cinema*. New York: Columbia University Press.

Kristeva, Julia. 1982. *Powers of Horror: An Essay on Abjection*. New York: Columbia University Press.

Kuhn, Annette, and Guy Westwell. 2012. "Chanchada." *Oxford Dictionary of Film Studies*. Oxford Reference. doi.org/10.1093/acref/9780199587261.001.0001.

Kulick, Don. 1998. *Travesti: Sex, Gender, and Culture among Brazilian Transgender Prostitutes*. Chicago: University of Chicago Press.

Labaki, Amir. 2003. "It's All Brazil." In *New Brazilian Cinema*, edited by Lucia Nagib. London: I. B. Tauris, 97–104.

Lacerda, Luiz Francisco Buarque, Jr. 2015. *Cinema gay brasileiro: políticas de representação e além*. PhD diss., Federal University of Pernambuco, Recife. repositorio.ufpe.br/handle/123456789/15772.

Lamas, Caio Túlio Padula. 2013. *Boca do Lixo erotismo pornografia e poder no cinema paulista durante a ditadura militar*. Master's thesis, University of São Paulo. doi.org/10.11606/D.27.2013.tde-10022014-164740.

Leitch, Vincent B., William E. Cain, Laurie A. Finke, John McGowan, and Barbara E. Johnson, eds. 2010. *The Norton Anthology of Theory and Criticism*. 2nd ed. New York: Norton.

Lévi-Strauss, Claude. 2011. *Tristes tropiques*. Translated by John Weightman and Doreen Weightman. London: Penguin Books.

Likosky, Stephan. 1992. *Coming Out: An Anthology of International Gay and Lesbian Writings*. New York: Pantheon Books.

Lima, Isabelle Moreira. 2014. "Tabu na TV." In *Observatório da Imprensa*. http://www.observatoriodaimprensa.com.br/tv-em-questao/_ed789_tabu_na_tv/.

Lima, Marcelo Guimarães da Silva. 1988. "Pau Brasil to Antropofagia: The Paintings of Tarsila do Amaral." PhD diss., University of New Mexico, Albuquerque.

Lobert, Rosemary. 1979. *A palavra mágica: A vida cotidiana do Dzi Croquettes*. Master's thesis, University of Campinas.

Lopes, Denilson. 2013. "Do entre-lugar ao transcultural." *UFRJ*. cutt.ly/pbnc6sV.

———. 2014. "Por una crítica cosmopolita." *Papel máquina* 4 (8): 25–36.

Love, Heather. 2007. *Feeling Backward: Loss and the Politics of Queer History*. Cambridge, MA: Harvard University Press.

Lugarinho, Mário César. 2002. "Al Berto, In Memoriam: The Luso Queer Principle." In *Lusosex—Gender and Sexuality in the Portuguese-Speaking World*, edited by Susan Canty Quinlan and Fernando Arenas, 276–300. Minneapolis: University of Minnesota Press.

———. 2010. "Antropofagia crítica: Para uma teoria queer crítica em português." *Revista olhar* 12 (22): 106–12.

Machado, Antônio Castilho de Alcântara. 1982. *Pathé-Baby*. São Paulo: Imprensa Oficial do Estado de São Paulo.

MacKenzie, Scott. 2014. *Film Manifestos and Global Cinema Cultures: A Critical Anthology*. Berkeley: University of California Press. JSTOR. www.jstor.org/stable/10.1525/j.ctt5vk01n.

Madureira, Luís. 2005. *Cannibal Modernities: Postcoloniality and the Avant-Garde in Caribbean and Brazilian Literature*. Charlottesville: University of Virginia Press.

———. 2011. "A Flat Carnivalesque Intention of Being a Cannibal, or, How (Not) to Read the Cannibal Manifesto." *Ellipsis: Journal of the American Portuguese Studies Association* 9:13–33. doi.org/10.21471/jls.v9i0.93.

Magalhães Filho, João Rocha. 1999. *Orgia ou o homem que deu cria: o radicalism estético no manifesto em celulóide de João Silvério Trevisan*. Master's thesis. Pontifical Catholic University of São Paulo.

Maia, Guilherme, and Euro Prédez de Azevedo. 2018. "Quanto vale uma Chanchada? Disputas conceituais e valorativas em torno das comédias cinematográficas brasileiras (1940–50)." *Brasiliana: Journal for Brazilian Studies* 6 (1): 105–25. tidsskrift.dk/bras/article/view/25279.

Maques, Maria Cristina da Costa. 2003. *A história de uma epidemia moderna: A emergência política da AIDS/ HIV no Brasil.* São Carlos: Rima Editora.

Mavrikakis, Catherine. 2009. *Deuils cannibales et mélancoliques.* Montreal: Héliotrope.

McClennen, Sophia A. 2011. "From the Aesthetics of Hunger to the Cosmetics of Hunger in Brazilian Cinema: Meirelles' City of God." *symplokē* 19 (1–2): 95–106.

Melo, Luís Alberto Rocha. n.d. "Orgia ou o homem que deu cria (1970)." *Contracampo* 30. www.contracampo.com.br/30/orgia.htm.

Mello, Christine. 2009. "Vídeo no Brasil 1950–1980: Novos circuitos para a arte." *Arte y políticas de identidad.* 1:185–220.

Mennel, Barbara. 2012. *Queer Cinema: Schoolgirls, Vampires and Gay Cowboys.* London: Wallflower.

Michel, Estève. 1972. *Le cinema nôvo brésilien.* Paris: Lettres Modernes.

Miskolci, Richard. 2012. *Teoria queer: Um aprendizado pelas diferenças.* São Paulo: Autêntica Editora.

Mogrovejo, Norma. 2011. "Lo queer en América Latina: ¿Lucha identitaria, post-identitaria, asimilacionista o neocolonial?" In *Cartografías queer: Sexualidades y activismo LGBT en América Latina*, edited by Daniel Balderston and Arturo Matute Castro, 231–49. Pittsburgh: Instituto Internacional de Literatura Iberoamericana, University of Pittsburgh.

Montero, Oscar. 1997a. "Modernismo and Homophobia: Darío and Rodó." *Sex and Sexuality in Latin America*, edited by Daniel Balderston and Donna J. Guy, 101–17. New York: New York University Press.

———. 1997b. "Notes for a Queer Reading of Latin American Literature." In *Queer Representations: Reading Lives, Reading Cultures: A Center for Lesbian and Gay Studies Book*, edited by Martin Duberman, 216–36. New York: New York University Press.

———. 1998. "The Signifying Queen: Critical Notes from a Latino Queer." In *Hispanisms and Homosexualities*, edited by Sylvia Molloy and Robert McKee Irwin, 161–76. Durham, NC: Duke University Press.

Moreira, Julia. 2010, August. "Dzi Croquettes: A história do polêmico grupo é relembrada e eternizada em documentário premiado." *Revista de História.* Accessed July 20, 2014. Website no longer available.

Moreno, Antônio. 2002. *A personagem homossexual no cinema brasileiro.* Rio de Janeiro: Ministério da Cultura, EDUFF.

Muñoz, Alfonso Ceballos. 2009. "Teoria Rarita." In *Teoría queer: Políticas boleras, maricas, trans, mestizas*, edited by David Córdoba, Javier Sáez, and Paco Vidarte, 165–77. Barcelona: Editoral Egales.

Nagib, Lúcia. 2003. *New Brazilian Cinema*. London: I. B. Tauris.

———. 2007. *Brazil on Screen: Cinema Novo, New Cinema, Utopia*. London: I. B. Tauris.

Nemi Neto, João. 2016. "Herbert Daniel e a luta contra o stigma da AIDS." *Intellèctus* 15 (1): 188–207.

Newcomb, Robert Patrick, and Richard A. Gordon, eds. 2017. *Beyond Tordesillas: New Approaches to Comparative Luso-Hispanic Studies*. Columbus: Ohio State University Press.

Nichols, Bill. 2010. *Introduction to Documentary*. Bloomington: Indiana University Press.

Nunes, Benedito. 1979. *Oswald Canibal*. São Paulo: Editora Perspectiva.

——. 2004. "Antropofagia e vanguarda—acerca do canibalismo literário." *Literatura e sociedade* 7:316–27.

Nunn, Amy. 2009. *The Politics and History of AIDS Treatment in Brazil*. New York: Springer.

Pannacci, Renato Coelho. 2013. "O cinema e a crítica de Jairo Ferreira." PhD diss., University of Campinas. repositorio.unicamp.br/jspui/handle/REPOSIP/284558.

Oliveira, Marco. Alexandre de. 2012. "Cannibal Logic: Latin America under the Sign of an Other Thinking." PhD diss., University of North Carolina–Chapel Hill. doi.org/10.17615/59eq-n412.

Ortiz, José Mario, and Arthur Autran. 2018. "O cinema brasileiro das décadas de 1970 e 1980." *Nova história do cinema brasileiro*. Vol. 2, edited by Fernão Pessoa Ramos and Sheila Schvarman. São Paulo: Edições SESC.

Parente, André. 2007. Cinema de vanguarda, cinema experimental e cinema de dispositivo. In *Filmes de artista no Brasil 1965–1980*, edited by Fernando Cocchiarale, 23–43. Rio de Janeiro: Contra Capa.

Parker, Richard. 1998. "'Within Four Walls': Brazilian Sexual Culture and HIV/AIDS." In *Reader on Culture, Society and Sexuality*, edited by Richard Parker, 253–66. London: Routledge.

———. 1999. *Beneath the Equator. Cultures of Desire, Male Homosexuality, and Emerging Gay Communities in Brazil*. New York: Routledge.

———. 2009. *Bodies, Pleasures, and Passions: Sexual Culture in Contemporary Brazil*. Nashville: Vanderbilt University Press.

Péret, Flávia. 2011. *Imprensa Gay no Brasil.* São Paulo: Publifolha.

Pérez-Oramas, Luis. 2018, February 28. "Part 1: Tarsila, Melancholic Cannibal." *Post: Notes on Art in a Global Context.* MoMA. post.moma.org/part-1-tarsila-melancholic-cannibal/

Perlongher, Néstor. 1988. El fantasma del sida. Beunos Aires: Puntosur S.R.L. Editores.

———. 1991. "Los devenires minoritários." *Revista de crítica cultural* 4:11–22.

———. 1997. *Prosa plebeya.* Buenos Aires: Ediciones Colihue S.R.L.

———. 2008. *O negócio do michê: Prostituição viril em São Paulo.* São Paulo: Editora Fundação Perseu Abrama.

Picabia, Francis. 2007. "Dada cannibal manifesto." In *I Am a Beautiful Monster: Poetry, Prose and Provocation.* Translated by Marc Lowenthal. Cambridge, MA: MIT Press.

Picchio, Luciana Stegagno. 1988. "Brazilian Anthropophagy Myth and Literature." *Diógenes* 36:116–25. doi.org/10.1177/039219218803614407.

Piontek, Thomas. 2006. *How Gay Theory and the Gay Movement Betrayed the Sissy Boy.* Urbana: University of Illinois Press.

Posso, Karl. 2003. *Artful Seduction: Homosexuality and the Problematic of Exile.* Oxford: Legenda.

Prado, Paulo. 2012. *Retrato do Brasil: Ensaio sobre a tristeza brasileira.* São Paulo: Companhia das Letras.

Preciado, Paul. 2005. "Multitudes queer: Notas para una política de los 'anormales.'" *Nombres: Revista de filosofía* 19:157–66. revistas.unc.edu.ar/index.php/NOMBRES/article/view/2338.

———. 2011a. *Manifesto contrasexual.* Barcelona: Editorial Anagrama.

———. 2011b. *Pornotopía: Arquitectura y sexualidad en "Playboy" durante la guerra fría.* Barcelona: Editorial Anagrama.

Puar, Jasbir K. 2007. *Terrorist Assemblages: Homonationalism in Queer Times.* Durham, NC: Duke University Press.

Quiroga, José. 2000. *Tropics of Desire: Interventions from Queer Latino America.* New York: New York University Press.

Rama, Ángel. 1998. *La ciudad letrada.* Montevideo: Arca.

Ramos, Fernão Pessoa. 1987. *Cinema Marginal (1968–1973): A representação em seu limite.* São Paulo: Ed. Brasiliense.

———. 2008. *Mas afinal . . . O que é documentário?* São Paulo: Senac.

———. 2018a. "A grande crise: Pós-modernismo, fim da Embrafilme e da pornochanchada." In *Nova história do cinema brasileiro.* Vol. 2, edited by Fernão Pessoa Ramos and Scheila Schvarman. São Paulo: Edições SESC.

———. 2018b. "Cinema Novo/ Cinema Marginal, Entre Curtição e Exasperação." In *Nova história do cinema brasileiro*. Vol. 2, edited by Fernão Pessoa Ramos and Sheila Schvarman. São Paulo: Edições SESC.

Ramos, Fernão Pessoa, and Sheila Schvarman, eds. 2018. *Nova história do cinema brasileiro*. 2 vols. São Paulo: Edições SESC.

Ramos, Guiomar. 2008. *Um cinema brasileiro antropofágico? (1970–1974)*. São Paulo: ANNABLUME.

———. 2014. "Um novo panorama para a história do cinema brasileiro." *Revista brasileira de estudos de cinema e audio visual* 3 (6). doi.org/10.22475/rebeca.v3n2.332.

Ramos, Julio. 2013. "Los viajes de Silviano Santiago." *Papel máquina* 4 (8): 191–212.

Reich, Wilhelm. *The Function of Orgasm*. London: Souvenir, 1983.

Retamar, Roberto Fernández. 2003. *Caliban*. San Juan: Ediciones Callejoón.

Ribemont-Dessaignes, Georges. 1974. *Manifestes, poèmes, articles, projets 1915–1930*. Paris: Editions Champ Libre.

Rich, B. Ruby. 2013. *New Queer Cinema: Director's Cut*. Durham, NC: Duke University Press.

Rivas, Jorge. 2015, March 1. "'Looking' Actor Says He's Glad He's Not One of Those 'Effeminate' Gays." Splinter. splinternews.com/looking-actor-says-hes-glad-he-s-not-one-of-those-eff-1793845813.

Rocha, Glauber. 1965. "The Aesthetics of Hunger." www.amherst.edu/media/view/38122/original/ROCHA_Aesth_Hunger.pdf.

———. 2003. *Revisão crítica do cinema brasileiro*. São Paulo: Cosac & Naify.

———. 2004. "The Aesthetics of Hunger." In *Film Manifestos and Global Cinema Cultures: A Critical Anthology*, edited by Scott MacKenzie, 218–20. Berkeley: University of California Press.

Rocha, João Cezar de Castro, and Jorge Ruffinelli, eds. 1999. *Anthropophagy Today? ¿Antropofagia hoje? ¿Antropofagia hoy? ¿Antropofagia oggi? Nuevo texto crítico* 23/24. Stanford, CA: Stanford University Press.

Rocha, João Cezar de Castro, David Shepherd and Tania Shepherd. 1999. "Let us Devour Oswald de Andrade. A rereading of the Manifesto antropófago." *Nuevo texto crítico* 12/1: 5–19.

Rodrigues, Geisa. 2013. *As múltiplas faces de Madame Satã: Estéticas e políticas do corpo*. Niterói: Editora da UFF.

Rouanet, Maria Helena. 2011. "Quando os bárbaros somos nós." In *Antropofagia Hoje, Oswald de Andrade em cena*, edited by Jorge Ruffinelli and João Cezar de Castro, 175–78. São Paulo: Realizações Editora.

Ruvalcaba, Héctor Dominguéz. 2016. *Translating the Queer: Body Politics and Transnational Conversations*. London: Zed Books.

Sadlier, Darlene J. 2003. *Nelson Pereira dos Santos*. Urbana: University of Illinois Press.

Said, Edward. 1983. *The World, the Text, and the Critic*. Cambridge, MA: Harvard University Press.

Salih, Sara. 2002. *Judith Butler*. London: Taylor & Francis.

Santiago, Silviano. 1978. *Uma literatura nos trópicos*. São Paulo: Editora Perspectiva.

———. 1985. *Stella Manhattan*. São Paulo: Editora Nova Fronteira.

———. 1989. *Nas malhas da letra—Ensaios*. São Paulo: Companhia das Letras.

———. 1992. "Oswald de Andrade ou elogio da tolerância racial." *Revista de ciências sociais* 35:165–76.

———. 2001. *The Space In-Between: Essays on Latin American Culture*. Edited by Ana Lúcia Gazzola. Translated by Tom Burns, Ana Lúcia Gazzola, and Gareth Williams. Durham, NC: Duke University Press.

———. 2002. "The Wily Homosexual." In *Queer Globalizations: Citizenship and the Afterlife of Colonialism*, edited by Arnaldo Cruz-Malavé and Martin F. Manalansan, 13–19. New York: New York University Press.

———. 2006. *As raízes e o labirinto da América Latina*. Rio de Janeiro: Rocco.

Santos, Boaventura de Sousa. 1997. *Pela mão de Alice: O social e o politico na pós-modernidade*. São Paulo: Cortez.

Santos, João Vieira dos. 2003. "Chronically Unfeasible: The Political Film in a Depoliticized World." In *New Brazilian Cinema*, edited by Lucia Nagib, 85–95. London: I. B. Tauris.

Schøllhamer, Karl Erik. 1999. "A imagem canibalizada: Tarsila do Amaral." *Nuevo texto crítico* 23/24:191–200.

Schroeder, Paul A. 2016. *Latin American Cinema: A Comparative History*. Oakland: University of California Press.

Schwartz, Jorge. 2008. *Vanguardas Latino-Americanas*. São Paulo: Edusp.

Scott, A. O. 2012, December 16. "25 Favorites from a Year When 10 Aren't Enough." *New York Times*. www.nytimes.com/2012/12/16/movies/a-o-scotts-25-best-films-of-2012.html.

Sedgwick, Eve Kosofsky. 1993. *Tendencies*. Durham, NC: Duke University Press.

Sganzerla, Rogério. 1970. "A mulher de todos para o seu autor." *Arte em revista*, no. 5. São Paulo: Kairós.

Shaw, Lisa. 2003. "The Brazilian Chanchada and Hollywood Paradigms (1930–1959)." *Framework: The Journal of Cinema and Media* 44 (1): 70–83. JSTOR. www.jstor.org/stable/41552353.

———. 2007a. "Afro-Brazilian Identity. Malandragem and Homosexuality in Madame Satã." In *Contemporary Latin American Cinema: Breaking into the Global Market*, edited by Deborah Shaw, 87–104. Plymouth: Rowman & Littlefield.

———. 2007b. "A imitação cultural na chanchada: O caso de *Quem roubou meu samba?* e *Rio, Zona Norte*." *Revista alceu* 8 (15): 69–81.

Shaw, Lisa, and Stephanie Dennison. 2005. *Latin American Cinema: Essays on Modernity, Gender and National Identity*. Jefferson, NC: McFarland.

———. 2007. *Brazilian National Cinema*. London: Routledge.

Siega, Paula Regina. 2014. "Breve, brevíssimo! O discurso cinematográfico brasileiro dos anos 1960 em sua veiculação externa." *Outra travessia* 17:149–67. periodicos.ufsc.br/index.php/Outra/article/view/2176-8552.2014n17p149/pdf_12.

Sifuentes-Jauregui, Ben. 2014. *Avowal of Difference Queer Latino American Narratives*. Albany: State University of New York Press.

Silva, Antônio Márcio da. 2013. "Gender." In *Directory of World Cinema: Brazil*, edited by Louis Bayman and Natália Pinazza, 81–85. Bristol: Intellect Books.

———. 2014. *The "Femme" Fatale in Brazilian Cinema. Challenging Hollywood Norms*. New York: Palgrave Macmillan.

Simões, Giuliana Martins. 2017. *Veto ao modernismo no teatro brasileiro*. São Paulo: Hucitec.

Smith, Paul Julian. 1996. *Vision Machines: Cinema, Literature and Sexuality in Spain and Cuba, 1983–93*. London: Verso.

———. 2011, December. "*Linha de passe*" (review). BFI Film Forever. *Sight & Sound*. old.bfi.org.uk/sightandsound/review/4494.

———. 2012. *Spanish Practices. Literature, Cinema, Television*. London: Legenda.

———. 2014. *Mexican Screen Fiction: Between Cinema and Television*. Cambridge: Polity Press.

———, and Emilie L. Bergmann, eds. 1995. *¿Entiendes? Queer Readings, Hispanic Writings*. Durham, NC: Duke University Press.

Smith, Verity, ed. 1997. *Encyclopedia of Latin American Literature*. London: Fitzroy Dearborn.

Soler, Marcelo. 2005. *Quanto vale um cineasta brasileiro? Sérgio Bianchi em palavras, imagens e provocações*. São Paulo: Editora Garçoni.

Sontag, Susan. 1988. *AIDS and Its Metaphors*. New York: Farrar, Straus & Giroux.

Stam, Robert. 1997. *Tropical Multiculturalism: A Comparative History of Race in Brazilian Cinema and Culture*. Durham, NC: Duke University Press.

———. 1998. "Hybridity and the Aesthetics of Garbage: The Case of Brazilian Cinema." *Estudios interdisciplinarios de América Latina y El Caribe* 9 (1): 9–26.

Sternheim, Alfredo. 2005. *Cinema da Boca: Dicionário de diretores*. São Paulo: Imprensa Oficial do Estado de São Paulo.

Subero, Gustavo. 2014. *Queer Masculinities in Latin American Cinema: Male Bodies and Narrative Representations*. London: I. B. Tauris.

———. 2016. *Representations of HIV/AIDS in Contemporary Hispano-American and Caribbean Culture Cuerpos SuiSIDAs*. London: Routledge.

Sullivan, Nikki. 2003. *A Critical Introduction to Queer Theory*. New York: New York University Press.

Tapia, Marcelo, and Telma Médici Nóbrega, eds. 2015. *Haroldo de Campos: Transcriação*. São Paulo: Editora Perspectiva, 2015.

Tejada, Luis. 1977. *Gotas de tinta*. Bogotá: Instituto Colombiano de Cultura.

Tenorio-Trillo, Mauricio. 2017. *Latin America: The Allure and Power of an Idea*. Chicago: University of Chicago Press.

Trevisan, João Silvério. 1998. *Seis balas num buraco só: A crise do masculino*. Rio de Janeiro: Editora Record.

———. 2004. *Devassos no paraíso*. Rio de Janeiro: Editora Record.

———. 2018. *Devassos no paraíso*. Rio de Janeiro: Editora Record.

———. 2019. *Pai, Pai*. Rio de Janeiro: Editora Record.

Veloso, Geraldo. 1995. "Oswald de Andrade e o cinema." In *Oswald Plural*, edited by Gilberto Mendaça, 75–78. Rio de Janeiro: Editora da UERJ.

Venkatesh, Vinodh. 2016. *New Maricón cinema: Outing Latin American film*. Austin: University of Texas Press.

Warner, Michael. 1993. *Fear of a Queer Planet: Queer Politics and Social Theory*. Minneapolis: University of Minnesota Press.

———. 2000. *The Trouble with Normal: Sex, Politics and the Ethics of Queer Life*. Cambridge, MA: Harvard University Press.

———. 2002. "Publics and Counterpublics." *Public Culture* 14 (1): 49–90.

———. 2012, January 1. "Queer and Then?" *Chronicle of Higher Education*. www.chronicle.com/article/queer-and-then/.

Williams, Linda. 1999. *Hard Core: Power, Pleasure, and the Frenzy of the Visible*. Berkeley: University of California Press.

Xavier, Ismail. 1993. *Alegorias do subdesenvolvimento: Cinema novo, tropicalismo, cinema marginal*. São Paulo: Editora Brasiliense.

———. 1997. *Allegories of Underdevelopment: Aesthetics and Politics in Brazilian Cinema*. Minneapolis: University of Minnesota Press.

INDEX

CPSIA information can be obtained
at www.ICGtesting.com
Printed in the USA
BVHW042328100322
631183BV00002B/22

9 780814 346099